HUMAN RESOURCE
MANAGEMENT AND TECHNOLOGY

HUMAN RESOURCE MANAGEMENT AND TECHNOLOGY

SHAHNAZ MIRZA

SERIALS PUBLICATIONS
NEW DELHI (INDIA)

First Published - 2010

ISBN: 978-81-8387-356-7

Published by

SERIALS PUBLICATIONS
4830/24, Prahlad Street, Ansari Road
Darya Ganj, New Delhi-110002 (India)
Phone : 23245225 Fax : 91-11-23272135
E-mail: serials@sify.com

CONTENTS

PREFACE

To select, coordinate, collate and furnish every topic with latest information, data, relevant to present needs, is difficult and complex for survival and most hazardous in this competitive age. I have selected seventeen such articles of writers of eminence and specialists in their respective fields, keeping in view the current needs and status of these articles. The contributors of these articles are well known authors. The articles are on different topics emphasize on human resource management and technology: The heart of the matter is the information, data, models, statistics and case studies furnished by the contributors.

The articles included in the book include-Relationship IT Network-Getting fit or Exhausted-Limits to Relationship Market, Buying Behaviour: A study of Children's influence on the purchase Decision Regarding Refrigerator, Contract Farming, The Practice of Untouchability in India, Sustainable Desertification-Management through Ecological Indicators: A Study of Gwalior Division, Community Participation for Rural Development in India, Financial Resources Mobilization strategies in India, Rural Social Work Practice: Prospective and Implications, Socio-Economic Dimensions of Retailing in India, The Function and Management of Railside Plantations: A case study of Central Railways-Bhopal Division, Training Approach: A Study with Reference to New Generation Bank: ICICI Bank Ltd, Indian Women workforce: Striking a Balance between Work-Life, Micro-Credit: A Way for Upliftment of the Rural Women, People's Participation in Rural Development Planning in Tripura, Participation of Women in Decentralized Rural Governance: A Study of Panchayati Raj Institutions in Uttar Pradesh, Performance of Joint Forest Management in Tamil Nadu, Fiscal Decentralization in India: An Overview.

Smita Singh's article, 'Indian Women Workforce: Striking Balance between Work-Life' aims at examining literature related to work life balance, special focus on Working Women. Work-life Balance has gradually become a major concern spreading across gender, generations and organization. There is substantial literature available which suggests that women experience greater work-life conflict as compared to men. The rapid increase of women in Indian workforce calls for attention to the issue of work life balance. It also discussed significance of work-life balance. Present work scenario makes greater demand on the personal resources, both time and energy, of women in professional roles. We may conclude that women, both at their work place and homes and all the world over, all exposed to diverse and greater number of stressors that men and this involves deeper examination of the issue.

P Sundara Pandian, in his eye opener article, 'Micro-Credit: A way for the upliftment of the Rural Women' highlights the importance and utility of Micro-Credit in these days all over the world. India's 75 per cent household depend on moneylenders to meet their financial needs, almost 90 per cent of people in rural India have no access to insurance; 50 per cent household are landless and need small credit to start some economic activity. The article defines Micro-Credit and Micro-Finance and works out how these work. Women are primary target of micro-finance services. Micro-credit took its birth in Bangladesh and the fther of the movement Dr. Mohammad Yunus, awarded with Nobel Prize, the world's most prestigious and covetous award. Micro-finance emerged in 1970, as social innovator began to offer financial services to the working poor. In India, Micro-credit has worked largely through self-help groups (SHGs), Predominantly by women, these are found with sample rules-Save, accumulate and give loan to each other. Micro-credit is a newly worked out technique to get rid of the rural folk from the clutches of moneylenders and other mafia like land grabbers.

Moinuddin Ahmed's article, 'Buying Behavious—Refrigerator, is a very fascinating article which studies and examines the market trends in the buying behavious and psychological, social, and traditional practices of buying new articles of consumption. Marketing is a ancient art, it has been practiced in one form or the other since the days of Adam and Eve. But as a management discipline, it is of recent origin. Marketing strategy is a set of objectives, policies and rules. It is the fine tuning of marketing mix to the target market. The article minutely studies the consumer behaviour, consumer research and the Indian Market and factors affecting consumers behavious, Socio-cultural environment, psychological field of Consumers. The study examines consumer behaviour towards purchase of refrigerators and identify the future which influence the purchase. It is concluded that before buying a consumer consults his relatives, other users of the articles and children have greater influence in the purchase of the refrigerators.

Surbhi Agarwal's article, 'Contract Farming: An implication for the Corporate World' is a timely article and reveals the new techniques in the agribusiness. In this era of globalization and liberalization, the agribusiness is changing at a fast pace. Various methods have been emerged like Contract Farming in which Companies are joining hands with the farmers and the whole agriculture activity is shaping the agriculture as the agribusiness. Many Companies like Reliance, Pepsi, ITC etc. have come up with their formulas to grasp the benefits existing in their business. Several national and multinational processors or fast food chains are increasingly entering into contract/alliances with the farmers to encourage them to cultivate farm products of desired quality by providing them not only seeds and other inputs but also assured procurement of the produce at pre-decided prices. Marketing tie-ups between farmers and processors or bulk purchasers have special significance for small farmers. The article is critical and detailed discussion is furnished for the wake-up readership. Also discussed various models.

Amit Singh's article, 'The Practice of Untouchability in India, discusses age old social evil of untouchability prevailed in India since time immemorial. It is a legal, moral and social wrong. It is the byproduct of caste system. The article delineates the historical development of untouchability and efforts generated since time of Buddha (500 BC). It shows how the great saints created spiritual equality and how social reformers, like Raja Rammohun Roy, Dada Panduranga, GD Deshmukh, etc. tried to abolish untouchability. Another social reformer Jotiba Phule's tireless efforts for the abolition of untouchability are discussed. Efforts of Lokmanya Tilak, Raja Shahu, VR Shinde, SM Mate, Gandhiji, Dr. BR Ambedkar, Kanshiram cannot be forgotten. The article beautifully discusses the topics in a convincing manner. It also details constitutional and other legal provisions provided in the Indian Constitution, various commissions appointed for scheduled Castes and Scheduled Tribes and other Backward Classes. The article completely and in details, highlights all the aspects of untouchability in India.

SP Singh's article, ' Sustainable Desertification Management through Ecological Indicators: A study of Gwalior Division' is a scientific and technical study of the problem. As per MAB (Man and Biosphere) Panel, it is very difficult to understand the process of desertification. Therefore, it is vital to understand and search remedy for the causes of desertification. SAARC Meeting on 7 December, 1990, on the Status of desertification in Africa and the methodology for its assessment, focused on the application of new Satellite based remote sensing technology, including NDVI Interpretations. The article has analyzed and brought forward subjects and results of several studies carried out on the subject, including the conventions by United Nations Organization and its other organs. UN Convention to Combat Desertification (CCD), provides a modern framework for international cooperation against desertification. The space limitations force me to limit all the conventions etc. here. The article studied only the problem in Gwalior Division. It is a field based study. Sampling framework has been chalked out from several villages of districts of Datia, Sheopur, Gwalior, Morena and Bhind. The article also assesses the Comparative Socio-economic impact of desertification in the studied villages. The research paper is stuffed with several useful tables/ statistics. Status of Wildlife is also studied. The author also gives several recommendations on the subject.

Therefore, as outlined earlier, all these research papers neatly and deeply streamline the subject matter and put forward use of new technology, latest topics of current use, which have been included in the collection of the book. Application of new models and statistics at internationally accepted norms, are used in all the research papers which can definitely prove of great help in the study of respective disciplines, since they include encyclopedic latest and scientific information. The book will prove an asset to Human Resource Management and technology research students. All the libraries and information centers will find the book extremely useful. I am also hopeful that the book will serve concerned readership to their best satisfaction. If some of these articles show their practical presence in the study of students and research scholars, we will consider our mission fulfilled.

Shahnaz Mirza

1

RELATIONSHIP IT NETWORKS GETTING FIT OR EXHAUSTED: LIMITS TO RELATIONSHIP MARKETING?

Abdulrahman Al-Juboori, Rashad Al-saed,
Neetham Sweedan& Syed Ahmad Rizwan

INTRODUCTION

Business to day is so complex and difficult, survival so hazardous, competitive and fraught with danger that existence depends upon the day-to day mobilisation of everybody's intelligence. Industry can on longer rely upon a system where managers plan, co-ordinate, motivate and organise.

How is the IT industry to release the undoubted potential of its people? What contracts need is some all-encompassing approach that taps into people's abilities. Employees want more than their pay and job security; they also want some meaning to their lives. If contractors can links this need for *meaning* to individual and organisational *purposes* we can begin to release the pent-up potential of staff. If people know what a company stands for and, most importantly, are convinced the company will stick by those beliefs then they are shielded form their worse fear-capriciousness. However, employees are intolerant of companies that don't walk the way they talk and quickly spot double standards. Employees put a lot of themselves into their jobs and if they are ignored, betrayed, or discarded it hurts, most companies do all these detrimental things, often through carelessness, and people build up defences against being hurt.

AN INTERNAL VERSUS AN EXTERNAL PERSPECTIVE

What is needed is a set of values that assure people the company will be true to its word. Yet firms struggle to honest articulate their values but without them commitment will be illusive. The value structure of an organisation is a set of informal role prescriptions indicating what behaviours, attitudes and characteristics are acceptable or unacceptable. However, although the value structure may exert a profound influence on decisions and actions by people they may not be fully aware of the nature of the value structure within which they operate. If, however, there is agreement between organisation members regarding good and bad role behaviour then the more effective on organisation is likely to be in achieving its goals. This agreement should not only be amongst superiors but also, amongst and subordinates and if there is consistency in viewing roles then conflict is at a minimum. A consistent value structure between individuals gives managers a clear picture of desired behaviour patterns and also enables them to act on this picture, assuming, of course, that the value structure contributes to goal attainments. Without a consistent value structure individuals are pulling and being pulled in conflicting directions, there is inconsistency. We also need to encourage trust by sticking to our values so that, not only does trust grow, but also the life of the organisation becomes more predictable.

Values and trust encourage people to think and improve what they do once they know what an organisation stands for and they believe it is sufficiently trustworthy to allow them to commit then they truly begin to extend themselves. Once this commitment has been achieved then by empowering people we can convert this commitment into contribution. The issue is whether this kind of change requires a shift in the structure of the organisation in the wake of the attitudes that underpin the culture. This will be returned to near the end of the paper.

CULTURE AND PERSPECTIVE

Culture has been defined as the way in which a group of people solves problems (Trompenaars, 1994). The problems were defined in terms of marketing as being narrow:

CULTURE AND MARKETING MIX

The concepts of the *marketing mix*, with its four Ps, have been with us for bouts 40 years (Grönroos 1993). Product, price, place and promotion remained the marketing truth, the "Holy Grail". The 4Ps are different factors of competition, which are blended into the marketing mix, which produces optimal profit. Mass market for consumer of the 1950s and 1960s suited the 4Ps because this limited number of marketing factors seemed to fit the typical situation of the time for distribution system and commercial mass media. It might be thought that those factors might vary in other markets, but nevertheless this marketing mix became and remained, the marketing model in almost every industry and economic sector. In the wake of this a marketing profession emerged. The profession developed its own *functional activity* with its own *marketing department*. This became quite separate from other functions. These specialists carried out tasks such as:

- *Marketing analysis*
- *Advertising*
- *Sales promotion*

From the perspective of others in the firm, the marketing department takes care of client *Needs* and *Want, the rest of us do not need to bother, we can leave the marketers to get on with their market research, market share and public relations, whilst we do the "real" work. Marketers joined this "conspiracy" with their attempts, often successful; to care out an "empire" within the organisation based upon micro-economic theory and behavioural sciences. Early criticism led to them attempting to extend their territory and, supported by academia the 4Ps soon became the 7Ps and the 15Ps (Gummesson, 1994). Kotler and others continually advocate extending the "empire", even claiming that everything is marketing. However, marketers did not seem to be addressing the pace of change in fast moving and fragmenting markets, perhaps the marketers empire had over-reached itself and was about to implode.*

The marketing miss model has therefore led to a loss of credibility by the marketing function in service industries which has been solved by downsizing or closing and banning the use of the word marketing. Perhaps we need to reconsider the 4Ps as:

- *Polemical:* given to disputing, controversial, "we are all marketers now".
- *Perspective:* prescribing laying down rules, custom or long continued use, "before we get down to business another double gin and tonic please"
- *Parable tic:* a false vision, "when may love swears that she is made of truth, I do believe her, though I know she lies" (Shakespeare, C 1596).
- *Problematical:* questionable, doubtful, "partnering is the future way"

THE RISE OF RELATIONSHIP MARKETING: THE KING IS DEAD

Instead of viewing clients as, someone *To* whom marketing is done we need to consider them as someone *For* whom marketing is done.

If the traditional form of marketing mix is more relevant to consumer packaged goods what might be more effective in this service-based IT industry? The suggestion, of course is relationship marketing. Marketing seen as relationship networks, interactive and holistic. Marketing is becoming or is about setting up informational and formal client alliances from which will develop enquiry, dialogue and empathy.

The picture has become more complex. The nature of problems has a far wider horizon that conceived. Marketing is not a hermetically sealed function in terms of concepts, profession nor functionally defined departments within the organisation. The culture is complex and the problem flow from this.

Culture problems have been defined as:

- Relationships with other people
- Passage of time
- Relationship with the environment (Trompenaars, 1994).

Taking the first category of relationships, there are relations internal to the corporate environment and external relations. One perspective that has become increasingly dominant is *relationship marketing*. Relationship marketing concerns external relations, derived from the Nordic School of Marketing, whose concern has been for focus upon business-to-business marketing in service environments (sees for example Grönroos. 1990:1993).

As a body of theory, relationship marketing proposes that the successful management of marketing in the external environment is dependent upon the way in which relations are conducted internally (Storbacka *et al*, 1994). Relationship marketing is about building long term relationships, identifying key business processes that help in training clients, developing trust. Clearly a relationship exists between culture and relationship marketing but is this relationship beneficial to firms in the IT industry or, indeed, even to clients? How can mutual loyalties and commitment be developed and maintained firms as constantly being re-designed or re-engineered?

CONTRADICTIONS OF CULTURE AND ECONOMICS

The Economical of Modern Management

In parallel to move towards relationship marketing, there have been other economic processes at work. As organisation in general responded to the changing external environment, a number of financially driven decisions emerged. These can be summarised as:

- Return to core business
- Delayering management to create flat structures
- Just-in-time.

The Focus of Marketing

Marketing on other hand demands a shift away from pure efficiency towards effectiveness. A shift of focused is required from an inward looking efficiency towards an external concentration on effectiveness, as well as efficiency.

In IT the internal-external focus has not followed the advocated theory.

Table 1. The Shift of Focus in IT Industry

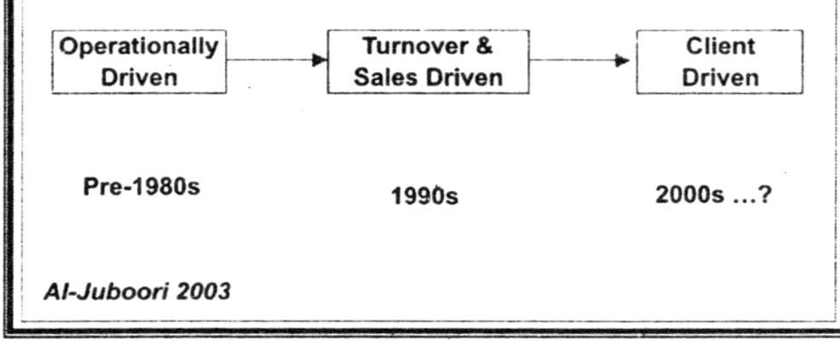

Being *Client driven* does not necessarily mean being *client orientation* (Abdulrahman Al-Juboori, forthcoming 2003). It is clients who have taken many of the key initiatives, for example in cost reductions and partnering.

Sheth *et al* (1988) identified some relationship marketing guidelines:

1. Create an obsession for quality internally and in external relationships.
2. Respond to client needs and requirements quickly and courteously.
3. Improve the price value to clients by reducing the cost of doing business.
4. Develop new products/services by anticipating future client expectations
5. Organise terms and functions around clients and markets.
6. Encourage active involvement of clients in product/service design and process improvement.
7. Build a client retention culture by basing reward and recognition systems on retention and loyalty.

For Sheth and other advocates relationship marketing success requires and increase in costs and investment with consequential restructuring (sees for example Storbacka, 1994 for service industries and IT construction specifically Abdulrahman Al-Juboori, forthcoming 2003). This creates a tension in general terms.

The Anorexic Contractor

Many companies have become so focussed on core activities and so lean production and services delivery; it could be argued that they do not have the economic capacity to adjust to the changing market. Perhaps they have become or are fast becoming company organisation. The visible evidence for this is the new wave of take-overs that has started in the financial sectors. Take-over becomes a prime means to overcome corporate resources of companies-it puts a bit of fat back into the system. In IT industry in general relationship marketing practice has followed the theory more precisely. In construction IT practice has fallen short of the theory and so has the outcome (Abdulrahman Al-Juboori, 2003). The investment has yet to be made and clients have yet to fully deliver mutual benefits (Abulrahaman Al-Juboori, 2003) the reason for this the drive to keep overheads down in order to survive recessive conditions. The essence of the argument is this:

In construction IT, there is therefor a ***contradiction*** *between the pursuit of Efficiency in terms of modern management practices and Effectiveness that embraces relationship marketing management. This has yet to be appreciated by IT industry and addressed in practice.*

Bulimia and Blame

Relationship marketing spans the organisation and encourages the blending of functional competencies through team oriented process management. The bottom line in trust, both within the organisation and between the organisation, clients, suppliers, sub-contractors, influence markets and recruitment markets. How are contractors to persuade people to trust each other and co-operate as through the concept of relationship marketing the attempts to transform companies to meet the demands partnering and other forms of relationship marketing for the future?

If IT industry in general is showing any evidence of IT company (for example ANOREXIA CORPORATION), then contracting must have reached advanced stages of bulimia. It does not even perceive its own condition with any degree of accuracy. The IT industry:

- Missed the opportunity to restructure into clients oriented businesses in the early 2000s.
- Continues to sees partnering as a means to sell services and not invest in service delivery and client satisfaction.
- Applies structural solutions to problems of marketing process by setting up separate divisions for each service.
- Still overall educates the client to select price despite its own protestations.

The cause rests with the analysis set out at the start of paper. The investment, if any, and most energy is directed towards the blame culture. It is this that has to be shifted before the process can be addressed. Only after that relevant structural change and economic budgets be prescribed that meet the requirements of relationship marketing is made. (A. Sh. Al-Juboori) has called this the culture of the Street Fighting Man:

I believe there has been something of an indulgence in being special and different. It provides an excuse when things do not go so well. This operates at a sector level. It also operates very powerfully within corporate hierarchies and for individuals. It is used on the one hand to stifle creativity and avoid change:

"We've always done it like that". It is used for individuals to avoid taking responsibility- a thin veil to hide behind. It is a type of posturing resonant of the street culture rather than corporate culture.

Gangs leaders posture at the street corners vying for fight. The bellboys always try to get other to do their dirty work for them. Verbal punches hit hard, physical ones are sometimes let loose, but cowardice lurks in the shadows and the heart is filled with fear. The management style of many in contracting companies is based upon the Street Fighting Man. Banter and joking, usually at the expense of others, is used for point scoring things are on a reasonably even keel. If that fails or the pressure is great, verbal abuse and shouting are the weapons to install fear and maintain power in the office corridor-a blame culture. This is the street corner expression of being special and different. It is an excuse for failing to address the insecurities the individual feels. It is an excuse for failing to address the shortcomings of the corporate body. Passing the buck and ruling fear is ultimately divisive both for the employer and for the individual who is torn apart in managing the conflicts and contradictions of their feelings. The Street Fighting Man knows that eventually he is to be replaced by someone throwing a harder verbal punch.

The solution lies in the external focus. Seeking to serve those in the organisation and seeking serve those in the external market:

The strong man rises above this. Overcoming the internal conflicts enable them to help others rather than focusing upon themselves. This paradox of focusing outside oneself to resolve internal conflict works because the individual is taking responsibility. Has this got anything to do with marketing? It is central for successful marketing. As a focus outside oneself encourages helping others, who are the groups who are to be helped? The client is the first group. A client orientation moves more to the fore. Posturing has yielded to delivering the goods. The staff is the second group. This helps them to overcome their Street Fighting mentality both through direct help, such as training, and indirectly through demonstration so that they too become more eager to serve. Contracting and consultant practice is, or should be, about working with people, not against them. Marketing too, especially relationship marketing which has relationship building rather than destruction at its core.

CONCLUSION

Failure to address these issues of internal focus will mean that relationship marketing will be consigned to the waste bin of fickle in It, sweeping partnering, alliances and all forms of co-operation with it.

The outcome will be a return to the marketing mix. "Long Live the King", as price dominates all and contracting remains fragmented IT industry of intense competition and unsatisfied clients, which experiences the occasional short lived boom of considerable instability. The solution in investment in relationship marketing in orders to deliver added value. This is effectiveness, although efficiencies will follow in the longer run (Abdulrahman Al-Juboori 2003). The path is a tortuous one, because the solution is nether neither structural nor budgetary in itself. The cultural approach has highlighted the need to address attitudes and processes as a prerequisite.

The question posed to you is this: "is your organisation getting IT fit or exhausted?"

References

Al-Juboori, Abdulrahman (forthcoming 2003), Key Concepts of the Strategic Industrial Marketing, Al Manahej-Jordan.

Grönroos, C. (1990), Service Management and Marketing: Managing the Moments of Truth in Service Competition, Free Press/ Lexington Books, Mass.

Grönroos, C. (1990), From Scientific Management to Service Management: A Management Perspective for the Age of Service Competition, *International Journal of Service Industry Management*, (5) 1 and pp. 5-20.

Shakespeare, W. (c 1596), Sonnet.

Sheth, J. N. Gardner, D. M. and Garrett, D. E. (1988), Marketing Theory: Evolution and Evaluation, Wiley, New York.

Storbacka, K., Strandvik, T. and Gronroos, C. (1994), Managing Customer Relationships for Profit: Dynamics of Relationship Quality, *International Journal of Services Industry Management* (5) 5, pp. 21-38.

Trompenaars, F. (1994), Riding the Waves of Culture, Nicholas Brealey, Publishing Ltd.

2

BUYING BEHAVIOUR: A STUDY OF CHILDREN'S INFLUENCE ON THE PURCHASE DECISION REGARDING REFRIGERATOR

Moinuddin Ahmad

INTRODUCTION

Marketing is indeed an ancient art; it has been practiced in one form or the other since the days of Adam and Eve. Its emergence as a management discipline, however, is of relatively recent origin. And within this relatively short period it has gained a great deal of importance and stature. In fact, to-day most management thinkers and practitioners the world over, regard marketing as the most important of all management functions in any business.[1]

Marketing strategies are concerned primarily with identifying opportunities to serve the target market profitably and this should be done so effectively that the competitors may find it difficult to take business away on a profitable basis. Formulation of strategy begins with the setting of company goals and can be undertaken after analysis of marketing situation.[2]

Study of consumer behavior is basic to all marketing activities and analysis of marketing opportunities must precede the formulation of strategies. Marketing strategy is a set of objective, policies and rules that guides overtime, the firms marketing effects——its' level, mix and allocation———partly independent and partly in response to changing environmental and competitive conditions, According to Kotler[3], marketing strategy is the fine tuning of marketing mix to the target market.

CONSUMER BEHAVIOUR

One of the few common denominators among all of us, despite our differences, is that, above all, we are consumers. That is, we use or consume on a regular basis food, clothing, shelter, transportation, education, brooms, dishes, vacations, necessities, luxuries, services, even ideas. In addition, as consumers, we play a vital, role in the health of the economy–local, national, and international.[4] The essence of the modern marketing concept is that all elements of business should be geared towards the satisfaction of consumers. This requires a thorough understanding of their behavior and buying motivations. This helps marketer to segment the market for effective penetration. The philosophy of a business should be such that every activity, operations & policy of a firm should have its root in consumer satisfaction. Thus, consumer behavior is an integral factor in the ebb and flow of all business[5] in a consumer-oriented society.

The term "consumer behaviour" refers to the behaviour that consumers display in searching for, purchasing, using, evaluating, and disposing of products and services that they expect will satisfy their needs. The study of consumer behaviour is the study of how individuals make decisions to spend their available resources (time, money, effort) on consumption related items. It includes the study of what they buy, why they buy it, when they buy it, where they buy it, how often they buy it. And how often they use it.[6]

Engell, Kollat and Black well have defined consumer behaviour as: "The acts of individuals directly involved in obtaining and using economic goods and services including the decision process that precede and determine those acts."

In a developed economy where the production and distribution system is complex, and the available range of goods and services is wide, a full under standing of the consumption decisions in such places requires the study of every aspect of a person's entire life time experience. Thus, in the broadest sense, consumer behaviour and human behaviour would be identified fields of study.[7]

Information on consumer behaviour is generally used to predict or diagnose consumer's action in markets, what he buys, why he buy and how he buy's what motivates him to buy, why he buy's a specific brand, why does he shifts his preferences from one brand to another, how he reacts to a new product introduced in the market etc. These are some of the questions that are of perennial interest to the marketing man. Because it is around these questions that the product and promotion strategies of the marketing man ultimately revolve. In all his plans he makes certain assumptions as to how the consumers would behave.[8] Knowledge of consumer and factors affecting buying behaviour is thus a fundamental necessity for a marketing man.

CONSUMER RESEARCH & THE INDIAN MARKET

The marketing concept is built on the premise that marketers first identify consumer needs and then develop products and services to satisfy those needs. Consumer research is used to better understand consumption behaviour. It is used to identify both felt and unfelt (latent) needs, to learn how consumers perceive products and brands and stores, what their attitudes are before and after promotional campaigns, and how and why they make their consumption decisions. Many of the applications of consumer research are managerial in perspective: they are designed to help a marketer make specific marketing decision concerning product, price, promotion, and distribution. Consumer research provides the basis for the development of new product and service concepts to meet targeted consumer needs. It also enables the marketer to build consumer "meaning" into the product or service by discovering which attributes are most important to the target market and integrating them into the product or service design.[9]

Theoretically consumer all over the world is the same as far as their basic needs and desires are concerned. However, the forces operating on consumers in developing countries like India, and the under developed countries of the third world, are far different from those that operate on consumers in the affluent west. Opportunities available to marketers are also very different.

As a result of government's planned efforts and more especially due to the bold policies initiated by the Government of India towards liberalization the Indian markets are undergoing rapid transformation. Household consumption of many products has grown fast both urban and rural India in recent years. It has cut across incomes irrespective of urban or rural markets. In addition Indian market has grown both in sophistication and variety. Gas stoves, microwave ovens, music systems incorporating the latest international features, electric pressure cookers, infrared superheat cookers, sophisticated scooters, motor cycles and other two wheelers, credit cards, jeans, designer shirts and a wide variety of services are being considered as indispensable necessities by middle and even lower classes across the country.

Till recently consumer research was a largely neglected field of study in the developing and under developed countries. Even in comparatively more industrially advanced and enlightened more industrially advanced and enlightened countries like India managements invested scarce effort and still lesser inclination to understand consumer behaviour. This was not surprising in a country where product markets were largely 'sellers' market-marked by perpetual shortages, where 'demarcating' was required more than marketing. But with the entry of multinationals, proliferation of brands and increase in advertising and promotion expenditure the situation dramatically changed form sellers to buyers market.

Earlier the manufacturers offered the consumers what they produced but after liberalisation it was the consumer who started dictating what the companies should offer. There was a demand for better quality of products and services improved performance, more information, and effective after sales service, greater variety and choice.

For the first time, companies started focusing on the customer. It was realized that to face the new economic realities and to survive and grow in a market that was becoming increasingly competitive, the corporations have not only to continuously monitor the changing customer needs but also delight the customer by delivering him unexpected additional benefits and value. It was also clear that they might have to devote greater efforts to market research, product development, distribution and advertising to answer the specific needs and requirements.

FACTORS AFFECTING CONSUMER BEHAVIOUR

Consumer decisions are affected by various factors listed below. Most of them are controllable for a marketer but must be taken into account for examining their influence on consumer behavior. Broadly we can divide them into two categories socio-cultural (external) environment and psychological field of consumer (individual determinant). However, the external environmental factors do not affect the consumer decision process directly, but filters through individual determinant to influence the decision process.

Socio-cultural (External) Environment

Culture

Sub culture

Social class

Reference & Social groups

Family

Personal influence and the opinion leadership process, diffusion of innovations.

Psychological Field of Consumer (Individual Determinist)

Motivation

Perception

Learning

Personality

Attitudes.

Wells & Reynolds[10] conducted a study in 1965 and they found that children's play influencing role on consumer behaviour of the families. Young children influence family decisions as soon as they possess the basis family members. Older children make more direct participation in family consumption activities. This takes place in various ways, viz. (1) by making personal purchase i.e. by spending small amount of money on their own. (2) by making direct requests in the store. (3) by making direct request at home and (4) by passive dictation (parents buy what children consume willingly and avoid buying what they resist).

Ward and Wackman[11] studied the influence of demographics; parent-child interaction and mothers mass communication behaviour on children's purchase influence attempts and parental yielding. The study was conducted for twenty-two products categorised as relevant foods, less relevant foods, durable, notions and toiletries other products.

The study found that the mediating influence of children varies across product categories, it is expected to be very high for relevant food products such as cereals and toys but lower in other products which usually they do not consume viz. Gasoline, vacuum cleaners, etc.

Carron & Ward[12] has examined the influence of mass media on children purchase desire & parents decision-making regarding children's desires. The study reveals that television is the most important source of information for children and parents both, followed by friends. Middle class children made more requests then upper class children & proved to be more influential. Yielding by parents however depend upon their social class & type of item requested.

Burr and Burr[13] in their study tried to find how do parents' responds to their children request and to their appeals attached with the products both durable & non-durable. They found that parents consider child's appeals attached with some prize/premium. Also, certain appeals like 'other's use it' or 'saw it on TV' or 'we want to learn/enjoy', etc., also falls in consideration zone. Not only this, parents combine it with information like economy, ease of use, safety, esteem, social etc. before making a purchase. Matching leads to purchase. The study concluded by saying that the mediating influence of children for specific brands increases with the increases in exposure to commercials as well as parents familiarity with the stimuli.

Kestorm, Tansuhaj & Foxmann[14] observed that socialization is a reciprocal process. Just as parents socialise children, children may also socialise their parents. Today's child is more informed & observant and is capable of learning "expressive" assets of consumption.

The refrigerator market in India has not only grown in numbers in last few years, but also witnessed a complete change in terms of market shares enjoyed by various players in the industry. Refrigerator's accounts for the largest segment of the Indian white-goods market since they are considered necessities by many middle-class families. The present study of the representative's sample is mainly descriptive type with the field study and partly causal in nature, as it seeks to find out the factors which influence the consumer decision making process and preferences, with respect to refrigerator's brands and correlate them with income, age, education, profession etc. In the present study, the element is a household because the focus is on buying behavior of consumer (regarding refrigerator) who is an inmate of a household.

HYPOTHESES

The following hypothesis was developed on the basis of the various studies made by other researchers.

H_0 The variable "Children's influence on the respondent's purchase decision regarding refrigerator" is independent of family income.

Introduction to the Problem

The refrigerator market in India has not only grown in numbers in last few years, but also witnessed a complete change in terms of market shares enjoyed by various players in the industry. The demand for refrigerators has grown from 11,000 units in 1969 to about 2.2 million units in 1996. Refrigerators account for the largest segment of the Indian white-goods market since they are considered necessities by many middle-class families. During 2002 Indians purchased about 3.4 m refrigerators. Compared with the double-digit growth of the 1990s, however, this represents flat demand. Sales actually declined in 2001. This was mainly because of the "wealth effect"—the depressed property and stock markets left everyone feeling poorer and this affected demand for consumer durables. Since 2001 demand has been rising steadily, though not at the high pace of earlier years. The factors affecting the demand for refrigerators are:

Growth in personal disposable income

Growth in urbanization

Growth in female work force

Trend towards smaller families

Behavior of a consumer is influenced by social, psychological and personal factors. *Social factors* that influence consumer decision making are social class reference groups, votes and family, and culture and sub culture. *Psychological factors* are internal forces within people that effect buying decisions; they are motives, perception, learning, and personality. *Personal factors* include situational and demographic factors and unique to each person. Situational factor are conditions or circumstances that exist when a consumer is making a purchase decision. *Demographic factors* are personal characteristics such as age, sex, race and ethnic group. The consumer vary in their consumption pattern based on geographical location, density of population, urban rural features of the consumer, age, literacy level, income level linguistic diversity, religion and dress, food habits and festival celebrated. Since consumer is one who will decide whether or not to buy a particular product, so it become relevant to explore why a common man buy's a refrigerator and how does he buy.

OBJECTIVES OF THE STUDY

1. To examine how consumer behaves towards purchase of refrigerator.
2. To identify, who in a family, influences and who makes a decision regarding purchase of refrigerator.

RESEARCH DESIGN

The present study of the representative's sample is mainly DESCRIPTIVE TYPE with the field study and partly CAUSAL in nature as it seeks to find out consumer preference with respect to refrigerator's brands and correlate them with income, age, education, profession etc. In other words, the present study attempts to describe the characteristic of certain groups of interest to the marketer; attempts to estimate the proportion of people in a given population who behave in a certain way; develop inference whether certain variables are associated for example income and price of refrigerators, status and special feature of refrigerator and makes specific predictions for specified future period.

Sample Design

Sample design was determined before the data was collected, and for developing the sampling design, following points were considered with regard to the present study:

(a) Population or Universe: Population or universe is the aggregate of all elements possessing certain specified characteristics which need to be studied and defined prior to sample population Since the present study is conducted in Lucknow city, the population is finite i.e. 2, 93,130 number of households, according to 1991 census.

Element	:	Household
Sampling Unit	:	Ward, Colonies, Household
Extent	:	Lucknow City
Time	:	2001–2002.

(b) Element: In the present study, the element is household because the focus is on buying behavior of consumer (regarding refrigerator) who is an inmate of a household.

(c) Sampling Units: It is that element or elements considered available for selection in some stage of the sampling process. A

decision has to be taken concerning a sampling unit before selecting sample. Sampling unit may be a geographical one such as state, district, village etc. or a construction unit such as house, flat etc. or it may a social unit such as family, club, school etc. or it may be an individual. In the present study, a sample of households is selected in three stages.

(d) Sampling Frame: It is also known as 'source list' from which sample is to be drawn. It contains the names of all items of a universe. Since, the present study undergoes multistage sampling process, hence a list of wards and a list of colonies/administrative areas was needed which was taken from Lucknow Nagar Nigam, Lucknow.

Although a lot of attention is paid to prepare this suitable frame, but certain shortcomings leading to frame error can not be avoided. The selected households may not necessarily posses a refrigerator. In some cases, refrigerator was not purchased, it was gifted to them. Still, in other cases, the selected households, possessing a refrigerator was found locked.

(e) Sampling Design: Representation of entire universe is only possible through the sampling technique. Considerable care has been taken in selecting the sample so that is convenient in terms of size and capable enough to represent the entire universe (which is Lucknow city in this case).

In the present study, sample has been derived on the basis of three consecutive stages, at the first stage and second stage probability sampling was applied and at the third stage, convenience sampling is done deliberately, because of non availability of definite number of households in each colony/administrative area. So the researcher ended up with what is known as 'Multi–Stage Sampling'.

Lucknow city is divided into 110 wards which are further divided into colonies/ administrative areas; a list of the same was obtained from Lucknow Nagar Nigam, Lucknow. From this list, cumulative totaling of the colonies/ administrative areas is done, and the cumulative total of the colonies/ administrative areas was found to be 856. In the present study, the scholar has used Multi Stage Sampling Design. In the first stage, simple random sampling is used in which random number 27 was selected as the first unit, as 27 is the district code of Lucknow.

ANALYSIS AND INTERPRETATION

Out of a total of 500 respondents, 297 (59.40%) fall in the age group between 21-30 years. Which is maximum followed by 83 (16.60%) respondents in the age group are between 41-50 years followed 78 (15.60%) in the age group 31-40 years and 42 (8.4%) respondents belong to the age group 51and above.

Family Income of Respondents

Nearly 10.60% of respondents belong to income category less than Rs. 50,000, 13.40%of respondents belong to income category Rs. 50,001 to 60,000, 46.40%respondents belong to Rs. 60,001 to 1,50,000 and the rest 29.60% belong to Rs. 1,50,001 and above.

Family Size of Respondents

Out of total 500 respondents, 3.20% are single, 50.40% have 2-4 members living in their family, 41.60% respondents have their family size 5-7 members and only 4.80% belong to large families of members 8 and above.

Occupation of Respondents

Out of 500 respondents 51.4 % belong to the service class, 34.8 % to business class, 8.6 % are Professional, 3.2% are Students and 2.2% are Housewives

Sex of Respondents

Sex	*No. of Respondents*	*Percentage*
Male	322	64.4 %
Female	178	35.6 %
Total	500	100.0%

Source: Opinion poll.

The above table is self–explanatory and needs no further explanation, besides the fact that respondents comprising of selected sample are taken from both the strata.

To test the awareness of the respondents about the different brand of refrigerators, they were asked to mention the name of the brand, which came to their mind. There was no respondent who could not recall any brand name. As many as fourteen brands were recalled.

The highest brand awareness is for Kelvinator (87per cent), followed by L.G (72.8 per cent).

The choice of the preferred brand is only indicative. Consumer choice and preference is highly complex, often tentative and hypothetical phenomenon. The only finality is when he actually buy's a brand. Nonetheless taken as an aggregate–it is certainly a definite pointer indicating the general popularity of a brand at a given point of time.

Table 1
Influence of Family Income on Capacity of Refrigerator

Family Income	*90 Ltr.*	*165 Ltr.*	*220 Ltr.*	*280 Ltr.*	*310 Ltr.*	*330 Ltr.*	*Total*
Below 50,000	2	17	17	10	2	5	53
	(3.77)	(32.07)	(32.07)	(18.8)	(3.77)	(9.43)	
50,001–60,000	1	23	21	8	11	3	67
	(1.49)	(34.32)	(31.34)	(11.9)	(16.4)	(4.47)	
60,001–1,50,000	0	87	80	20	23	22	232
	(0.0)	(37.5)	(34.48)	(8.62)	(9.91)	(9.48)	
1,50,001 & Above	0	43	38	30	14	23	148
	(0.0)	(29.05)	(25.67)	(20.3)	(9.45)	(15.5)	
Total	3	170	156	68	50	53	500

Source: Opinion Poll.

Out of 53 respondents in the family income group below Rs. 50,000. 32.7per cent of respondents prefer 165 Lit. capacity and 220 Lit. respectively18.8 per cent of respondents preferred 280 Lit. 9.4 per cent 330 Lit. and 3.7 per cent to 90 Lit. For 67 respondents in the family income group of Rs. 50,001-60,000, 34.3 per cent of respondents prefer 165 Lit, 31.4 per cent 220 Lit, 16.4 per cent 310 Lit, 4.4 per cent 330 Lit, and 1.4 per cent 90 Lit. In the family income group of Rs. 60,001-1,50,000 having 232 respondents, 37.5 per cent 165 Lit, 34.4 per cent 220 Lit, 9.9 per cent 310 Lit, 9.4 per cent 330 Lit, and 8.6 per cent 280 Lit, and non preferred 90 Lit.

Out of 148 respondents belonging to the income group Rs. 1,50.001 and above, 29.5 per cent preferred 165 Lit, 25.6 per cent preferred 220 Lit, 20.2 per cent preferred 280 Lit, 15.5 per cent preferred 330 Lit, and 9.4 per cent preferred 310 Lit, but non preferred 90 Lit.

It can be said that preference for 165 Lit. refrigerator is irrespective of family income. Also from the table it is evident that as the family income increases the preference for larger capacity refrigerator increases but for 90 Lit, it declines.

Table 2
Pre–Purchase Consultation

	No. of Respondents	
Elements of Consultation	*Yes*	*No*
Father	283	217
	(56.6)	(43.4)
Mother	260)	240
	(52.0	(48.0)
Wife	145	177
	(45.03)	(54.97)
Husband	69	109
	(38.67)	(61.24)
Children	91	409
	(18.2)	(81.8)
Friends/ Relatives	260	240
	(52.0)	(48.0)
Dealers of the Product	216	284
	(43.2)	(56.8)
Dealers who are competitors	112	388
	(22.4)	(77.6)
Users of the Product	292	208
	(58.4)	(41.6)

Base: 322 for element no. 3 (wife) as there are 322 males, and 178 for element no. 4 (Husband) as there are 178 females, and 500 for all other elements of consultation.

Table 2 highlights the pre purchase behaviour of the respondents with emphasis on elements being considered for consultation, surprisingly out of 500 respondents 322 were males and 178 females, in which all of them were married. It is found that 56.6per cent consult their friend relative, 43.2 per cent consult their mother, 18.2per cent their children 52 per cent their friends relative 43.2 per cent consulted the dealer of the product and 58.4 per cent consulted the user or the product. Out of 322 males 45.3 per centconsulted their wives, where else out of 178 females 38.7per cent consulted their husbands.

Hence we can conclude that before purchasing a refrigerator, consultation by maximum number of respondents is made through user of product, Friend relative, father & mother, wives, user and dealer of product. Hence they could be said as opinion leaders secondly children also play an important role in pre purchase consultation, thirdly all the females buyers have not consulted their husbands in buying such a big thing, as the possibility is that women are considered better in managing homes.

Through Table 3 an attempt is made to examine the influence of family income on respondents pre-purchase consultation and also to examine the trend. There are 53 respondents who belong to the family income group below Rs. 50,000, 58.4per cent consult the User of the product, this is the largest per cent of the total, 56.6per cent consult their Father and Mother, 13.2per cent consult Wife, 11.3per cent consult Husband, 9.43 per cent Children, 47.1per cent consult their Friends and Relative, 26.4per cent Dealer of the product and 20.7 per cent consult Dealer who is competitor.

In the income group of Rs. 50,001 to 60,000 there are 67 respondents, 61.9 per cent consult their Father, 50.74 per cent Mother, 37.31 per cent Wife, 10.44 per cent Husband, 22.39 per cent Children, 49.25per cent Friends Relative, 55.22per cent dealer of product, 16.41 per cent consult Dealer who is a competitor and 52.23 per cent consult User of product.

Out of 232 respondents belonging to the family income of Rs. 60,001-1,50,000, 56.3 per cent consult Father, 53.1 per cent consult Mother, 32.32 per cent Wife, 16.81 per cent Husband, 20.25 per cent Children, 55.17 per cent Friends and Relatives, 47.84 per cent Dealer of product, 25.8 per cent Dealer who is a competitor and 62.5 per cent which is the largest per cent of the total consult User of product (refrigerator).

Among the 148 respondents in the income group Rs 1, 50,001 and Above, 55.4per cent consult Father, 49.3 per cent Mother, 25.6 per cent Wife, 11.48 per cent Husband, 16.2 per cent Children, 50 per cent Friends and Relative, 36.4 per cent Dealer of product (refrigerator), 20.2 per cent Dealer who is a competitor and 54.7per cent consult the User of the product (refrigerator).

It is observed that as family income rises, the trend of Father & Mother consultation declines, and as it moves from upper middle to higher income group it is seen that the wife consultation with their husband also decreases and the respondents of the other family income groups consult the Users before purchasing a refrigerator.

Table 3
Influence of Family Income on Pre–Purchase Consultation

Family Income (p.a)	*Elements of Family Income on Pre–Purchase Consultation*								
	Father	*Mother*	*Wife*	*Husband*	*Children*	*Friends/ Relatives*	*Dealer of Product*	*Dealer of Comp. Prod.*	*Users*
50,001–60,000	4	34	25	7	15	33	37	11	35
	161.19%	50.74%	37.31%	10.44%	22.39%	49.25%	55.22%	16.41%	52.23%
60,001–1,50,000	130	123	75	39	47	128	11	60	145
	56.03%	53.01%	32.32%	16.81%	20.25%	55.17%	147.84%	25.86%	62.5%
150,001–& above	82	73	38	17	24	74	54	30	81
	55.40%	49.32%	25.67%	11.48%	16.21%	50.0%	36.48%	20.27%	54.73%
Total	283	260	145	69	91	260	216	112	292

Note: Since the same respondent has consulted more than one element hence grand total of row is not mentioned.

In this question the respondents were asked to tick only one element, which influenced them most to go in for refrigerator. From the figure we can say that for 36 per cent of respondents it is self-decision to purchase a refrigerator and they are not influenced by any one. 14.6 per cent are influenced by Father, 15.2 per cent by Mother, 12.2 per cent by Wives, 3.4 per cent by Children 5 per cent by Husband, 7.6 per cent by friends 4.6 per cent by Relatives and a very small segment is influenced by Children.

Thus on analyzing the table it is found that Mother's are the major influencer in decision making for a particular brand of refrigerator, followed by Father and Wife.

Table 4 was made to find out the impact of family income of the respondents on influences to go in for refrigerator purchase. Out of 53 respondents belonging to the income group less than Rs 50,000, 33.9 per cent are influenced by Father, 11.32 per cent by Mother, 9.43 per cent by Wife, 5.66 per cent by Husband and 3.77 per cent by Relatives. It was observed that 30.19 per cent of respondents belonging to this group were not at all influenced by any one it was their own decision.

In the family income group of Rs. 50,001-60,000 there are 67 respondents out of them 10.4 per cent are influenced by their Father, 11.94 per cent by Mother, 114.93 per centby wife, 7.46 per cent by Children, 4.48 per cent by Friends, 10.45 per cent by Relatives, 1.49 per cent by Neighbour, and 38.81 per cent were not at all influenced by any one it was their own decision.

In the family income group of Rs. 60,001-1,50,000 there are 232 respondents out of them 15.9 per cent are influenced by their Father, 17.24 per cent by Mother, 14.23 per cent by Wife, 3.45 per cent by Children, 7.76 per cent by Husband, 9.49 per cent by Friends, 5.60 per cent by Relatives, 43 per cent by Neighbour and 26.72 per cent took their own decision.

In the income group of Rs. 1,50,001 and above there are 148 respondents out of them 8.78per cent are influenced by father, 14.87 per cent by mother, 8.78 per cent by wife, 2.70 per cent by children, 3.38 per cent by husband, 6.76 per cent by friends, 67 per cent by relatives, 2.7 per cent by neighbor and 51.35per cent took their own decision.

Thus an analysis of the table reveals that most of the respondents are not influenced by any one and it is their self decision to purchase

Table 4
Impact of Family Income of Respondent on Influencers to Go in for Refrigerator Purchase

	Elements Who Influenced the Most to Go in for Refrigerator Purchase								
Family Income	*Father*	*Mother*	*Wife*	*Children*	*Husband*	*Friends*	*Relatives*	*Neighbors*	*my own decision*
Below 50,000	18	6	5	0	3	3	2	0	16
	33.96%	11.32%	9.43%	0.0%	5.66%	5.66%	3.77%	0.0%	30.19%
50,001–60,000	7	8	10	5	0	3	7	1	26
	10.45%	11.94%	14.93%	7.46%	0.0%	4.48%	10.45%	1.49%.	38.81%
60,001–150,000	35	40	33	8	18	2	13	1	62
	15.09%	17.24%	14.93%	3.45%	7.76%	29.49%	5.60%	0.43%	26.72%
1,50,001& above	13	22	13	4	5	10	1	4	76
	8.78%	14.87%	8.78%	2.70%	3.38%	6.76%	0.67%	2.70%	51.35%
Total	73	76	61	17	26	38	23	6	180

refrigerator, irrespective of the family income group to which they belong. The other elements which influenced the respondents in making decision to purchase refrigerator are Father, Mother, Wife and Children.

TESTING OF HYPOTHESIS

H_0: *The variable "children's influence on the respondent's purchase decision regarding refrigerator" is independent of family income.*

Testing of Hypothesis

Application of Chi-square test of significance to test the null Hypothesis (Ho)

Contingency Table

	Family Income PA. (In Rs.)				
Children's influence on respondents purchasing decision of refrigerators	*Below 50,000*	*50,001-60,000*	*60,001-150,000*	*Above 150,001*	*Total*
Yes	0	5	8	4	17
No	53	62	224	144	483
Total	53	67	232	148	500

$$\text{Estimated Value} = \frac{\text{Corresponding Row Total} \times \text{Corresponding Column Total}}{\text{Grand Total}}$$

Worksheet for calculation of chi-square

$$\chi^2 = \Sigma\,(O - E)^2/E$$

Observed Value(O)	*Estimated Value (E)*	*(O-E)²*	*(O-E)²/E*
0	1.802	3.2472	1.802
53	51.198	3.2472	0.06342
5	2.278	7.4092	3.25253
62	64.722	7.4092	0.11447
8	7.888	0.0125	0.00159
224	224.112	0.0125	0.00005
4	5.032	1.0650	0.21165
144	142.968	1.0650	0.00744
Total			5.45315.

Calculated value of Chi-Square = 5.45315.

The H_0 was tested by applying the chi-square test of significance in a 2 × 4 table the degree of freedom is (2-1) (4-1) = 3. The calculated value of chi-square is 5.45315. The critical value of chi-square with 3 degree of freedom at 5% level of significance is 7.815. Since the calculated chi-square is less than the critical value. Hence the hypothesis (null) H_0 is accepted. Thus it can be stated that family income had no positive effect "on the respondent's whose purchase decision were influenced by the children".

Findings

In the contemporary business environment it is need less to say that buyer/consumer holds the key for the success of any business. Therefore understanding of the buying behavior and of the target market is the essential task of the marketers who believe in the modern marketing concept.

Understanding of the consumer behavior becomes more complex when despite of overriding similarities, we find no two consumers are alike. Under the same set of drives they prefer differential products. It shows that each consumer, being a complex entity, has its own sets of special needs and priorities. Complexity results because of demographic, psychographics, cultural social and personal factors related to the consumers. The degree of complexity increases when the purchase of highly specialized durable products, such as Refrigerator is involved. The widespread development of new taste, likings and preferences, shift in the life-styles, decision making patterns, changing roles in the families, their habits etc. provides the impetus for the study of consumer behavior with respect to purchase of durable product, "Refrigerator".

The consumer durable industry consists of a large number of household use items like refrigerators, washing machines like refrigerators, washing machines, air-conditioners, desert coolers, televisions, audio equipment, videos and a large number of household and kitchen appliances like mixers-grinders, electric irons, toasters immersion rods etc., of these refrigerators, washing machines and air-conditioners are known as the white goods industry.

The demand for refrigerators has grown from 11,000 units in 1969 to about 2.2 million units in 1996. The factors affecting the demand for refrigerators are:

- Growth in personal disposable income
- Growth in urbanization
- Growth in female work force
- Trend towards smaller families

The refrigerator market in India has not only grown in numbers in last few years, but has also witnessed a complete restructuring in terms of market shares enjoyed by various players in the industry.

The market which was restricted to six players (Voltas, Allwyn, Godrej, Kelvinator, Videocon and BPL) in 1995 nas become wider in the recent past with the entry of new multinational players like Whirlpool, L.G., Samsung, Daewoo and Electrolux.

Interestingly, the new entrants in the industry have snatched around one third of the total market (32 per cent in 1999) and are poised to increase their market shares further in the coming years with the launch of new generation products in the Indian market.

The consumers demand for refrigerators peaks at two distinct periods during the year: (i) just before the summer season, i.e. March-April; and (ii) festival season (Dusshera- Diwali), i.e. October/ November and is the lowest during the monsoons. The total capacity of refrigerator manufactures has never been fully utilized because of the strong seasonality in the industry.

Marketers who understand consumer behavior towards the purchase of refrigerators enjoy a great competitive advantage in the market place .It can also help them to carve out new market segments based on variables that emerged as important discriminations among consumers for refrigerators.

The study basically attempts to explore the factors responsible for particular behavior also the effects and relationship between various parameters viz. age, family, income, education, sex, background etc. to that of other factors related to consumer perception, learning, personality, need patterns, lifestyle, social class determinants etc. by ignoring consumers. Those firms who take due consideration of consumers, their needs and preferences certainly emerge as winners. The consumers can certainly add "Midas touch" to the sales of a product or can even ruin them. Thus a keen and careful timely study of changing consumer buying behavior, their needs and preferences becomes necessary for a marketer. The present study aims to investigate thoroughly the changing behavior, buying decision influencers and identifying the decision makers for purchase of refrigerators. Besides endeavour has been made to find out those social, economic and cultural factors which acts as catalysts for actual purchase of product.

A sincere effort has been made to extract interesting facts about buying behavior. which may be of great importance for the marketer, by becoming aware of the subtle influences that persuade a consumer, marketers can certainly make an endeavor to fill the gap amidst consumer requirement and manufacturers of refrigerators.

The results of this study have been influenced by consumer's background and family size because most of the respondents belong to family size 2-4 and urban background as well.

Therefore we infer that respondents' opinions, preferences, attitudes, values and aspirations, in this study, must be contingent upon these two parameters. Also. service man, being the largest percentage of respondents, surely is affecting the results very much. The percentage of service class respondents is higher in Lucknow city.

Considering that the chosen sample owned refrigerators of different brands, sizes, and costs one can conclude that there is very high level of satisfaction among the refrigerator owners. It indicates that for durable and specialty, people go in for maximum information search and they put in enough efforts before committing their resources for a particular committing their resources for a particular product / venture and this concept has been fully vindicated here. It categorically reiterates the fact that refrigerators technology in India has come of age and the quality of Refrigerators produced in India are of high order.

Before buying a refrigerator buyers had discussed with the users of the product, their father and their mother's, friends and relatives. Hence it can concluded that before purchasing a refrigerator, consultation by maximum number of respondents is made through user of product, Friend relative, father & mother, wives, user and dealer of product. Hence they could be said as opinion leaders secondly children also play an important role in pre purchase consultation, thirdly all the females buyers have not consulted their husbands in buying such a big thing, as the possibility is that women are considered better in managing homes.

Children's influence on the respondents purchase decision regarding refrigerator is independent of family income is proved at 0.05 level of significance on applying chi-square test.

Notes and Reference

1. Kotler Philip, *Marketing Management-Analysis Planning and Control,* Prentice Hall of India, New Delhi, IV Ed., p. 130.
2. Bell Martin, L. (1972), *Marketing–Concepts and Strategy,* H.M.Co., Boston, 1972, p. 905.
3. Kotler Philip: *Ibid.*, p. 131.
4. Schiffman Leon, G. and Kanuk, L. L. (1995), *Consumer Behaviour,* Prentice Hall of India (P) Ltd., New Delhi, V. Ed., 1995, p. 6-7.
5. Schiffman & Kanuk, *Ibid.* p. 7.
6. Schiffman & Kanuk, *Ibid.,* p. 7.
7. Engell J. F., Kollat D. T. and Black Well, R. D. (1973), *Consumer Behaviour,* Holt, Rinehart and Winston Inc. II Ed. 1973, p. 5.
8. Ramaswamy V. S. and Namakumari, S. (1995), *Marketing Management–Planning Implementation and Control,* Macmillan India Ltd. New Delhi, II Ed. 1995, p. 179.
9. Schiffman & Kanuk, *Ibid.,* p. 25.
10. Wells, William D. & Reynolds, Fred. D. (1977), *Consumer Behaviour,* Mc Graw Hill Co,. 1977, p. 49-74.
11. Ward, Scott and Wackman, Daniel. B. (1972), "Children's Purchase Influence Attempts and Parental Yielding." *J. of Marketing Research,* Vol. IX (Aug. 1972), p. 312-319.
12. Carron, Andre and Ward, Scott (1975), Gift Decisions by Kids and Parents, *J. of Advertising Research,* Vol. 15, No. 4 (Aug. 1975), p. 15-20.
13. Burr, Pat. L. and Burr, Richard, M. (1977), "Parental Responses to Child Marketing", *J. of Advertising Research,* Vol. 17 No. 6, (Dec. 1977), p. 17-20.
14. Kestorm, Karin, Tansuhaj, Patriya and Foxmann, Ellen (1987), *"Children's Influence in Family Decisions and Consumer Socialization: A Reciprocal View",* Advances in Consumer Research XIV, Mellanic Wallend of and Paul Anderson (eds), Provo, Utah: Association for Consumer Research, 1987, p. 283-287.

3

CONTRACT FARMING: AN IMPLICATION FOR THE CORPORATE WORLD

Surabhi Agarwal

INTRODUCTION

In this era of globalization and liberalization, the agribusiness is changing at a fast pace. Now a day, various methods have been emerged like, contract farming in which companies are joining the hands with the farmers and the whole agriculture activity is shaping the agriculture as the agribusiness. Many companies like Reliance, Pepsi, ITC Ltd, etc have come up with their formulas to grasp the benefits existing in this business. Apart from linking the farmer to consumer through farmers' organizations, another initiative for reducing transaction cost is establishment of direct channel between farmer-processor/bulk consumers, through contract farming. Several national and multinational processors or fast food chains are increasingly entering in to contract/alliance with the farmers to encourage them to cultivate farm products (fruit, vegetables, etc.) of the desired quality by providing them not only seeds and other inputs but also assured procurement of the produce at pre-decided prices. Marketing tie-ups between farmers and processors or bulk purchasers have special significance for small farmers, who have small-marketed surplus and do no have staying power. Such arrangements are being encouraged to help in reducing price risks of farmers and to also expand the markets for farm products.

Contract Farming (CF) can be defined as a system for the production and supply of agricultural and horticultural produce by farmers/primary producers under advance contracts, the essence of such arrangements being a commitment to provide an agricultural commodity of a type, at a specified time, price, and in specified quantity to a known buyer. In fact, CF can be described as a halfway house between independent farm production and corporate/captive farming and can be a case of a step towards complete vertical integration depending on the given context. Owing to the efficiency (coordination and quality control in a vertical system) and equity (smallholder inclusion) benefits of this hybrid system, it is being promoted aggressively in the developing world by various agencies. It basically involves four things– pre-agreed price, quality, quantity or acreage (Minimum/maximum) and time.

The contracts could be of three types; (i) procurement contracts under which only sale and purchase conditions are specified; (ii) partial contracts wherein only some of the inputs are supplied by the contracting firm and produce is bought at pre-agreed prices; and (iii) total contracts under which the contracting firm supplies and manages all the inputs on the farm and the farmer becomes just a supplier of land and labor. The relevance and importance of each type varies from product to product and over time and these types are not mutually exclusive. Whereas the first type is generally referred to as marketing contracts, the other two are types of production contracts. But, there is a systematic link between product and factor markets under the contract arrangement as contracts require definite quality of produce and, therefore, specific inputs. Also, different types of production contracts allocate production and market risks between the producer and the processor in different ways. The price of the contracted produce can be growers' fixed price, residual (profit/loss) sharing by sponsor and grower, open market based price, spot market price, consignment based two-part split price, tournament price (fixed plus variable based on relative performance), base price plus quality based incentive price, or administered price.

For different reasons, both farmers and farm product processors/ distributors may prefer contracts to complete vertical integration. A farmer may prefer a contract that can be terminated at reasonably short notice. Also, contracting gives access to additional sources of capital, and a more certain price by shifting part of the risk of adverse price movement to the buyer. Farmers also get an access to new technology and inputs, including credit, through contracts which otherwise may be beyond their reach. For a processor or distributor, contracts are more flexible in the face of market uncertainty, make smaller demands on scarce capital resources, and impose less of an additional burden of labor relations, ownership of land, and production activities, on management. The firm even gets an access to unpaid family labor and can make use of state funds indirectly through agricultural production sector, which are directed at farmers by development agencies. Also, food processors can minimize their overhead costs per unit of production by operating their plants at or near fully capacity as contracting gives assured and stable raw material supplies from farms. The firm can also project an image of working with local producers as a partner when it undertakes CF and may even obtain state and international agency incentives for its activities as developmental projects, instead of corporate farming. Contracts also help improve product quality by directly introducing incentives and penalties as there are problems of adverse selection and moral hazard in any contractual arrangement resulting in under investment or shirking by any of the parties.

At more macro economic level, contracting can help to remove market imperfections in produce, capital (credit), land, labor, information and insurance markets; facilitate better coordination of local production activities which often involve initial investment in processing, extension etc.; and can help in reducing transaction costs. It has also been used in many situations as a policy step by the state to bring about crop diversification for improving farm incomes and employment. CF is also seen as a way to reduce costs of cultivation as it can provide access to better inputs and more efficient production methods. The increasing cost of cultivation was the reason for the emergence of CF in Japan and Spain in the 1950s and in the Indian Punjab in the early 1990s.

Some recommend CF as the only way to make small scale farming competitive, as the services provided by contracting agencies cannot be provided by any other agencies. Contract farming also lowers transaction costs for the farmers as the procuring firm internalizes many of the transactions. CF is also an alternative to corporate farming which may be costly, risky, and difficult to manage and still not viable. Further, in India, supermarket chain growth including FDI in retail, international trade and quality issues like SPS, organic trade, fair trade, and ethical trade, promotion by the central and state agencies, banking and input industry push for CF, farming crisis and reverse tenancy, and failure of traditional cooperatives, are helping CF spread across crops and regions as they provide new space to this arrangement in the context of withdrawal of state from agricultural space. Even new IPR regime that encourages protection and exploitation of proprietary genetics is likely to accelerate contract-farming practice.

But, generally, contracting agencies especially private, tend to prefer large farmers for CF because of their capacity to produce better quality crops due to the efficient and business oriented farming methods, large volumes of produce which reduces the cost of collection for the firm, their capacity to bear risk in case of crop failure, and various services provided by these large producers like transport, storage, etc. On the other hand, firms for contracts pick up small farmers only when they dominate the area, there is government directive to do so or they are found to be low cost producers in certain areas and crops.

Further, firms may work with small farmers to make use of the state support (financial and technical) to these producers under various development programs and to benefit from lower cost of production on these farms as these farmers have access to cheaper family labor, and being residual claimants of their labor, work more conscientiously than hired labor. In fact, some of them even use large growers, rural elite, and local small processors as sub-contractors to procure from the small growers for the company. The seed companies in India use small companies as subcontractors to procure seeds produced under contracts. In gherkin small and marginal farmers carry out CF as the crop requires plenty of labor inputs, which these farming families can provide from within. Also, working with many small farmers in the case of small processors gives the required flexibility in procurement schedule helping to extend the processing season and use the equipment efficiently; and helps spread risk of supply failure as compared to working with a few large farmers.*(httpp://planningcommission.nic.in/ aboutus/committee/ wrkgrp11/wg11_agrpm.pdf)*

MODELS OF CONTRACT FARMING

Multinational corporations, smaller private companies, individual entrepreneurs and, in some cases, farmer cooperatives can all act as sponsors and financial investors for CF activities. In nearly all instances, the sponsors are also responsible for management of the venture.

CF can be structured in a variety of ways depending on the crop, the objectives and resources of the sponsor and the experience of the farmers. Contracting out production is a commercial decision to facilitate an adequate supply within a designated period and at an economic price. Any crop or livestock product can theoretically be contracted out using any of the models; however, certain products favor specific approaches. Broadly speaking, CF arrangements fall into one of five models:

1. The centralized model.
2. The nucleus estate model.
3. The multipartite model.
4. The informal model.
5. The intermediary model.

Decisions by sponsors on the type of model to follow should be made on the basis of market demand, production and processing requirements and the economic and social viability of plantation versus smallholder production.

Where market requirements necessitate frequent changes to the farm technology with fairly intensive farm-level support from the sponsor, the permanent organization and maintenance of a production chain under a centralized model is vital. Organizations that require stringent processing standards rely largely on the centralized model. For crops such as tea, sugar and oil palm, with which farmers may have had little or no experience, sponsors are more likely to follow, where possible, the nucleus estate approach. Such crops require a significant long-term investment and, generally, immediate processing after harvest. However, the lack of adequate land or political opposition to estate development may dictate a centralized rather than nucleus estate approach.

Where quality control is not the predominant concern, the informal model may suffice. In some examples, sponsors use third parties or intermediaries to subcontract production out to farmers.

If the sponsor considers that a field trial is warranted prior to the introduction of a crop to farmers or that a guaranteed minimum throughput is required for the processing facility, a nucleus estate model is often most appropriate. Where capital investment in processing facilities is considerable and the number of contract farmers is high, either the centralized or the nucleus estate structures can be used, accompanied by strong managerial inputs and backed by formal contracts. Seasonal, short-term crops characterize the informal model, which may become more widespread in the future, with only minimal material support to farmers.

Often, the operational structure of projects changes over time. For example, the distinctions between the centralized model and the informal model are sometimes blurred. Successful individual informal developers may expand their operations into activities that eventually evolve into the centralized category. One successful small-scale developer in Indonesia started a small operation in 1970 with a few greenhouses. By 1996 the company had grown into a $US6.4 million business supplying fresh vegetables to local supermarkets and frozen vegetables for export, with the produce originating from hundreds of contracted farmers.

THE CENTRALIZED MODEL

This is a vertically coordinated model where the sponsor purchases the crop from farmers and processes or packages and markets the product. Except in a limited number of cases, farmer quotas are normally distributed at the beginning of each growing season and quality is tightly controlled. A sponsor may purchase from tens of thousands of small-scale farmers within a single project. The centralized scheme is generally associated with tobacco, cotton, sugar cane and bananas and with tree crops such as coffee, tea, cocoa and rubber, but can also be used for poultry, pork and dairy production. Where fresh vegetables and fruits are grown under contract, the term "processing" may include grading, sorting and packaging as well as the provision of cool storage facilities.

In Africa, the contracting out of crops to farmers under centralized structures is common. These are often called "out grower" schemes. For example, in Zambia the multinational corporation, Lonhro, considered the system preferable to growing cotton on a plantation basis. In the late 1980s it initiated a smallholder project where over 15 000 farmers grew cotton under contract for the company's ginnery.

The level of involvement of the sponsor in production can vary from a minimum where, perhaps, only the correct type of seed is provided, to the opposite extreme where the company provides land preparation, seedlings, agrochemicals and even harvesting services. The extent of the sponsor's involvement in production is rarely fixed and may depend on its requirements at a particular time or its financial circumstances. In India, a tomato-processing factory in the Punjab was transferred in 1997 from one multinational company to another. The previous owners had supplied seed, supervised production and harvesting operations and provided technical advice when needed, but the new owners only provided seeds. In the Philippines, a vegetable canning company operating close to Manila decided to cease advancing fertilizer and chemicals to its contract farmers because these were being diverted to other crops and farmers were also making extra-contractual sales. The company changed to a policy of supplying only seeds unless it was convinced of the farmer's honesty.

The centralized model

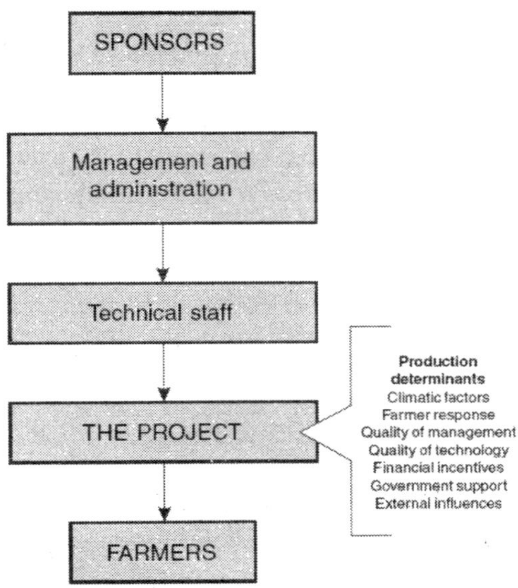

THE NUCLEUS ESTATE MODEL

Nucleus estates are a variation of the centralized model. In this case the sponsor of the project also owns and manages an estate plantation, which is usually close to the processing plant. The estate is often fairly large in order to provide some guarantee of throughput for the plant, but on occasion it can be relatively small, primarily serving as a trial and demonstration farm. The British-based Commonwealth Development Corporation (CDC) was a pioneer of the nucleus estate model although it no longer develops such estates. A common approach is for the sponsors to commence with a pilot estate then, after a trial period, introduce to farmers (sometimes called "satellite" growers) the technology and management techniques of the particular crop. Nucleus estates have often been used in connection with resettlement or transmigration schemes, such as in Indonesia and Papua New Guinea, for oil palm and other crops. While mainly used for tree crops, there are examples of the nucleus estate concept with other products. Indonesia, for example, has seen the operation of dairy nucleus estates, with the central estate being primarily used for the rearing of "parent stock".

THE MULTIPARTITE MODEL

The multipartite model usually involves statutory bodies and private companies jointly participating with farmers. Multipartite contract farming may have separate organizations responsible for credit provision, production, and management, processing and marketing. In Mexico, Kenya, and West Africa, among other countries, governments have actively invested in contract farming through joint ventures with the private sector. Multipartite structures are common in China where government departments as well as township committees and, at times, foreign companies have jointly entered into contracts with village committees and, since the early 1980s, individual farmers.

In this particular case, the county branches, through their agronomists and field technicians, were responsible for implementing and maintaining the terms and specifications of the agreement. There were formal contracts between the joint venture and the branches, and written contracts between the counties and the village committees, but only a verbal understanding between farmers and their respective committees. In theory, farmers were expected to carry out cultivation as specified by the joint venture. In practice, however, county officials only followed instructions from the joint venture if to do so was in the county branch's immediate economic interest, irrespective of quality standards and long-term production objectives. The lack of coordination between the joint venture and the county management, village cadres and farmers eventually resulted in the collapse of the venture.

In Colombia, a company started buying passion fruit in 1987, using the centralized model. The company ran into difficulties, however, because it proved impossible to control extra-contractual marketing. It therefore developed a multipartite model in which all farmers were expected to belong to associations or cooperatives, and public institutions became involved as providers of credit and extension. This arrangement significantly reduced both the risk of extra-contractual marketing and the company's costs of dealing with individual farmers, while being generally welcomed by farmers. Problems remained, however, most notably in relation to the lack of management skills on the part of the farmer associations and cooperatives.

The multipartite model
– A joint-venture contract farming project in China

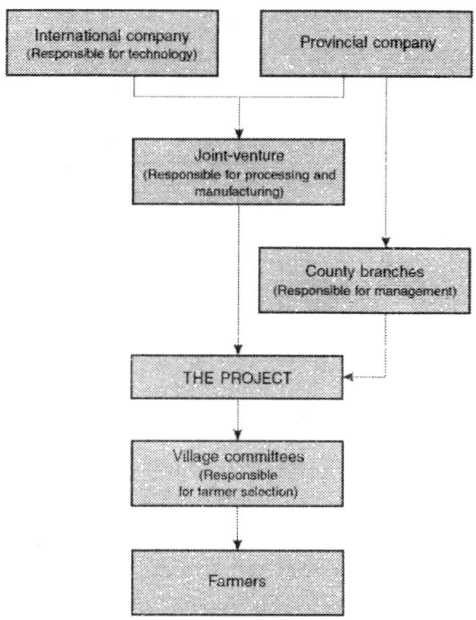

THE INFORMAL MODEL

This model applies to individual entrepreneurs or small companies who normally make simple, informal production contracts with farmers on a seasonal basis, particularly for crops such as fresh vegetables, watermelons and tropical fruits. Crops usually require only a minimal amount of processing.

Material inputs are often restricted to the provision of seeds and basic fertilizers, with technical advice limited to grading and quality control matters. A common example of the informal model is where the sponsor, after purchasing the crop, simply grades and packages it for resale to the retail trade. Supermarkets frequently purchase fresh produce through individual developers and, in some cases, directly from farmers. Financial investment by such developers is usually minimal. This is the most transient and speculative of all contract-farming models, with a risk of default by both the promoter and the farmer. Nevertheless, in many developing countries such developers are branches, and written contracts between the counties and the village committees, but only a verbal understanding between farmers and their respective committees. In theory, farmers were expected to carry out cultivation as specified by the joint venture. In practice, however, county officials only followed instructions from the joint venture if to do so was in the county branch's immediate economic interest, irrespective of quality standards and long-term production objectives. The lack of coordination between the joint venture and the county management, village cadres and farmers eventually resulted in the collapse of the venture.

In Colombia, a company started buying passion fruit in 1987, using the centralized model. The company ran into difficulties, however, because it proved impossible to control extra-contractual marketing. It therefore developed a multipartite model in which all farmers were expected to belong to associations or cooperatives, and public institutions became involved as providers of credit and extension. This arrangement significantly reduced both the risk of extra-contractual marketing and the company's costs of dealing with individual farmers, while being generally welcomed by farmers. Problems remained, however, most notably in relation to the lack of management skills on the part of the farmer associations and cooperatives.

THE INTERMEDIARY MODEL

Throughout Southeast Asia the formal subcontracting of crops to intermediaries is a common practice. In Thailand, for example, large food processing companies and fresh vegetable entrepreneurs purchase crops from individual "collectors" or from farmer committees, who have their own informal arrangements with farmers. In Indonesia, this practice is widespread and is termed *plasma*.

The use of intermediaries must always be approached with caution because of the danger of sponsors losing control over production and over prices paid to farmers by middlemen. In addition, the technical policies and management inputs of the sponsors can become diluted and production data distorted. In short, subcontracting disconnects the direct link between the sponsor and farmer. This can result in lower income for the farmer, poorer quality standards and irregular production. *(www.fao.org/ag/ags/AGSM/ contract/cfchap3.pdf)*

Contract Farming: Different Perspectives

Different types and models of CF lead to different situations. It is important that the right model and type of contract be chosen. Since farmers are not always well informed, they could end up signing contracts that exploit them.

Companies can sign contracts with big capitalist farmers who use wage labor, with small peasant farmers who use family labor, and even with the landless who lease land for contract farming. Most agribusiness companies, however, favor big farmers who can deliver in bulk and are better equipped to withstand risk. Small farmers are favored when they dominate a region, or when they benefit from government support.

Various studies have shown that there is adverse fallout of the contract system. For example, agribusiness firms have been found to overprice their services, pass on the risk to the producers, offer low prices for produce, and delay payments. Some firms look at contracts only as a management tool and a strategy to overcome procurement and related business problems.

CF tends to shift production in favor of export-oriented and cash crops at the cost of basic food crops for the poor. This could lead to higher prices for food commodities and products, especially for non-contract farmers. The contract system could also lead to over-

Characteristics of contract farming structures

STRUCTURE – MODEL	SPONSORS	GENERAL CHARACTERISTICS
Centralized	Private corporate sector State development agencies	Directed contract farming. Popular in many developing countries for high-value crops. Commitment to provide material and management inputs to farmers.
Nucleus estate	State development agencies Private/public plantations Private corporate sector	Directed contract farming. Recommended for tree crops, e.g. oil palm, where technical transfer through demonstration is required. Popular for resettlement schemes. Commitment to provide material and management inputs to farmers.
Multipartite	Sponsorship by various organizations, e.g. • State development agencies • State marketing authorities • Private corporate sector • Landowners • Farmer cooperatives	Common joint-venture approach. Unless excellent coordination between sponsors,internal management difficulties likely. Usually, contract commitment to provide material and management inputs to farmers.
Informal developer	Entrepreneurs Small companies Farmer cooperatives	Not usually directed farming. Common for short-term crops; i.e. fresh vegetables to wholesalers or supermarkets. Normally minimal processing and few inputs to farmers. Contracts on an informal registration or verbal basis. Transitory in nature.
Intermediary (tripartite)	Private corporate sector State development agencies	Sponsors are usually from the private sector. Sponsor control of material and technical inputs varies widely. At time sponsors are unaware of the practice when illegally carried out by large-scale farmers. Can have negative consequences.

Source: www.fao.org/ag/ags/AGSM/contract/cfchap3.pdf.

exploitation of resources. Firms tend to move on to new growers and land after exhausting local resources such as land and water.

CF has serious implications for existing agribusiness cooperatives. They will now have to compete with the multinational firms in terms of providing competitive prices and other incentives to retain their producer members. *(www.centad.org/cwp/02.asp)*

The Indian Experience

CF in India is currently being led by multinationals such as Unilever (tomato, chicory, tea, milk), Pepsi (potato, chillies, groundnut), Cadbury (cocoa), ITC Ltd. (tobacco, wood trees, oilseeds), Cargill (seeds), domestic corporate like Ballarpur Industries Ltd, JK Paper and Wimco (eucalyptus and poplar trees), and many more. CF models involve two or more players, with banks, state corporations and franchisees being involved as well, in some cases. *(www.centad.org/cwp/02.asp)*

CF has various models/variants being practiced in India at present. It is found that contract production gave much higher (almost three times) gross returns compared with that from the traditional crops of wheat, paddy, potato, tomato and onion in the case of gherkin and cotton due to higher yield and assured price under contracts. The studies of tomato contract production in Punjab and Haryana, of cucumber in Andhra Pradesh and cotton in Tamilnadu also found the net returns from these crops under contracts being much higher than those under non-contract situations though production cost in tomato was higher under the contract system. A more recent study across crops, companies and locations in Punjab also confirms this. In case of cotton in Tamilnadu, the contract growers had lower input cost, lower interest loans, faster payment for produce, and the crop insurance facility. The studies in the states of Punjab and Haryana reveal that contract growers faced many problems like undue quality cut on produce by firms, delayed deliveries at the factory, delayed payments, low price and pest attack on the crop. More recently, DSCL run input supply and CF program (Haryali Kisan Bazaar) for potato in Haryana also showed higher net returns for growers compared with non-growers due to higher yields and higher prices, though the cost of cultivation was also higher (17-24%).

It was also found by all of the studies that most of the firms work mostly with large and medium farmers with the exception of firms in Karnataka, Tamilnadu, and Andhra Pradesh which worked with small and marginal farmers due the nature of the crops (cucumber/gherkin, and broiler chicken). Gherkin contracting was also smooth as there was no local market for the crop, there was flexibility in contracts due to the short-term nature of the crop, and farmers maintained alternative sources of income. Similar was the case of iceberg lettuce grown for McDonalds in India, which had a very thin market. This bias in favor of large/medium farmers is perpetuating the practice of reverse tenancy in regions like Punjab where these farmers lease in land from marginal and small farmers for contract production.

Breach of contracts by farmers as well as firms has also been reported. Some of these studies recommend further expansion and promotion of CF system due to its benefits. The eligibility criteria for participation in CF projects/schemes like irrigated land, suitable land, land near main road, literacy level of the farmer are themselves discriminatory in terms of who can be a contract grower. In fact, in CF everywhere, private agribusiness firms have less interest and ability to deal with small scale farmers on an individual basis.

The more recent models of CF like franchising being practiced by the Tatas (Tata Kisan Sansar) for wheat in states of UP, Haryana and Punjab; and by the Mahindra Shubhlabh Services Limited (Mahindra Krishi Vihar) for paddy in Tamil Nadu, Andhra Pradesh, Karnataka and basmati and maize in Punjab and Haryana are also not delivering as expected. Mahindra & Mahindra's recent involvement in Punjab agriculture has not worked to the advantage of the farmers. In fact, this model creates a monopsony where a single buyer buys produce of hundreds and thousands of farmers. This system works to the disadvantage of those farmers who lack adequate information about the market, which is termed as asymmetry of information. This model increases the buyer's power disproportionately and puts seller entirely at the buyer's mercy. Small and marginal farmers have not gained from these experiments. Wherever any gain has been reported, it is reported for the farmers in general and distinction between big/rich and small/poor farmer's gains is not reflected in any way. The interests of the poor farmers are not synonymous with those of large/rich farmers. One of the limiting factors in performance of the contract scheme in Punjab seems to be the minimum support price (MSP), which introduces price rigidity and acts unfavorably for the buyers and exporters. On the other hand, because Basmati is out of the purview of the MSP, its contracting performance has been quite favorable for the processors and exporters as they could discover a market price. Also, being an export crop, it enjoys a well-established high value market, which in turn has created a lot of comfort for the exporters. The performance of CF in Punjab has been tardy despite the fact that the state (PAFC) has been reimbursing the extension service fees to the companies, on behalf of the growers.

Further, the contracts protect company interest at all costs to the farmer and do not cover farmer's production risk e.g. crop failure, retain the right of the company to change price, and generally offer prices which are based on open market prices. Even organic produce buyers offer conventional produce market price based prices to their growers. This is a serious issue, as even a significant premium over market price may not help a farmer if open market prices go down significantly which is not uncommon in India. The market price based price is offered to avoid grower defaults as they can, otherwise, sell the produce in the open market due to availability of alternative market due to product symmetry.

Some firms also manipulate provisions of the contracts in practice, e.g. in the case of broiler chickens in Tamilnadu where they picked up birds before due date or delayed it depending on the demand which meant losses for contract growers.

They also delayed payments up to 60 days. But, growers were locked into these contracts due to the firm specific fixed investments they had made. Thus, many of the CF projects also failed due to either poor design of the project or default by any of the contracting parties.

Even state sponsored program of CF did not deliver in Punjab. The contracted winter maize failed almost completely due to inclement weather and poor quality seeds. In case of green peas, the contract growers were forced to dump their produce in open market, after being rejected by the PAIC on quality ground as per the contract specification, as there had been fungus infection due to inclement weather which was marked by heavy rains in winter season and then sudden rise in temperature. An area of 500 acres under contract production of green peas in Patiala and Fatehgarh Sahib districts had been affected. Some farmers found fault with the fungicide supplied by the contracted company in this regard. The dumping of contract-produced crop in open market led to fall in local market prices and it was being sold at Rs. 3 per kg now as against a promised price of Rs. 5 per kg by the PAIC. In general, across crops and regions, the CF program could not achieve the stated area goal. Not only it fell short in terms of contracted area being less than that stated by the agency, but also the farmers did not plant the entire contracted area with the contract crops. Most of the problems farmers faced related to production and quality (like quality of seed and extension) and not marketing of produce (except peas) as open market could take care of contract produce. Due to this experience, a large majority (60%) was not willing to enter into CF arrangement again. There have also been instances of corruption and malpractice in the PAFC run CF program due to conflicts of interest among implementing agencies and lack of monitoring.

It is not incidental that most of the CF projects are in the states of Punjab, Haryana, Gujarat, Maharashtra, Karnataka and Tamilnadu which are agriculturally developed states. On the other hand, vast areas of the country such as Bihar, Jharkhand, Chhatisgarh, Orissa, West Bengal, the entire northeast India and areas of Uttaranchal, Himachal Pradesh, Kerala and Jammu & Kashmir have been bypassed by CF projects. Does it mean that these areas and farmers would not benefit from commercialization and vertical integration of agriculture? These are areas with highest concentration of small and marginal farmers. This essentially means that contracting companies do not encourage the participation of those who need to be helped to participate as risk preference and innovativeness require not just attitude but also resources and risk taking capability to undertake risky crops and ventures. The aspects of contracting which contribute to CF excluding small producers are: enforcement of contracts, high transaction costs, quality standards, business attitudes and ethics like non/delayed/reduced payment and high rate of product rejection, and weak bargaining power of the small growers. CF also reinforces reverse tenancy where in small and marginal farmers lease out land to large and medium farmers who are often contract growers for the companies as was the case in the Indian Punjab. *(httpp://planningcommission.nic.in/aboutus/committee/wrkgrp11/wg11_agrpm.pdf)*

Contract Farming: Bane or Boon?

Companies engaged in processing and marketing of agricultural products are entering into contracts with the farmers. The CF is done with the view to fulfill the following objectives:

- To reduce the load on the central & state level procurement system.
- To increase private sector investment in agriculture.
- To bring about a market focus in terms of crop selection by Indian farmers.

- To generate a steady source of income at the individual farmer level.
- To promote processing & value addition.
- To generate gainful employment in rural communities, particularly for landless agricultural labor.
- To flatten as far as possible, any seasonality associated with such employment.
- To reduce migration from rural to urban areas.
- To promote rural self-reliance in general by pooling locally available resources & expertise to meet new challenges. *(www.ficci.com/media-room/speeches-presentations/200/oct/wheat/workshop1/Seth.ppt)*

The companies provide the farmers with the inputs and buy back the product with a rate specified in advance. Following are the inputs normally provided by the CF company:

- The variety of seeds needed for processing/ marketing.
- Guidelines to grow the crop.
- Pesticides, which does not result in residual toxicity.
- Extension services, free of cost.
- Fertilizers, hormones required for crop growth
- Other materials not available locally

The terms of the contract are well designed and spelt out in advance and a consent letter is obtained from the farmer. The company monitors the arrangements from "seed to shelf". *(www.etagriculture.com/mar_april2002/farming2.html)*

Well-managed CF is an effective way to coordinate and promote production and marketing in agriculture. Nevertheless, it is essentially an agreement between unequal parties: companies, government bodies or individual entrepreneurs on the one hand and economically weaker farmers on the other. It is, however, an approach that can contribute to both increased income for farmers and higher profitability for sponsors. When efficiently organized and managed, contract farming reduces risk and uncertainty for both parties as compared to buying and selling crops on the open market. Critics of CF tend to emphasize the inequality of the relationship and the stronger position of sponsors with respect to that of growers. CF is viewed as essentially benefiting sponsors by enabling them to obtain cheap labor and to transfer risks to growers. However, this view contrasts with the increasing attention that contract farming is receiving in many countries, as evidence indicates that it represents a way of reducing uncertainty for both parties. Furthermore, it will inevitably prove difficult to maintain a relationship where benefits are unfairly distributed between sponsors and growers. *(www.fao.org/ag/AGSM/contract/ cfchap1.pdf)*

BENEFITS TO FARMERS

The prime advantage of a contractual agreement for farmers is that the sponsor will normally undertake to purchase all produce grown, within specified quality and quantity parameters. Contracts can also provide farmers with access to a wide range of managerial, technical and extension services that otherwise may be unobtainable. Farmers can use the contract agreement as collateral to arrange credit with a commercial bank in order to fund inputs. Thus, the main potential advantages for farmers are:

- Provision of inputs and production services;
- Access to credit;
- Introduction of appropriate technology;
- Skill transfer;
- Guaranteed and fixed pricing structures; and
- Access to reliable markets. *(www.fao.org/ag/AGSM/contract/ cfchap1.pdf)*

Provision of Inputs and Production Services

Many contractual arrangements involve considerable production support in addition to the supply of basic inputs such as seed and fertilizer. Sponsors may also provide land preparation, field cultivation and harvesting as well as free training and extension. This is primarily to ensure that proper crop husbandry practices are followed in order to achieve projected yields and required qualities. There is, however, a danger that such arrangements may lead to the farmer being little more than a laborer on his or her own land.

It is often difficult for small-scale farmers outside the contract-farming context to gain access to inputs. In Africa, in particular, fertilizer distribution arrangements have been disrupted by structural adjustment measures, with the private sector having yet to fill adequately the void created by the closure of parastatal agencies. In many countries a vicious circle has developed whereby the low demand for inputs provides no incentive for the development of commercial distribution networks and this, in turn, further adversely affects input availability and use. Contract farming can help to overcome many of these problems through bulk ordering by management. *(www.fao.org/ ag/AGSM/ contract/ cfchap1.pdf)*

Access to Credit

The majority of smallholder producers experience difficulties in obtaining credit for production inputs. With the collapse or restructuring of many agricultural development banks and the closure of many export crop-marketing boards (particularly in Africa), which in the past supplied farmers with inputs on credit, difficulties have increased rather than decreased.

CF usually allows farmers access to some form of credit to finance production inputs. In most cases it is the sponsors who advance credit through their managers. However, arrangements can be made with commercial banks or government agencies through crop liens that are guaranteed by the sponsor, i.e. the contract serves as collateral. When substantial investments are required of farmers, such as packing or grading sheds, tobacco barns or heavy machinery, banks will not normally advance credit without guarantees from the sponsor.

The tendency of certain farmers to abuse credit arrangements by selling crops to buyers other than the sponsor (extra-contractual marketing), or by diverting inputs supplied by management to other purposes, has caused some sponsors to reconsider supplying most inputs, opting instead to provide only seeds and essential agrochemicals. The policies and conditions that control advances are normally described in attachments to contracts. *(www.fao.org/ag/AGSM/contract/cfchap1.pdf)*

Introduction of Appropriate Technology

New techniques are often required to upgrade agricultural commodities for markets that demand high quality standards. New production techniques are often necessary to increase productivity as well as to ensure that the commodity meets market demands. However, small-scale farmers are frequently reluctant to adopt new technologies because of the possible risks and costs involved.

They are more likely to accept new practices when they can rely on external resources for material and technological inputs. Nevertheless, the introduction of new technology will not be successful unless it is initiated within a well-managed and structured farming operation. Private agribusiness will usually offer technology more diligently than government agricultural extension services because it has a direct economic interest in improving farmers' production. 6 Most of the larger sponsors prefer to provide their own extension rather than rely on government services. *(www.fao.org/ag/AGSM/contract/ cfchap1.pdf)*

Skill Transfer

The skills the farmer learns through CF may include record keeping, the efficient use of farm resources, improved methods of applying chemicals and fertilizers, a knowledge of the importance of quality and the characteristics and demands of export markets. Farmers can gain experience in carrying out field activities following a strict timetable imposed by the extension service. In addition, spillover effects from contract farming activities could lead to investment in market infrastructure and human capital, thus improving the productivity of other farm activities. Farmers often apply techniques introduced by management (ridging, fertilizing, transplanting, pest control, etc.) to other cash and subsistence crops. *(www.fao.org/ag/AGSM/contract/cfchap1.pdf)*

Guaranteed and Fixed Pricing Structures

The returns farmers receive for their crops on the open market depend on the prevailing market prices as well as on their ability to negotiate with buyers. This can create considerable uncertainty that, to a certain extent, CF can overcome. Frequently, sponsors indicate in advance the price(s) to be paid and these are specified in the agreement. On the other hand, some contracts are not based on fixed prices but are related to the market prices at the time of delivery. In these instances, the contracted farmer is clearly dependent on market volatility. *(www.fao.org/ag/AGSM/contract/cfchap1.pdf)*

Access to Reliable Markets

Small-scale farmers are often constrained in what they can produce by limited marketing opportunities, which often makes diversification into new crops very difficult. Farmers will not cultivate unless they know they can sell their crop, and traders or processors will not invest in ventures unless they are assured that the required commodities can be consistently produced. CF offers a potential solution to this situation by providing market guarantees to the farmers and assuring supply to the purchasers.

Even where there are existing outlets for the same crops, CF can offer significant advantages to farmers. They do not have to search for and negotiate with local and international buyers, and project sponsors usually organize transport for their crops, normally from the farm gate. *(www.fao.org/ag/AGSM/contract/cfchap1.pdf)*

PROBLEMS FACED BY FARMERS

For farmers, the potential problems associated with CF include:

- Increased risk;
- Unsuitable technology and crop incompatibility;
- Manipulation of quotas and quality specifications;
- Corruption;
- Domination by monopolies; and
- Indebtedness and over reliance on advances.

Efficient management can usually minimize these potential problems that consults frequently with farmers and closely monitors field operations *(www.fao.org/ag/AGSM/ contract/ cfchap1.pdf)*

Increased Risk

Farmers entering new CF ventures should be prepared to balance the prospect of higher returns with the possibility of greater risk. Such risk is more likely when the agribusiness venture is introducing a new crop to the area. There may be production risks, particularly where prior field tests are inadequate, resulting in lower-than-expected yields for the farmers. Market risks may occur when the company's forecasts of market size or price levels are not accurate. Considerable problems can result if farmers perceive that the company is unwilling to share any of the risk, even if partly responsible for the losses. In Thailand, for example, a company that contracted farmers to rear chickens charged a levy on farmers' incomes in order to offset the possibility of a high chicken mortality rate. This was much resented by the farmers, as they believed that the poor quality of the day-old chicks supplied by the company was one reason for the problem. *(www.fao.org/ag/AGSM/contract/cfchap1.pdf)*

Unsuitable Technology and Crop Incompatibility

The introduction of a new crop to be grown under conditions rigorously controlled by the sponsor can cause disruption to the existing farming system. For example, the managers may identify land traditionally reserved for food crops as the most suitable for the contracted crop. Harvesting of the contracted crop may fall at the same time as the harvesting of food crops, thus causing competition for scarce labor resources. Particular problems may be experienced when CF is related to resettlement programs. In Papua New Guinea, for example, people from the Highlands were resettled in coastal areas to grow oil palm and rubber. This required the farmers, who were traditionally sweet potato eaters, to learn cultivation techniques for new food crops and to adapt their dietary practices accordingly.

Two factors should be considered before innovations are introduced to any agricultural environment. The first is the possible adverse effect on the social life of the community. When tobacco growers in Fiji were encouraged to cure tobacco themselves rather than sell it in the fresh green form, it was found that they were unable to handle the highly technical curing operation with any degree of continuity. This was attributed to intermittent social commitments and customary obligations that overrode contractual responsibilities and eventually resulted in the cancellation of their contracts.

The second factor is the practicality of introducing innovations or adaptations. The introduction of sophisticated machines (e.g. for transplanting) may result in a loss of local employment and overcapitalization of the contracted farmer. Furthermore, in field activities such as transplanting and weed control, mechanical methods often produce less effective results than do traditional cultivation methods. Field extension services must always ensure that the contracted crop fits in with the farmer's total cropping regime, particularly in the areas of pest control and field rotation practices. *(www.fao.org/ag/ AGSM/contract/cfchap1.pdf)*

Manipulation of Quotas and Quality Specifications

Inefficient management can lead to production exceeding original targets. For example, failures of field staff to measure fields following transplanting can result in gross over planting. Sponsors may have unrealistic expectations of the market for their product or the market may collapse unexpectedly owing to transport problems, civil unrest, change in government policy or the arrival of a competitor. Such occurrences can lead managers to reduce farmers' quotas.

Few contracts specify penalties in such circumstances. In some situations management may be tempted to manipulate quality standards in order to reduce purchases while appearing to honor the contract. Such practices will cause sponsor-farmer confrontation, especially if farmers have no method to dispute grading irregularities. All contract farming ventures should have forums where farmers can raise concerns and grievances relating to such issues. *(www.fao.org/ag/AGSM/contract/cfchap1.pdf)*

Corruption

Problems occur when staff responsible for issuing contracts and buying crops exploits their position. Such practices result in a collapse of trust and communication between the contracted parties and soon undermine any contract. Management needs to ensure that corruption in any form does not occur. On a larger scale, the sponsors can themselves be dishonest or corrupt.

Governments have sometimes fallen victim to dubious or "fly-by-night" companies who have seen the opportunity for a quick profit. Techniques could include charging excessive fees to manage a government-owned venture or persuading the government and other investors to set up a new contract farming company and then sell that company overpriced and poor quality processing equipment. In such cases farmers who make investments in production and primary processing facilities run the risk of losing everything. *(www.fao.org/ag/AGSM/contract/cfchap1.pdf)*

Domination by Monopolies

The monopoly of a single crop by a sponsor can have a negative effect. Allowing only one purchaser encourages monopolistic tendencies, particularly where farmers are locked into a fairly sizeable investment, such as with tree crops, and cannot easily change to other crops. On the other hand, large-scale investments, such as for nucleus estates, often require a monopoly in order to be viable. In order to protect farmers when there is only a single buyer for one commodity, the government should have some role in determining the prices paid.

Drucker suggests that privately managed monopolies under public regulation are preferable to non-regulated private or public monopolies. The greatest abuses do tend to occur when there are public monopolies, where the government sets buying prices, or where farmers have made long-term investments in perennial crops. In 1999 the Kenya Tea Development Authority experienced serious unrest amongst its growers, reportedly because of the Authority's inefficient extension services and alleged "manipulation" of farmers. There was also discontent in Kenya among sugar farmers because the price set by the government did not change between 1997 and 1999. *(www.fao.org/ag/AGSM/ contract/cfchap1.pdf)*

Indebtedness and Over Reliance on Advances

One of the major attractions of CF for farmers is the availability of credit provided either directly by the company or through a third party. However, farmers can face considerable indebtedness if they are confronted with production problems, if the company provides poor technical advice, if there are significant changes in market conditions, or if the company fails to honor the contract. This is of particular concern with long-term investments, either for tree crops or for on-farm processing facilities. If advances are uncontrolled, the indebtedness of farmers can increase to uneconomic levels.

In one-venture "compassionate" advances for school fees, weddings and even alimony resulted in many farmers receiving no payments at the end of the season. Dropout rates for farmers in that particular project were high, as they thought contract farming did not pay. *(www.fao.org/ag/AGSM/contract/cfchap1.pdf)*

BENEFITS TO SPONSORS

Companies and government agencies have a number of options to obtain raw materials for their processing and marketing activities. The benefits of CF are best examined in the light of the other alternatives, namely spot market purchases and large-scale estates. The main potential advantages for sponsors can be seen as:

- Political acceptability;
- Overcoming land constraints;
- Production reliability and shared risk;
- Quality consistency; and
- Promotion of farm inputs. *(www.fao.org/ag/AGSM/contract/cfchap1.pdf)*

Political Acceptability

It can be more politically expedient for a sponsor to involve smallholder farmers in production rather than to operate plantations. Many governments are reluctant to have large plantations and some are actively involved in closing down such estates and redistributing their land. CF, particularly when the farmer is not a tenant of the sponsor, is less likely to be subject to political criticism. As a result of the restructuring of their economies, many African governments have promoted contract farming as an alternative to private, corporate and state-owned plantations. In Zimbabwe, for example, CF is actively encouraged, particularly in the sugar-cane, tea and cotton industries.

In recent years many countries have seen a move away from the plantation system of production to one where smaller-scale farmers grow crops under contract for processing and/or marketing. In Central America, for example, multinational corporations have moved from banana plantation production to purchasing bananas grown by contracted farmers, with the corporations providing technical advice and marketing services. This trend is also found in the international tobacco industry; smallholder tobacco production through CF has replaced estates in several countries. Similar changes have occurred with other crops. In Kenya, the tea industry, originally founded on the plantation model, now provides extension services and inputs to tens of thousands of contracted farmers.

The decision to choose CF does not make a company totally immune from criticism. For example, the considerable opposition to the role of multinational corporations in India in the late 1990s had a negative effect on investment in CF by foreign agribusiness corporations. *(www.fao.org/ag/AGSM/contract/cfchap1.pdf)*

Overcoming Land Constraints

Most of the world's plantations were established in the colonial era when land was relatively plentiful and the colonial powers had few scruples about either simply annexing it or paying landowners minimal compensation. That is, fortunately, no longer the situation. Most large tracts of suitable land are now either traditionally owned, costly to purchase or unavailable for commercial development. Moreover, even if it were possible for companies to purchase land at an affordable price, it would rarely be possible to purchase large enough parcels of land to offer the necessary economies of scale achieved by estate agriculture. CF, therefore, offers access to crop production from land that would not otherwise be available to a company, with the additional advantage that it does not have to purchase it.

Although it may be considered that plantation agriculture on a large scale is generally more cost-effective than small-scale production that is not always the case. Estate production involves both direct labor costs and indirect costs of labor in terms of hiring, training and supervising. It is often necessary to provide accommodation and meals for estate workers. As noted above, land can be very expensive and difficult to obtain, thus CF can often be competitive, particularly for crops where large-scale economies of scale are difficult to achieve. As already noted, experience in some developing countries indicates that plantation models of crop production can evolve successfully into cost-effective smallholder contract farming ventures. *(www.fao.org/ag/AGSM/ contract/cfchap1.pdf)*

Production Reliability and Shared Risk

The failure to supply agreed contracts could seriously jeopardize future sales. Plantation agriculture and CF both offer reasonable supply reliability. Sponsors of CF, even with the best management, always run the risk that farmers will fail to honor agreements. On the other hand, plantation agriculture always runs the risk of labor disputes. In the case of horticultural production some companies do prefer estate rather than contracted production. In Gambia and Ghana, for example, a number of crops are grown under the estate model, as are strawberries and flowers in Kenya.

Working with contracted farmers enables sponsors to share the risk of production failure due to poor weather, disease, etc. The farmer takes the risk of loss of production while the company absorbs losses associated with reduced or non-existent throughput for the processing facility. Where production problems are widespread and no fault of the farmers, sponsors will often defer repayment of production advances to the following season. The use of crop insurance may be possible, and this is discussed in.

Both estate and CF methods of obtaining raw materials are considerably more reliable than making purchases on the open market. The open market is rarely an acceptable option for organizations that have significant assets tied up in processing facilities and need to have guaranteed quantities of raw material to justify their investment. For example, it is hardly ever an acceptable option for companies who make regular shipments of horticultural produce to supermarkets and for export. Companies must ensure that crops are harvested and sold on a carefully scheduled and consistent basis: a factor that is normally assured under a well-directed CF scheme. *(www.fao.org/ ag/ AGSM/ contract/cfchap1.pdf)*

Quality Consistency

Markets for fresh and processed agricultural produce require consistent quality standards. Moreover, these markets are moving increasingly to a situation where the supplier must also conform to regulatory controls regarding production techniques, particularly the use of pesticides. For fresh produce there is an growing requirement for "trace ability", i.e. suppliers to major markets increasingly need to be confident of identifying the source of production if problems related to food safety arise. Both estate and contracted crop production require close supervision to control and maintain product quality, especially when farmers are unfamiliar with new harvesting and grading methods. Often, large numbers of crops within a single project have to be transplanted, harvested and purchased in a uniform manner so as to achieve product consistency.

Distinct varieties of produce in the desired quality and quantities are often not available on the open market. For example, a multinational that invested in the Indian State of Punjab found that the local varieties of tomatoes were unsuitable for processing into paste or ketchup. This was one of the factors that made it decide to go into CF.

Agribusinesses producing for markets demanding high quality standards, such as fruits and vegetables for export, often find that small-scale farmers and their families are more likely to produce high-quality products than farmers who must supervise hired labor. Also CF makes quarantine controls more manageable. It is easier for quarantine authorities to inspect a limited number of exporters of a single commodity, who closely supervise farmers, than to inspect hundreds, or sometimes thousands, of individual producers selling through open markets. Much of the production of "organic" foods is being done on contract, as an integrated operation facilitates a clear crop identity from farmer to retailer. In some highly sophisticated operations, containers are now being loaded on the farm for direct delivery to the supermarket. *(www.fao.org/ag/AGSM/ contract/cfchap1.pdf)*

Promotion of Farm Inputs

An example of an unusual but, nevertheless, interesting benefit for sponsors comes from the Philippines. A feed milling company experienced difficulties in marketing its feed, which was more expensive than that produced by competing companies. To solve this problem it developed rearing schemes for pigs and poultry under contract in order to provide a market outlet for its feeds and to demonstrate their performance to other farmers living near the contracted farmers. *(www.fao.org/ag/AGSM/contract / cfchap1.pdf)*

PROBLEMS FACED BY SPONSORS

The main disadvantages faced by CF developers are:

- Land availability constraints;
- Social and cultural constraints;
- Farmer discontent;
- Extra-contractual marketing; and
- Input diversion. *(www.fao.org/ag/AGSM/contract/ cfchap1.pdf)*

Land Availability Constraints

Farmers must have suitable land on which to cultivate their contracted crops. Problems can arise when farmers have minimal or no security of tenure as there is a danger of the sponsor's investment being wasted as a result of farmer landlord disputes. Difficulties are also common when sponsors lease land to farmers. Such arrangements normally have eviction clauses included as part of the conditions. In Gambia, land rights are determined not only by gender but also by the historic manner of land use. When international donor organizations insisted on having a legal titleholder for contracted crops, resistance to giving women formal titles to land was shown by male household heads. The objection was based on the fear of permanent land alienation that could occur as the result of matrimonial disputes.

Some CF ventures are dominated by customary land usage arrangements negotiated by landless farmers with traditional landowners. While such a situation allows the poorest cultivator to take part in CF ventures, discrete management measures need to be applied to ensure that their landlords do not exploit landless farmers. Before entering into contracts, the sponsor must ensure that access to land is secured, at least for the term of the agreement. *(www.fao.org/ag/AGSM/contract/cfchap1.pdf).*

Social and Cultural Constraints

Problems can arise when management chooses farmers who are unable to comply with strict timetables and regulations because of social obligations. Promoting agriculture through contracts is also a cultural issue. In communities where custom and tradition play an important role, difficulties may arise when farming innovations are introduced. Before introducing new cropping schedules, sponsors must consider the social attitudes and the traditional farming practices of the community and assess how a new crop could be introduced. Customary beliefs and religious issues are also important factors.

For example, Easter for some Christians is an inappropriate time for sowing vegetable crops. Harvesting activities should not be programmed to take place during festivals, and failure to accommodate such traditions will result in negative farmer reaction. It must also be recognized that farmers require time to adjust to new practices. *(www.fao.org/ag/AGSM/contract/cfchap1.pdf).*

Farmer Discontent

A number of situations can lead to farmer dissatisfaction. Discriminatory buying, late payments, inefficient extension services, poor agronomic advice, unreliable transportation for crops, a mid-season change in pricing or management's rudeness to farmers will all normally generate dissent. If not readily addressed, such circumstances will cause hostility towards the sponsors that may result in farmers withdrawing from projects. This emphasizes the importance of good management to the success of CF. Ways in which management can avoid such problems are addressed in. *(www.fao.org/ag/AGSM/contract/cfchap1.pdf).*

Extra-contractual Marketing

The sale of produce by farmers to a third party, outside the conditions of a contract, can be a major problem. Extra-contractual sales are always possible and are not easily controlled when an alternative market exists. For example, a farmer cooperative in Croatia bought cucumbers, red peppers and aborigines on contract. The cooperative's advances to the farmers included all necessary production inputs. Unfortunately members often sold their vegetables to traders at higher prices than the cooperative had contracted. The outside buyers offered cash to farmers as opposed to the prolonged and difficult collection of payments negotiated through the cooperative. Sponsors themselves can sometimes be a cause of extra-contractual practices. In Colombia, a company purchased passion fruit from a competitor's growers when production shortfalls occurred. A similar situation was also experienced in Indonesia where a number of sponsors competed for quality tobacco by surreptitious means. This led to a "tobacco war" between various sponsors that eventually forced the local provincial government to intervene.

In another case, a tobacco project diversified into off-season maize to provide farmers with additional income. In the first season some farmers sold their maize crops to traders for cash. Over 60 per cent of the first season's maize crop was estimated to have been sold outside the agreement. The repayment of loans advanced for inputs was thereby circumvented, making the diversification venture uneconomical for the sponsor. The sponsor imposed strict penalties the following year as part of the maize registration formula. If the

State and Contract Farming matrix

State/ Institution	*Nomenclature of the Scheme*	*Short Details of the Scheme*	*Benefit to Farmers/ Benefit to Private House*	*States/Districts where it is being implemented*
1. Assam				
Hindustan Paper Mill	Area Development Scheme	The Scheme envisages cultivation of Bamboo on wastelands.	Farmers would be benefited in terms of production and income	8 Districts of Assam– Cachar, Hailakandi, Karimganj, Nagaon, Kamrup, Morigaon, Udalguri and Darrang
2. Bihar				
1. Sarvodaya Krishak Sewa Swablambi Sahkari Samiti	Seed production	Minimum Rs. 100 per quintal	Rs. 100 per quintal to Samiti	Ara district
2. Doon Valley through Aditya Kumar, entrepreneur	Basmati rice	Assured procurement	Crop grown through organic farming methods prescribed by it.	Munger district
3. Chhatisgarh				
MSSL Mahindra Krishi Vihars		Supply of quality inputs, technical guidance, buy back of produce at pre decided price.	Assured availability of quality produce in required quantities at pre decided rates	Chhatisgarh
4. Himachal Pradesh				
Himalayan International Limited	3 herbs being cultivated	Assured purchase of crop by the company at a prefixed price	Assured supply	Paona block of Solan district

Contd...

State/ Institution	*Nomenclature of the Scheme*	*Short Details of the Scheme*	*Benefit to Farmers/ Benefit to Private House*	*States/Districts where it is being implemented*
5. Karnataka				
1. M/s Bharati Associates	Gherkin Processing	Assured market, good price, 1000 farmers benefited.	Assured supply of quality produce	Hassan, Karnataka
2. M/s Sai Agro Tech				Kolar, Karnataka
6. Madhya Pradesh				
1. ITC Ltd.	e-Choupal for Soybean & Wheat	Information on best agricultural practices Supply of farm inputs Supply of information on weather forecasting Price discovery of commodities	Availability of quality Soybean & Wheat at reasonable prices to ITC Ltd. for captive consumption	MP
2. Hindustan Lever Ltd.	Wheat (Durum & Sharbati wheat)	Supply of farm inputs	Availability of quality wheat at reasonable prices for captive consumption	MP
3. Cargil India Pvt. Ltd.	Wheat (Durum & Sharbati wheat)	Supply of farm inputs	Availability of quality wheat at reasonable prices for captive consumption	MP
4. Rallies India Pvt. Ltd.	Wheat (Durum & Sharbati wheat)	Supply of farm inputs	Availability of quality wheat at reasonable prices for captive consumption	MP
5. Reliance Bio-Sciences Ltd.	Aromatic oils (Lemon grass, Palmarosa, Citronella, Tulsi)	Purchase is affected through traders. No direct benefit to farmers.	Availability of aromatic oils for export purposes	MP

Contd...

State/ Institution	*Nomenclature of the Scheme*	*Short Details of the Scheme*	*Benefit to Farmers/ Benefit to Private House*	*States/Districts where it is being implemented*
7. Punjab and Haryana				
1. TATA Chemicals	TATA Kisan Sansar (TKS) through TATA Krishi Vikas Kendra (TKVK)	Enhanced farm productivity & income	(i) achievement of leadership by delivering value to agriculture (ii) Social engineering through community service (iii) Serving as a complete solution provider to farmers & building lasting relationship (iv) establishment of new identity and enhanced brand image (v) Increased sale of company's products (fertilizers, chemicals etc.) leading to enhanced revenue	TKVK set up in Sunam in Sangrur district of Punjab and proposed to cover 2700 villages in Punjab & Haryana
2. Vardhaman led consortium of spinning mills of North India & State Bank of Patiala	Village cluster adoption programme	(i) Productivity of cotton increased from 4.6 quintals in 2002-03 to 9.6 quintals per acre. (ii) Expenditure reduced from Rs.7995 per acre in 2002-03 to Rs. 7112 in 2003-04.	Increased production & hence better capacity utilization of plants & machinery.	Bathinda & Muktsar districts of Punjab

Contd...

State/ Institution	*Nomenclature of the Scheme*	*Short Details of the Scheme*	*Benefit to Farmers/ Benefit to Private House*	*States/Districts where it is being implemented*
8. West Bengal				
M/s Fritoley India	Cultivation of Processable Grade potato (with low sugar contents)		Farmers get all critical inputs through the company at right time in right quantity. Further, they also get technical know-how from the company. Company get assured supply of the raw material, as the key input supply is under their regulation, the quality of the raw materials are more or less as per their specification.	Hooghly, Bardhaman and Medinipur (West) of West Bengal State.
9. Maharashtra				
Tata Chemicals Ltd.	Grapes-Nashik district	(i) Assured quality of grapes for export and improving brand name 'Tata Grapes"	(i) Easy availability of crop loan (Rs. 55000 / acre). (ii)Availability of technical know-how and supply of required inputs (iii) No marketing problem for farmers. Farmers are also resorting to direst sale whenever local processes are attractive.	(i) Scheme implemented through SBI.

Contd...

State/ Institution	*Nomenclature of the Scheme*	*Short Details of the Scheme*	*Benefit to Farmers/ Benefit to Private House*	*States/Districts where it is being implemented*
2. S. H. Kelkar Group of companies	Patchouli (Aromatic oil plant)	(i) Availability of tissue culture planting material (ii) Marketing facility by the company	Availability of assured quality raw material	Ratnagiri & Sindhudurg districts
3. Champagne India Limited	Production of grape wine- Pune distrit	(i) Easy availability of planting material (@Rs.65-70 /.	Assured supply of quality raw material	2500 acres of Wine grapes under contract
4. Venkate shwara Hatcheries Private Ltd.	Contract Broiler Farming in Maval Block of Pune district	(i) Technical inputs and marketing of product is assured. (ii) All recurring expenditures are borne by the company	Assured availability of marketable product. The Company is saving on the investment cost as well as management cost	(i) Being implemented through Pune DCCB. (ii) 120 units of 5000 birds each are envisaged

Source: www.nabard.or farm_sector contract_farm.asp

farmers were found to be selling their maize outside the agreement, their highly profitable tobacco agreement was cancelled.

Where there are several companies working with the same crop (e.g. cotton in some southern African countries), they could collaborate by establishing a register of contracted farmers. Managers must be aware of produce being sold outside the project and also be aware of produce from outside being channeled into the buying system. This occurs when non-contracted farmers take advantage of higher prices paid by an established sponsor. Outside farmers through friends and family who have crop contracts filter non-contracted crops into the buying system. Such practices make it difficult for the sponsor to regulate production targets, chemical residues and other quality aspects. *(www.fao.org/ag/AGSM/contract/cfchap1.pdf)*

Input Diversion

A frequent problem is that farmers are tempted to use inputs supplied under contract for purposes other than those for which they were intended. They may choose to use the inputs on their other cash and subsistence crops or even to sell them. Clearly this is not acceptable to the sponsor, as the contracted crop's yields will be reduced and the quality affected. Steps to overcome such problems include improved monitoring by extension staff, farmer training and the issuing of realistic quantities of inputs. However, the knowledge that a contract has the advantages of technical inputs, cash advances and a guaranteed market usually makes the majority of farmers conform to the agreement. Unless a project is very poorly managed, input diversion is usually an annoyance rather a serious problem. *(www.fao.org/ag/AGSM/contract/cfchap1.pdf)*

CONCLUSION

The system helps eliminate the chain of middlemen and brings the producers and processors face-to-face. For the processing firm, it is an important step in supply-chain management. Spot market purchases are fraught with uncertainties *vis-à-vis* quality, quantity and price. The search and information costs for the right quality and quantity are high under open market purchases, whereas CF takes care of all these uncertainties. The advantages to the farmers are in terms of assured market, access to technology, supply of inputs and extension services.

In India, CF is confined to certain crops in select pockets. But there is immense potential. The increasing income has created quality and health consciousness among consumers who demand food products of certain specifications. The only way the demands of niche domestic and export market can be met is by having control over production of the crops at different stages. CF allows firms to have such controls.

Despite these advantages, farming under contract has many constraints. Though CF is basically a way of allocating risk between the firm and its farmers, the distribution of risk depends largely on such factors as bargaining power, availability of alternatives and access to information. The advantage export - that is, after the investment has been made to one party- leads to reneging on contract and exploiting the other party with the disadvantage. When, say, the vendor and the firm are locked in asset-specific investments with no room for either party to use the resource alternatively, the contract is fairly smooth. Especially in short- term crops such as vegetables, farmers tend to divert the produce to the open market rather than supply to the processing firm when the prices are high. The cost calculations of the firm crumble, as they are forced to arrange supply of raw materials from alternative sources with attendant uncertainties.

Similarly, in long-duration crops such as plantation crops, the firms often fail to honor the contract, as they know that farmers have no alternative but to sell the, products to them at lower prices. The latter often succumb to the firm's diktats. The solution to these problems must be found within the framework of the contract so as to ensure a smooth relationship between the firm and the farmer.

The firm can avoid to an extent the opportunistic behavior of the farmer by adopting an innovative price policy. CF is viewed aptly as an important tool to increase private corporate involvement in agro-processing, and help improve rural employment and income. However, to ensure smooth functioning of contract, innovative features need to be built in. *(www.etagriculture.com/mar_april2002/farming2.html)*

For the effective working of the CF it is necessary to aware the farmers about it. The prior information should be given to each party so that a healthy contract can be made and followed. On the other hand, the companies can grasp the profits through CF but keeping in mind the social responsibility of its and should try to turn it as two way process that benefits everybody including the farmers, the sponsor, and the society. It will create a good image of the company in the eyes of everyone and this will further leads to fast growth and increased market share of the company.

References

http://agmarknet.nic.in/ConFarm.htm (assessed on January 07, 2008).

www.centad.org/cwp/02.asp (assessed on January 07, 2008).

www.etagriculture.com/mar_april2002/farming2.html (assessed on January 08, 2008).

www.fao.org/ag/ags/AGSM/contract/cfchap3.pdf (assessed on January 08, 2008).

www.fao.org/ag/AGSM/contract/cfchap1.pdf (assessed on January 20, 2008).

www.ficci.com/media-room/speeches-presentations/200/oct/wheat/workshop1/Seth.ppt (assessed on December 28,2007).

www.nabard.or/farm_sector/contract_farm.asp (assessed on January 06, 2008).

httpp://planningcommission.nic.in/aboutus/committee/wrkgrp11/wg11_agrpm.pdf (assessed on January 06, 2008).

4

THE PRACTICE OF UNTOUCHABILITY IN INDIA

Amit Singh

> *"I do not want to reborn but if I am reborn I wish I would be reborn as a harijan, as an untouchable, so that I may lead a continuous struggle against the oppression and indignities that are heaped upon these classes of people."* **Mahatma Gandhi**

HISTORICAL DEVELOPMENT

Untouchability is a legal, moral and social wrong. It is repugnant to reason and to the instinct of pity or love. The tyranny and the oppression caste upon the socially backward classes by certain historically prevalent practices attaching stigma upon them led to the cancerous growth of social inequality affecting the vitals of the nation. Untouchability is the by product of caste system. The first reference of cast system has found in Manusmriti written by 'King Manu'. He has divided Hindu society into four compartments i.e. "chaturvarna". The caste system has to characteristics[1].

(i) Its membership is confined to those who are born in it.

(ii) Its member are forbidden to marry outsiders.

The lowest castes in this hierarchy are often referred to as untouchables and are described variously as Avarna, Antyaja, Himshudra, Harijans, Dalit, Untouchables and so forth. The word untouchables as a name generally applied to persons in the lowest classes of Hindu Society is a literal translation of the Hindi word

"Achhut". The websters dictionary vividly describes untouchables as–

> *"member of a large hereditary group in India having traditional Hindu belief and quality of defiling by contact the persons, food or drink of a member of a high caste, and formely being strictly degraded and restricted to menial work. From its very inception the term has been hated as it amounted to a degrading appellation for the people concerned."*

It is believed that untouchability was practised in India since Manu's times. They are expected to do the lowliest Jobs-sweepers and scavengers, attendants at cremation grounds etc. They are subjected to severe restrictions and disabilities and have very few privileges. In daily life the practice of untouchability often takes the form of denial of access to common water sources place of worship, village schools, communal dinners and celebrations and social and religious functions[2].

ATTEMPTS TO CURB UNTOUCHABILITY

Energetic efforts to free the Hindu society from the evil system of untouchability were going on since the time of the Buddha (500 B.C.). He initiated them into his new religion. The ideological and spiritual attempts to abolish untouchability and establish social equality were going on for centuries. Chakradhar, Ramanand, Kabir, Chaitanya, Ekanath, Tukaram, Rabidas and other saints succeeded to a great extent in establishing spiritual equality[3].

Earlier invaders and conquerors did not dare to interfere with this compartmentalised social order. They rather opted to reconcile and adjust themselves to this social stratification. When in the 19th century the British established their rule over most of India, their policy too was one of non-interference but there was pressure on them to change the social order of India[4]. In the early British period Raja Ram Mohan Roy, Dadaha Panduranga, G.D. Deshmukh and Vishnubhuva Barahmachari spoke against inequality in Hinduism and supported the cause of the lower castes and women.

Another social reformer "Jotiba Phule" founded the 'Satyashodhak Samaj' (Society for the search of truth) in 1873. He started a school for untouchables in 1854. He organized non Brahmin Sections in Poona and challenged the supremacy of the Brahmins[5].

Lokmanya Tilak: ilak had strongly opposed the caste system in India. Tilak gave a speech in a caste eradication meeting in 1878 he declared "Even if God stood in the line of advocating caste system, I would not accept it[6].

Raja Shahu: The Prince of Kolhapur state Chhatrapati Raja Sahu took inspiration from Jotiba Phule and founded Satyashodhak Samaj (1912) in Kolhapur. He criticized "chaturvarna" casteism and untouchability. He gave employment to Mahars, a dominant untouchable caste in Maharashtra, in different to an end, put a stop to "balutendari' and 'Vethbigari' systems and gave equal rights to the untouchables in his state[7].

V. R. Shinde: Popularly known as "Karmaveer" Shinde was a man of foresight. It was he who first raised the issue of untouchability at the national level and asked the Indian national congress to pass a resolution to that effect. As a result in 1977, the Congress adopted a resolution on the abolition of untouchability in Calcutta. He founded the "Depressed Class Mission" for the untouchables in 1903.

S. M. Mate: He founded the "Asprushyata Nivarak Mandal" (society for the removal of untouchability) in 1917 in Poona. He used to visit the colonies of untouchables and started a school for them. He specifically pointed out and criticized references to untouchability in the Hindu religious books[9].

Gandhi Ji: The man was a class by himself. By virtue of his many sided personality he defined classification. He was religious by nature. He organized the "Harijan Sevak Sangh" in Feb. 1933 and started publication of the weekly Harijan which become a most important journal and the forum through which he propagated his ideas on political and social reforms. Shortly afterwords he decided to arrange marriages between caste Hindus and Harijans. Gandhi described untouchability as an ugly outgrowth of Hinduism and appealed to caste Hindus to do penance and purify themselves and Hinduism.

Dr. B. R. Ambedkar: Ambedkar devoted his whole life against fighting with untouchability. He launched an active movement against untouchability during Indian Freedom Struggle. In 1920 he started the publication of the weekly 'Mooknayak' (Leader of the silent) in Bombay. In 1920 he became a nominated member of Bombay Legislative council. He started with public movements and marches to open up and share public drinking water resources, also he began a struggle for the right to enter Hindu temples. In 1932 on issue of Separate electorates he made an agreement 'Poona pact' with Mahatma Gandhi. In 1947 he became the head of drafting committee to frame constitution of India. After Independence he became the first law minister of India.

Kashiram: Popularly known as 'Manyawar' born in 1934 at Ropar in Punjab. After completing his education, he got a reputed government job in Puna. Caste based discrimination in job forced him to leave the job and follow Ambedkar's ideology for the uplift of Dalits. He sacrificed his family to devote his life for the Bahujan Samaj. He vowed to place the employed Dalits under a single banner, "BAMCEF'. He laid stress on education, organization, and agitation. He espoused the cause of Dalits for a separate electorate and fought against injustice, and humiliation meted out to Dalits by the Manuvadies through the weapons of assertion. His five doctrines struggle, self-respect, independence, equality, and brotherhood became widely popular. BSP came up as a party of the oppressed and repressed people. The Bahujans includes SCs, OBCs, STs, and the other minorities in India. BSP strives for social, economic, political equality. 85% Bahujans have power to dismantle 15% of Manuvadies. He plans to implement 'Hukmshan', to convert the Bahujan Samaj into Hukmshan Samaj, and spread Buddhism in India. He continues to be a source of inspiration for Dalits.

Mayawati Naina Kumari: Properly known as 'Bahenji', born in 1956 at Cuttack. After meeting with Manyawar Kashiram in 1977, she gradually come under his patronage and was part of his core team when he founded the BSP in 1984 as a party to represent Dalits, Mayawati was one of the key people in the new organization. She became Chief Minister of Uttar Pradesh four times in 1995, 1997, 2002 and 2007. When she become Chief Minister, she was the fist Dalit women to hold the high office in India. U.S. magazine 'Newsweek' has profiled him one of the top 8 women leaders of the world. Despite all odds with the dalit leader narrating her struggle to rally the oppressed community. In her tenures as Chief Minster, Mawayati has erected a number of monuments to Dalit heroes like Bhimrao Ambedkar, Chhatrapati Shahuji Maharaj, Gautam Budda and Manyawar Kashiram and others.

Contrary to some poll predictions, BSP won a majority in 2007 election. Mayawati managed to attract support from Brahmins, thakurs, muslims and OBCs voted for the first time for a Dalit party. This was accompanied by colourful slogans : "Hathi Nahi Ganesh Hain, Brahma, Vishnu, Mahesh hai." She has made the Bahujan Party into Sarvajans. Her announced agenda is focused on social justice through laws and other means for weaker sections providing employment instead of distributing money to unemployed, her slogan is to make Uttar Pradesh into an Uttam (excellent) Pradesh.

LAWS IN BRITISH INDIA

The British Law in principle did not recognize the caste structure. They established a nation wide legal system, which resulted in the movement of disputes from caste and village tribunals to the governments courts which supported the norm of equality before the law[10].

By the early 20th century, the communal quota began to be viewed as a step towards equality. Though the state of Mysore inaugurated the first regime of communal quota in 1918 the reservations were only for the non Brahmin "backward castes". Some relief was given by the 1919 reforms. In 1938 for the first time in British India, governments intervened to secure the opening of temples when the Bombay and Madras legislatures passed temple entry acts. Encouragement to the education of the untouchables increased and measures were taken to secure for them some posts in Government Service. Before independence 27 Acts had been enacted by various legislatures to give more legal rights to those who had till then experienced social and religious disabilities due to the practice of caste[11].

LAWS IN INDEPENDENT INDIA

At the transfer of power in 1947, it was widely accepted that caste system would have no place in Independent India. The framers of the Indian constitution took care to safeguard the interests of the minorities. Particularly untouchables to give them a sense of security to protect them against any discrimination, and to help them to get integrated in the main stream of national life. Consequently the Indian constitution in its very preamble assures every citizen of social, economic and political justice and equality of status and opportunity. Various provisions has been incorporated in constitution for prohibiting discrimination on grounds of caste and to promote the interests of weaker section especially untouchables.

In Indian constitution untouchables are known as scheduled castes. The constitution does not specify the castes which are to be called as the scheduled castes. It leaves the power to list those castes and tribes to the president, i.e. the Central Executive. Schedule castes, according to article 366 (24) read with article 341 are those castes, races or tribes or groups these of in each state and union Territory would be regarded as the scheduled castes for the purposes of the constitution in relation to that state or Union Territory. Thus the lists of the scheduled castes may vary from state to state and one Union Territory to another as regards the states, the president issues the notification after constitution with the Governor of the State concerned. It is not open to anyone to include any caste as scheduled caste. It is therefore not possible to give evidence that a particular caste is a Scheduled caste even though not mentioned in the Presidential order[12]. Even the court cannot modify, add or subtract any entry in the Presidential order. The function of the court is to interpret what an entry in the Presidential order is intended to mean[13]. The important constitutional safeguards for the schedule caste are as follows:

Developmental and Protective Safeguards

(i) Article 14 – right to equality for all persons.

(ii) Article 15 (1) – Prohibits discrimination or ground of race or caste etc.

(iii) Article 15 (2) – Prohibits both the state and private individuals from making any discrimination on caste to use public places and public utilities.

(iv) Article 15 (4) – State has power to make special provision for advancement of the Scheduled Caste.

(v) Article 15 (5) – State have power to make special provisions related to admission to educational institutions including private educational institutions for the advancement of S.C.

(vi)	Article 17	– Forbids the practice of untouchability in any form.
(vii)	Article 23, 24	– Prohibits Traffic in Human beings and 'bagar' and other similar forms of forced labour, which are one of the form of exploitation of S.C.
(viii)	Article 25 (2) (b)	– Throwing open of Hindu religious institutions of a public character to all classes and sections of Hindus.
(ix)	Article 46	– State will promote special care for educational and economic interests of the weaker section especially the S.C.
(x)	Article 244	– Administration of Scheduled Areas.
(xi)	Fifth Schedule	– Provisions as to the administration and control of scheduled areas.
(xii)	Article 29 (2)	– Prohibits discrimination on the base of caste in admission into any educational institution maintained or aided by state.

Political Safeguards

(i)	Article 164 (1)	– There shall be a Minister incharge of tribal welfare who may in addition be incharge of the welfare of the Scheduled Castes in State of Chhattisgarh, Jharkhand, Madhya Pradesh and Orissa.
(ii)	243 'D' and 'T'	– In every Panchayat and municipality seats shall be reserved for the Scheduled Castes. 1/3 of the total number of seats shall be reserve for women belonging to the S.C.
iii)	Art. 330, 332, 334	– Seats shall be reserved for Schedule Castes in house of People and legislative assemblies.

Service Safeguards

(i) *Article 16*– Article 16 (1) guarantees equality of opportunity in matters of appointment or employment in state services clause

(2) says that no citizen shall on grounds only of caste etc. discriminated in employment under the state. Clause (4) says that state have power for the reservation of appointments or posts in favour of any backward of citizens which is not adequately represented in the services of State. Clause 4A enables the state to make provision for reservation in matters of promotions for S.C. Clause (4B) empowers state to end the 50% limit for scheduled castes in backlog vacancies which could be filled up due to non availability of eligible candidates of these categories in the previous years[15].

(ii) *Article 335*– This provision imposes a constitutional obligation on the various governments to take steps to ensure that the claims of members of the S.C. are duly considered in making appointments to government services. In provides that the claims of S.C. are to be taken into consideration consistently with the maintenance of efficiency of administration in making appointments to services and posts in connection with the affairs of the Union or of a State.

NATIONAL COMMISSION FOR SCHEDULED CASTE (ARTICLE 338)

Article 338 provides a National Commission for the Schedule Castes. The commission shall consist of a chairman, vice chairman and three other members, appointed by the President of India. The Commission investigates and monitors all matters relating to the safeguards provided for S.C. under constitution, any law or any other by govt. The commission is to inquire into specific complaints with respect to deprivation of any rights and safeguards of these people and to participate and advise on the planning process of socio-economic development of the S.C. The central and every state government are required to consult the commission on all major policy matter affecting S.C.[16]

The commission is to make an annual report to the President. It can also make a report as and when it thinks necessary. Commission has been given power of the a civil court trying a suit and, in particular in respect of such matters as summoning and examination of witnesses, discovery and production of documents. The Commission has several state offices located in different states and Union territories. These offices serve as the "eyes and ears" of the commission as these offices keep the commission informed of all important activities, decisions and orders of the state government concerning scheduled caste[17].

PARLIAMENTARY COMMITTEE FOR S.C.

In 1968, Parliament appointed a committee as the welfare of the S.C. The committee consists of 20 members elected from Lok Sabha and 10 elected from the Rajya Sabha. It has been invented with powers to criticize, guide and control the government of India in the matter of S.C. It considered the reports of the commission of S.C. The committee reports to both Houses of Parliament on the action to be taken by the Government for the Welfare of these people. The committee also goes into the question of their employment in services under the central government including the public sector undertakings. The committee could thus go deeper into the major recommendations made by the commissioner and could assess how far these recommendations has been implemented[18].

LEGAL SAFEGUARDS FOR S.C.

There are a number of laws both central and state which provide for Safeguards to SCs. Some of these emanate from the various constitutional provisions. An illustrative list of such laws is given below:

1. The protection of civil rights Act 1955 and its Rules.
2. The S.C. / S.T. (Prevention of Atrocities) Act 1989 and its Rules (1995).
3. The Bonded Labour system (Abolition) Act, 1976 (in respect of SCs).
4. The child labour (Prohibition and Regulation) Act 1986 (in respect of SCs).
5. The minimum wages Act 1948 (in respect of SCs).
6. Acts and regulation inforce in different states to prevent alienation of land belonging to SCs for example– U.P. Zamidari Abolition and Land reforms Act, 1950. In some states such provision exists in the land Revenue Code.

THE PROTECTION OF CIVIL RIGHTS ACT 1955

Article 17 of Indian constitution abolishes "untouchability" and forbids its practice in any form. The enforcement of any disability arising out of untouchability is to be an offence punishable in accordance with law. This article is included in Part-III of the constitution which catalogues our fundamental rights. The abolition of untouchability is a right in as much as it provides a remedy against a disability. In the word of Dr. Ambedkar–

> *"it is a great fundamental right, a charter of deliverance of 1/6th of the Indian population from perpetual subjugation and despair from perpetual humiliation and disgrace. Abolition of untouchability in itself is complete and its effect is all pervading applicable to state action as well as acts or omissions by individuals, institutions or juristic body of persons*[19].

In exercise of power conferred by article 35 (a) (ii) parliament has enacted the "Untouchability (offences) Act, 1955. Due to many loopholes this law was not effective in eradicating the practice of untouchability. Hence to review its working, a committee was constituted under the chairmanship of Shri L. Elayaperumal in 1965[20] its report submitted in 1969. The report revealed clearly the poor implementation of the Act. After that, Act was amended by the 'Untouchability (offence) Amendment Act 1976 and this was renamed as *"The Protection of Civil Right Act, 1955"*. The Act which came into being on the 19th Nov., 1976. The Act defines civil right as "any right accruing to a person by reason of the abolition of untouchability by Article 17 of the consittution[21]. The Act provides penalties for preventing a person, on the ground of untouchability from entering a place of public worship and offering prayers, or taking water from a sacred tank, well or spring. Penalties are also provided for enforcing any kind of social disability such as denying access to a shop, restaurant, public hospital or educational institution, hotel or any place of public entertainment, or denying the use of any road, river, well, tank, water, tap bathing ghat, cremation ground, sanitary convenience, dharamshala or utensils kept in such institutions and hotels and restaurants[22]. The Act also lays down penalties for refusal to sell goods or render services to a person on the ground of untouchability or molesting, injuring or annoying a person or ganising of boycott of a person who has exercised the rights accuring to him as a result of the abolition of untouchability[23].

The offence under the Protection of civil rights act are cognizable as well as non compoundable.[24] The striking feature of this legislation is that where an offence is committed under the Act to any scheduled caste, the cost shall presume, unless the contrary is proved, that Such an act is committed on the ground of untouchability[25]. A public servant who willfully neglects the investigation of any offence punishable under the Act is deemed to have committed an offence under the Act. State Government are authorized to impose collective fines of the inhabitants when people in an area are involved in offences of untouchability[26]. *In Asiad project workers case*[29], the Supreme Court has held that the fundamental right under article 17 is available against private individuals and it is the constitutional duty of the state to take necessary steps to see that these fundamental rights are not violated.

In State of Karnataka Vs. Appa Balu Ingale[28], the respondents were tried for offences under Sec. 4 and 7 of the Protection of Civil Rights Act, 1955. The charge against the respondents was that they restrained the complaint party by show of force from taking water from a newly dug up tubewell on the ground that they were untouchables. The Supreme Court upheld the conviction and held that Abolition of untouchability in itself is complete and its effect is all pervading applicable application to state action as well as acts or omissions by individuals institutions or juristic body of persons.

SC/ST (PREVENTION OF ATROCITIES) ACT 1989

Due to lack of proper implementation PCR Act 1955 has not come to its means. Untouchability instead of becoming weak has received a re-birth in this period and has gained new strength and vitality[29]. It has loosened its grip on the religious sphere but tightened its hold on the secular sphere. This reformulation of caste system has given to it a fresh lease of life. To cut the most monstrous caste discrimination in the whole India, Parliament has enacted. *"The Scheduled Castes and Scheduled Tribes (Prevention of Atrocities) Act, 1989.* This Act is complementary to PCR Act 1955. The objects and reasons accompanying the corresponding Bill stated as follows:

> *"Despite various measures to improve the socio economic conditions of the Scheduled Castes and the Scheduled Tribes, they remain vulnerable. They are denied number of civil rights. They are subjected to various offences, indignities, humiliations and harassment. They have in several brutal incidents, been deprived of their life and property. Serious crimes are committed against them for various historical, social and economic reasons....."*

The Act was made to fulfil three purposes–

(i) To Prevent the commission of atrocities against the members of the SC and ST.

(ii) To provide for setting up of special courts for the trial of offences under the Act.

(iii) To provide for the relief and rehabilitation of victims of such offences.

The SC/ST Act 1989 was brought into force from 30th January 1990 in order to check and deter crimes against SC/ST by persons belonging to other communities. These enactments have extended the positive discrimination in favour of SC/ST to the field of criminal law in as much as they prescribe penalties that are more stringent than the corresponding offences under Indian Penal Code or PCR Act. The Act contains a list of such acts as fall within the category of atrocity. These acts have been made punishable with imprisonment for a term of six months to five years and with fine. Provisions has been made for designating special courts for the purpose of providing for speedy trial of offences under the Act.[50] Provision has also been made for imposing collective fines.[31]

Provisions of this Act over side the provisions of any other Act[32]. Every year the central government has to lay on the table of each House of Parliament a report on the measures taken by itself and the State Governments in pursuance of this Act[33]. The State Governments are required to make provision for the economic and social rehabilitation of the victims of atrocities, and provide them legal aid.[34]

SHORTCOMINGS OF THE LAW

Inspite of numerous movements, constitutional provisions and legislative measures the reality of the untouchables is for from encouraging. Caste prejudices and practice of untouchability is still continue in Indian Society specially in ruler areas as one can see from Table 1.

The year 2006 has witnessed an increase of 36 per cent in crime against Scheduled Castes as 26127 case reported in 2005 have increased to 270270 cases in 2006. Cases registered under PCR Act showed a considerable increase of 39.2 per cent in 2006 over 2005.

Table 1
Comparative Incidence of Crime Against Scheduled Castes

Crime-Head	*Years*					
	2002	*2003*	*2004*	*2005*	*2006*	*% Variation in 2006 over 2005*
(1)	*(2)*	*(3)*	*(4)*	*(5)*	*(6)*	
Murder	739	581	654	669	673	0.6
Rape	1331	1089	1157	1172	1217	3.8
Kidnapping & Abduction	319	232	253	258	280	8.5
Dacoity	29	24	26	26	30	15.4
Robbery	105	70	72	80	90	12.5
Arson	322	204	211	210	226	7.6
Hurt	4491	3969	3824	3847	3760	-2.3
Protection of Civil Right Act	1018	634	364	291	405	39.2
S/St (Prev. of Atrocities) Act	10770	8048	8891	8497	8581	1.0
Others	14383	11401	11435	11077	11808	6.6
Total	33507	26252	26887	26127	27070	3.6

Source: National Crime record Bureau Annual Report 2007.

Experience with sixty years of social reform has shown that many of the worst evils of caste system have been done away with partly by legal measures and partly by socio-economic programmes. Data's of 2006 crime report clearly shows that despite of different constitutional and legal laws untouchability is increasing. Northern belt of the India has most number of cases reported in 2006 under PCR Act and SC/ST Act 1989. This increase can be seen in Table 2.

The Hindi belt states has highest number of cases recorded. Cases registered from Uttar Pradesh and Madhya Pradesh accounted for 18.3% and 15.6% of the total cases (27070) reported in the country followed by Rajasthan 14.4 per cent.

These datas clearly shows that our laws are not upto mark. Some of the major shortcoming of the laws are–

(i) The guardians of the Law who are expected to take cognizance of the offences under laws were mostly ignorant of it. Copies of the Acts were not available at many of the district offices.

(ii) Delay in the disposal of cases by the Police and courts under Laws is another big problem. Upto 2006; more than 80 per cent of the cases are pending in the courts and are delayed for a long time. Thus the victims do not get justice early

Table 2
Crime against SC/ST Statewise During 2006-05

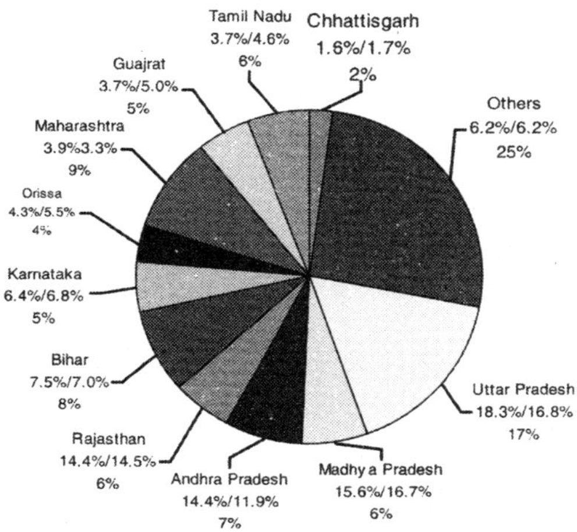

Percentage of Crime w.r.t. to All India for 2005
Percentage of Crime w.r.t. to All India for 2006
Percentage of Population w.r.t. to All India for 2006

Source: National Crime Record Bureau Annual Report 2007

enough. Special courts under SC/ST Act 1989 and other regular courts are not doing well, this we can see from Table 3.

(iii) Legal procedures that are not geared to the needs of the poor. National crime record Annual Report 2007 shows that 81.2 per cent cases under PCR Act and 83.4 per cent cases under SC/ST Act 1989 is pending comparatively to the gross total of 79.9 per cent which is lessor than the two previous ones. Out of hundred cases only 27.6 per cent convicted for offences which is again very low rate.

(iv) Prosecution under the Act is under taken by government pleaders and in most cases it has resulted in the acquittal of the accused persons who usually belonging to the affluent sections of society and are able to secure services of competent lawyers to twist the facts or cover up the guilt.

(v) The amended article 338 provides for the establishment of a National Commission for the Schedule Caste. Commission has power to investigate, inquire and recommend the matters.

Table 3

Percentage of Cases by Courts Disposed of for Crimes Committed Against Scheduled Castes During 2006

Crime Head	*No. of Cases*						
	Cases With-drawn by Govt.	*Compounded or With-drawn*	*Convicted*	*Acquitted or Discharged*	*Total [(6)+(7)]*	*Pending Trial at the end of the year*	*Conviction Rate (5/7×100)*
(1)	*(2)*	*(3)*	*(4)*	*(5)*	*(6)*	*(7)*	*(8)*
Murder(Sec. 302, 303 IPC)	0.0	0.0	9.8	10.1	19.9	80.0	49.2
Rape (Sec. 376 IPC)	0.0	0.1	6.7	14.9	21.6	78.3	30.8
Kidnapping & Abduction (Sec. 363-369, 371-373 IPC)	0.0	0.1	7.2	12.8	20.0	79.9	36.2
Dacoity (Sec. 395-398 IPC)	0.0	0.0	1.9	21.2	23.1	76.9	8.3
Robbery (392-394, 397, 398 IPC)	0.0	0.0	5.3	17.8	23.1	76.9	22.9
Arson (Sec. 435, 436, 438 IPC)	0.0	0.1	5.4	15.4	20.9	79.0	26.0
Hurt (Sec. 323-333, 335-338 IPC)	0.0	1.6	6.1	13.9	20.1	78.3	30.6
PCR Act, 1955 for SCs	0.0	0.1	2.9	15.8	18.7	81.2	15.5
SC/ST PREV. of Atrocities Act, 1989 for SCs.	0.0	0.6	3.8	12.2	16.0	83.4	23.6
Other Crime	0.0	1.3	6.2	15.6	21.9	76.9	28.6
Total	0.0	0.9	5.3	13.9	19.2	79.9	27.6

Source: National Crime Record Bureau Annual Report 2007.

Practice of untouchability and its related atrocities are offences of criminal nature but the commission has been given power of civil court only i.e. trying of a suit and in particular in respect of such matters as summoning and examination of witnesses discovery and production of documents. This is only an eye wash to the requirements of the constitution now the time has come that commission has to be vested with powers to punish the offenders.

CONCLUSION AND SUGGESTIONS

To curb "untouchability' the cancer of society, we may take following important steps–

1. The Law Commission should constantly fall back upon feedback from research institutes specializing in the problems of the SCs and itself interview groups of SCs and hear the various parties; and amend procedures accordingly. If socially conscious persons are appointed such simplied procedure can be helpful in enabling the SCs to use the law as a support in their struggle to demand their rights.
2. The escalating cost of litigation and the painfully slow and complicated judicial procedure have to be streamlined and simplified if law is to make any sense to the SC victims most of whom are illiterate, poor and powerless.
3. Ignorance of their rights has been another bottleneck in bringing justice and equality to millions of untouchables in India. A concerted drive to spread legal literacy among the weaker sections would be a solution to this. This would include knowledge of various laws such as Minimum Wages Act, Land Reform Laws, Bonded Labour (Abolition) Act, PCR Act etc. which are relevant to them. This campaign will support the section of the SCs who are beginning to wake up to their situation.
4. In this context of bringing Judicial Power to the gross roots level and spreading legal literacy, the role of para-legal personal can never be over emphasized. The para legal personal must be chosen preferably from among the scheduled castes and their training programmes should be adopted to the specific needs of the community.

5. Governmental action alone cannot be relied upon for the emancipation of the Scheduled Castes, voluntary groups i.e. NGO's, Civil Societies have to play a major role. Active assistance and support in this direction can be provided by voluntary organisations who can set up social justice cells in the rural and urban areas. The cell may enroll advocates, journalists, social activists and other interested persons from various professions and human rights organisations on and when required.
6. Radical land reforms are needed to break up monopoly hold of land lords specially in the State of Bihar and Jharkhand. Some states has done good job like West Bengal and U.P. They have to be made as models for the other ones.
7. Since most cases of untouchability affects poor and vulnerable individual of society. They are not able to use assistance and legal aid by special public prosecutor and special court established under SC/ST Act 1989. There is great scope in this connection if the liberal interpretation of locus standi i.e. public interest litigation should be extended to all special courts set up under Sec. 14 of SC/ST Act 1989. These will very helpful if by reason of poverty or disability, the victims cannot approach the court for judicial redress, any public spirited individual or institution acting in good faith can move in special courts for judicial redress.
8. People participation in the administration of justice with the help of "Nyaya Panchayats' must be encouraged. This alternative forum is helpful for the resolution of disputes of untouchability at the grass root level. The Nyaya Panchayats should rely on the indigenous justice potentiality of the People and their sense of justice. A part from promoting accessibility to the institution of justice for the poor person the Nyaya Panchayats can adopt a simple informal procedure.
9. The Joint Committee of both Houses of Parliament recommended, small committees at state and district levels to guard the working of the PCR and SC/ST Act, 1989, known as "Sentinels". The SC/STs Commission in its Fifth report, apart from other suggestions, recommended: "It is found that

> mostly State Govt's have not established "sentinels". Thus watch has not kept on the working of the Acts which are very essential for the removal of social disabilities. So it is recommended that for effective and powerful implementation of the Laws. 'Sentinel Committees' have to formed in all states."

Thus, at last we find that lack of political will, the apathy of the administration and the ignorance of the scheduled castes regarding their basic human rights have contributed to the present state. To curb untouchability the system of justice needs to be brought nearer to the SCs and the downtrodden. Law is only a door substitute in the combat against social evil. A vigilant watch upon the wrong doers, the mastering of public opinion, the enlargement of the hearts of the higher classes and above all the ethical and moral condemnation of the existing system are necessary to uproot this evil from the body of our social system.

Notes and References

1. Katkar, Dr. S. V. (1919), The History of Caste in India, Rawat Publication: Jaipur, p. 4.
2. Bose N. K. (1975), The Structure of Hindu Society, Orient Longman, New Delhi, p. 166.
3. Srinivas M. N. (1972), Social Change in Modern India, orient Longman, New Delhi (Indian Ed.), p. 93.
4. Mathew, P.D. and Stephen, Simson (1986), *"Untouchability and the Law"*, Vol. 36 April–June *Social Action* 183-194 at p. 183.
5. Dr. Ambedkar B.R. (1969), "The Untouchable who were they and why they become untouchables". Bharatiya Buddha Shiksha Parishad, Second ed. 1969, p. 8.
6. Chandra, Prof. Ramesh & Mitra, Dr. Sangh (2003), Dalit Identity in the New Millenaium" (Ajay Verma, New Delhi, 2003) Vol. 3 p. 74.
7. *Ibidem*, at 75
8. *Ibid.*
9. *Ibid.*
10. *Supra n.* 3 at 93.
11. *Supra n.* 4 at 184.

12. Jain M. P. (2003), Indian Constitutional Law, (Wadhwa and Company, Nagpur, 2003) at p. 1662.

13. Srish Kumar Chaudhaury Vs. State of Tripura, AIR 1990 SC 191, Vimal Ghosh Vs. State of Kerala, AIR 1997 Ker. 237.

14. *Supra n.* 12 at 1661.

15. Pandey Dr. J. N. (2007), Constitution of India (Central Law Agency, Allahabad, 2007) at p. 136.

16. *Ibidem,* at 689

17. *Supra n.*-12 at 1661.

18. *Ibid* at 1659

19. Gitanath Ganguli (1978) , "*Laws on Untouchability*", Vol. 15, JILI 304-306 at 304.

20. *Supra n.* 4 at p. 185.

21. Sec.–2 (A) Civil Rights Act, 1976.

22. Sec. 4 Civil Rights Act, 1976

23. Sec. 6 Civil Rights Act, 1976

24. Sec. 15 Civil Rights Act, 1976

25. Sec. 12 Civil Rights Act, 1976

26. Sec. 10 (A) Civil Rights Act, 1976.

27. People's Union for Democratic Rights Vs. Union of India, AIR 1982 SC 1473.

28. AIR 1993 SC 1126.

29. Nayar, P. K. B. (1974), "Untouchability *vis-a-vis* The caste System", *Journal of Constitutional and Parliamentary Studies,* Vol-VII, 66-70 at 66.

30. Sec. 14 SC/ST Act 1989.

31. Sec. 16 SC/ST Act 1989.

32. Sec. 20 SC/ST Act 1989.

33. Sec. 21 (4) SC/ST Act 1989.

34. Sec. 21 SC/ST Act 1989.

5

SUSTAINABLE DESERTIFICATION MANAGEMENT THROUGH ECOLOGICAL INDICATORS: A STUDY OF GWALIOR DIVISION

S. P. Singh, M. Mishra & Deepak Tripathi

INTRODUCTION

In Indian Peninsular the rainfall is received by the two major Branches an example for Bay of Bengal and Arabian Sea, which results in a moisture retainment in the soil. The regions, which have been receiving very, low rainfall or less than the average rainfall continuously for a long period results in eco-disequilibrium.

The ecology of such regions gets adverse due to certain types of forces in the ecological relationship, nature provides the base, lay down limits of freedom and indicates the direction along with optimum appropriation through social labour is possible in the long run. Technology aids natural process, bends to human purpose modifies them and thus extends the range of freedom. Institutions are either conducive or restrictive of man nature interaction, we concern with ecology with in the frame work of an eco-systemic approach is directed to optimizing (not maximizing) development so as to extricate our people from the vicious stranglehold of hunger and poverty; for hunger continues to be dangerous pollutant of an eco-destructive force of tremendous magnitude for it destroys man, the crucial component of the contemporary eco-system.

The report of planning commission in its five year plan, indicates clearly that the Thar (Rajasthan) desert has been advancing at the rate of ½ a mile per year is indeed a menace for the eco-climatic and agro-climatic regions where it has started crawling towards. Every year the Barren land is increasing and fertile land in coming future may tends to get convert in desert. The news live telecast on 24th Jan. 93 at 12.30 IST by BBC states that the fertile land has converted in desert has attracted the attention not only of the scientists, planners but also of the general people to check or to evolve a planning to cope with such a problem of natural hazard.

As per the MAB (Man and Biosphere) Panel it is very difficult to understand the process of desertification. Therefore it becomes very vital at the top to tackle the new area under desertification and to find out the causes responsible for its spread before making a plan.

Desertification, defined by the United Nations Convention to Combat Desertification as "land degradation in arid, semi-arid and dry sub-humid areas resulting from various factors, including climate variation and human activities" (UNCCD 1995), is a major global concern. The USA 'Dust Bowl' during the 1930s dislocated and impoverished many thousands. The collapse of the Soviet Union revealed land degradation on a large scale in the Central Asian drylands caused by inappropriate, mechanized over-farming (Holzel et al. 2002). The diversion of water flowing into the Aral Sea for crop irrigation during the Soviet era triggered catastrophic desertification over a large area (Saiko and Zonn 2000).

Archaeological evidences suggest that the onset of aridity was the major cause of the extinction of the Riparian and Harappa Kalibangan civilization. A well-knit river system existed in the desert until recent times. The deterioration of climate the rise of the Himalayas, the lowering of the Aravallis, important changes in the system, e.g. the diversion and disappearance of three classical rivers (the Yamuna, the Saraswati and the Ghaggar), and the lowering of the underground water-table caused increased aridity in the area (Wadia, 1960). (Krishnan, 1952) observed that arid conditions might have set in between 4000 BC. And 1000 BC. Palynological evidences indicate that the desertification process set in during the late cretaceous. (Lukose, 1972); Gurdip Singh, pers comm.) Biotic interference of the natural resources further accentuated the xeric conditions at a latter stage.

The first usages of the term desertification emerged in the 1920s/ 30s to express a concern that the Sahara might be marching southwards, swallowing Sub-Saharan Africa in its wake (Aubréville 1949; Stebbing 1938). Other urged caution though as more careful studies could not substantiate an advancing Sahara (Anglo-French Commission 1973; Helldén 1991; Mortimore 1989). Nevertheless, the frightening image of a creeping burial by sand triggered urgent calls for action from international aid organizations, donor countries and governments (Swift 1996). As the 'advancing deserts' narrative faded in the absence of convincing data, attention shifted towards human actions that were demonstrably degrading lands, such as deforestation, over cultivation, over-grazing, and salinity-inducing irrigation practices, frequently aggravated by droughts.

The notion that the Rajasthan desert has been advancing at the rate of ½ a mile per year for the last 50 years, as claimed by the planning commission in its first five year plan report, is fairly widespread but lacks scientific unanimity, mostly because of terminological controversies. The increase and decrease in the wind blown surfaces have been illustrated by a comparison of old and recent survey maps which indicated an extension of the desert towards the east (Singh, 1952). However, the fact is that in some areas sand formations have developed, whereas others they have diminished or vanished is no conclusive proof of the movement of desert.

The palaeobotanical evidence indicates an increasing trend in aridity since the Miocene times in Western India. It is during the early to mid-quarter nary most probably that the repeated fluctuations in temperature and precipitation caused the formation of the desert and over all aridity in Western India. (Vishnu Mittre 1975). The geo-morphological evolutionary history of the region has revealed that the landforms of the pre-quartenary eras in the Rajasthan desert have evolved through long periods subaerial degradation and interrupted by short-periods of tectonic activities (Ghose, Singh, 1977).

Work done by (Meher-Homji 1972) points towards the bio-climatic change and vegetational aspect, whereas (Satyanarayan 1964) has studied the plant communities of Indian desert and (Shankar 1977) measured the desertification through plant indicators. (Jain, 1988, 91) points out the desertification in Malwa Platua.

SAARC meeting held from 5 to 7 December, 1990 on the STATUS OF DESERTIFICATION IN Africa and the methodology for its assessment" focused on the application of new satellite based remote sensing technology, including NDVI interpretation, for the assessment and monitoring of desertification. The need was expressed for further development of the methodology to assess the dynamic process and to collect reliable data by actual measurements using a combination of remote sensing and ground surveys and employing a standardized set of desertification parameters.

(Singh 1993) highlighted, how the velocity of wind and direction of wind helps in spreading desertification and how the depleted forest coverage, increasing temperature, population, cattle and live stocks affects the rate of increasing desertification. In the same paper some suggestions were also made to combat crawling desertification.

Singh *et. al.*(2006) organized an awareness generation program related to desertification control through NAEB sponsored workshop on the eve of "World Desertification Day" on 17 June 2006, at Krishi Vigyan Kendra, Rajgargh, M.P. The program was organized to combat desertification and to suggest remedial measures.

Some of the studies were conducted by Singh (1989); Joshi (1997) highlighted the impact of drought and documented the perception of drought in the tribal region of Ratlam and Jhabua district of Madhya and found that occurrence of drought may led to desertification condition. In another study of FAO and UNEP (2006), which was the Joint effort in accordance with arrangements agreed to by the Inter-Agency Committee on Sustainable Development. It reflects extensive consultations and information exchange between United Nation agencies, interested Governments, non-governmental organizations and a range of other institutions and individuals on desertification. The present report reviews progress in the implementation of chapter 12 of Agenda 21, on combating desertification and drought, in the context of integrated land resource planning and management. It also reviews the implications of the implementation of the United Nations Convention to Combat Desertification in Countries Experiencing Serious Drought and/or Desertification, Particularly in Africa for the integrated planning and management of land resources in the affected countries. It is submitted to the Commission on Sustainable Development as an addendum to the report of the Secretary-General on integrated planning and management of land resources. The desertification and drought remain crucial issues for the sustainability of land use, having economic and social consequences and causing environmental degradation. The problems are worldwide, with more than 100 countries affected, but they are particularly evident in the poorest regions of the developing countries, especially in Africa. At least one quarter of the total land area of the world, or 3.6 billion hectares, is affected by desertification. Recent estimates suggest that almost 1.6 billion people live in arid and semi-arid countries and that nearly half of the world's poor people live in dry land regions with fragile soils and irregular rainfall.

This report also focuses on major trends and developments in achieving the objectives of the Convention to Combat Desertification with regard to the sustainable management of drylands. More detailed information on progress in the implementation of the Convention was reported to the Conference of the Parties at its third session (Recife, Brazil, 15-26 November 1999) and is available on the Convention web site (*www.unccd.de/*). The report had also addressed the issue related to , Improving knowledge, understanding and assessment of land resources, present land use and land degradation; Developments and trends in integrated land resource planning and management in drylands; and Emerging challenges and priorities for sustainable land resource management.

The ratification of the Convention to Combat Desertification by 159 countries is a binding commitment to combat desertification and related degradation problems and to integrate its initiatives into broader development policies and mechanisms. International agencies, including the International Fund for Agricultural Development (IFAD), UNSO, UNEP, FAO, the World Bank, the United Nations Educational, Scientific and Cultural Organization (UNESCO) and the World Meteorological Organization (WMO), play a key role in assisting countries to prepare their national action plans and to implement Conference-related activities. In most signatory countries, the process of elaborating national, regional and/or sub- regional action plans is under way with variable results and progress.

Study conducted by Winslow, Shaprio, *et. al.* (2004) deals with the research lessons and opportunities related to desertification, drought poverty and agriculture. This report has highlighted the issues related to drought desertification its causes and how affects the livelihood of people living in the arid and semi-arid regions in the world and raises the six high priority areas for research to combat dry land degradation.

The United Nations Convention to Combat Desertification (CCD) provides a modern framework for international cooperation against desertification. In response to severe droughts in Africa during the late 1960s/70s in Sub-Saharan Africa that killed approximately 200,000 people and millions of animals, the United Nations organized the first global Conference on Desertification (UNCOD) in Nairobi in 1977, which produced an ambitious Plan of Action. Although it did not generate the hoped-for global commitment of resources, it rekindled a sense of urgency that carried forward to the United Nations Conference on Environment and Development (UNCED, or the Earth Summit) in Rio de Janeiro in 1992.

The Earth Summit raised the profile of the problem by catalyzing negotiations for an International.

Convention to Combat Desertification (CCD): The CCD was especially favored by developing countries who saw it as more closely aligned with their development priorities than its more environmentally-oriented sister Conventions on Biodiversity and Climate Change, also initiated at that Summit. The CCD entered into force in 1996 and had been ratified or accepted by 191 nations by early 2004.

The CCD urges a wide range of development efforts and policy reforms, supported by increased scientific and technical cooperation (Horstmann 2002; Humphreys and Carr 2001; Hoven 2002; UNCCD 1995). The United Nations reiterated its call for support for the CCD in its Millennium Declaration, signed by 189 Member States (UN 2000 and 2001). The 2002 Johannesburg World Summit on Sustainable Development also reinforced the call to action.

In India efforts has been made by several department to combat Desertification by Science and Technology, NAEB , MoeF, Department of Rural development, Ministry of water resources, Irrigation department, NGOs etc.

The importance of the study-In a developing country like India, there are three facets of any natural hazard, namely the problem as perceived by the planners and experts, the problem as perceived by the people and the problem, which really is.

Desertification or new areas, which are converting or tends to get convert in future, needs a in-depth analysis to evaluate planning and management strategies.

However, no study or a research paper has been traced on Gwalior Division, as such to know what the factors, which are responsible for crawling desertification and why the vegetation is changing in time and space? How the planning management and developmental strategies could be developed to combat it.

Therefore it becomes very vital at the top priority to know how desertification takes place, how an exogenous and endogenous factors are responsible in spreading desertification? How the eco-system is changing with reference to time and space in pre-stage of desertification? Why the natural vegetation, crops which were grown earlier, were not found now, in the area where desertification has started crawling? (as the vegetation and crops could be grown a decade earlier).

Tropical forest is vital for social, economic and ecological reasons. They play an important role in eco-system processes (such as biogeochemical and hydrological cycles), they provide habitat for wildlife and serve as source of bio-diversity, and they offer protection against soil erosion (Kermenet *et. al.*2000, Sala *et al.*2000, Pandey 2001, Condit et al.2002). In this era of global warming (Forest et al.2002), tropical forest help mitigate the effects of climate change (Phillips *et al.* 1998, Schimel *et al.* 2001), and maintain bio-diversity and ecosystem functioning (Loreau *et al,* 2001). Therefore, we need broader strategies to maintain resilience and regenerative capacity of these tropical forests to ensure their sustainability (Elmqvist *et al,* 2002). The regenerative capacities of disturbed, fragmented, or harvested tropical forests provide hope and a clear message about how to prevent further species loss (Chazdon 1998).

Singh and Singh (2006) found that the eco regional Modeling is very important for the ecological sustainability in the villages. The ecological sustainability could be restored through regeneration and plantation of the species in the waste land or degraded areas.

The tropical forests are vital for social, economic and ecological reasons. The core questions of sustainability science in context of tropical forests and design robust policy and practice for adaptive tropical forest management if we are to mitigate the negative effects of human intervention in these ecosystems (Pandey, 2002).

Study conducted by (Sankar, *et al.* 2000) has tested and developed criteria and indicators for sustainable management of Tropical Plantation Forests in India. The Report find out the relevance of eight set of criteria and 43 indicators in context of sustainable plantation. Hence, the eco- regional modeling is essentially required in the region to restrain the ecological sustainability. Thus, ecological sustainability is very important for the community and the rural people to come out from the clutches of vicious circle of poverty. (Singh and Singh, 2006).

The important indicators related to the spread of desertification could be judged by the Ecological Indicators first, followed by social, Agricultural and economic indicators. (Singh and Mishra: 2008).

Thus the objective of this paper is as follows:

OBJECTIVES

- To develop criteria and indicators for ecological sustainability.
- To assess the changes in attributes related to ecology of the Gwalior division in spatial and temporal dimension.
- To assess the changes in water resources, vegetation and wildlife status in the forest area.
- To suggest a strategies to combat desertification in the study area

METHODOLOGY

The present project is a field based one. The methodology to be adopted is therefore aimed at making qualitative and quantitative assessment of the following during the intensive survey.

1. Identification of the area under desertification in the districts.
2. A detailed analysis was made of ecology with reference to temporal and spatial change, which had occurred during the last decade.
3. A time series analysis was made to judge how the forest coverage, rainfall, temperature, humidity winds etc. affects the barran and uncultivable land, current fallow and old fallow land why our permanent pastures and grazing lands are contracting. (Three dimensional analysis).
4. To analyze why the natural vegetation were not found now in the area, where desertification has started crawling.

Universe of Study

The North-West region of Gwalior Region/ Division is the universe of the present study.

Unit of Study

The present study is based on an intensive field work/ survey carried out in the selected area of the Universe in the four districts of Gwalior division - comprises of Datia, Sheopur, Morena, Bhind and adjoining portion of Gwalior District. From the selected district ranges were selected based on the criteria of availability of water resources viz. surface and ground water.

Sampling Framework

Firstly with the help of Government records, pilot surveys, and based on the list of areas, where desertification has started spreading or characteristics has been found were identified. From Gwalior Region 24 villages were selected randomly for intensive study. The following villages were selected for in depth study from Datia District-*Hinotia Lariata, Dangra, Dangra Ka Khuan, Raori*; Sheopur District-*Gurja Village: Raori, Ranawad, Bangroud, Itwai, Gohra*; Gwalior District-*Ghatigaon-Range; Berkheda, Dursedi; Ghatigaon–West–Mohana Sahasari, Dadori*; Morena district-*Usad, Gaudhoupura, Dimini Khurd, Nand Ka Pura, Nayapura-*; Bhind district- *Bilaw, SitaRam Ka Pura, Soai, Sapad, Kadaura.*

1. General discussions/ Focus group discussion with the people of different sections and their responses was organized in each village with forest depart.
2. Interviewing 10 households per villages with the help of structured schedules. Total 240 respondents were interviewed.
3. The pre testing of Questionnaire and Village profile and Group discussion schedule was done in the five villages of Datia district in the year of Nov 2006 with the team members of the project.

Documentation of perception responses of Villagers and Forest department and other officials has been done by pre tested format in the study area of Gwalior Region consisting of Five districts, Datia, Morena, Gwalior, Bhind, Sheopur. From Each district One DFO, SDO, 3 rangers and 3-4 Dy. rangers and 2-3 Forest guards have been concerted.

The perception of the respondents was also documented to understand the impact of the problem. "Before" and "after" analysis of 240 households from selected VFCs/ FPCs were under taken to assess the comparative socio-economic impact of desertification in the study area.

Collection and Compilation of Three-dimensional Data: Variable and Indicators Tested in the Study Area

The three dimensional data has been gathered through structured and pre-tested schedules. The three dimensional data was based on the 26 variables and its related indicators and sub-attributes from the selected 24 villages. The three dimensional data and changes taken place in the time frame of 60 years, of each selected variables and indicators have been tested. These attributes were mainly categorized under the following heads. The percentage change during last six decades has analyzed. The Key Informant are the old persons, villagers and staff of forest department.

DEMOGRAPHIC PROFILE

As per Census 2001, the population of Madhya Pradesh was 60,385,118 which consists of male 31,45,6873 and females 28,928,246 while decadal growth rate 91-2001 was 24.34% which is greater than National growth rate. It is evident from the Table 1 that India's 5.87% of Population is living in Madhya Pradesh. The male female ratio in Madhya Pradesh as compared to India is less by 13 persons per thousand. While density of population per sq. km is 196 which is less by 128 persons per sq km than the density of our country. It is also clear from the table that 9.65 per cent of population of Madhya Pradesh Lives in Gwalior Region.

Table 2 shows the forest cover in the study area of Gwalior region of Madhya Pradesh . It is clear from the table that the highest forest cover consisting of Very dense, Moderate dense and open forest was recorded in Sheopur district with 54.98% followed by Gwalior, Morena with 29.01 and 15.57% respectively. The lowest forest cover was found in the Bhind district with 2.71%. The overall changes recorded in Gwalior region were -208 Sq. K.M, while the per capita forest cover area was recorded less than, 0.001031 sq.km. which less than the per capita area of M.P.

PROFILE OF THE STUDY AREA OF GWALIOR REGION

On the basis of criteria adopted for the selection of VFCs from the study area of Gwalior Region. The following is the status of JFM

Table 1
Population of India, Madhya Pradesh, and study area of Gwalior Region

India and State/ Union territory/ District	Code No.	Population 2001			Decadal growth rate		Sex ratio		Density	
		Persons	Males	Females	81-91	91-2001	1991	2001	1991	2001
India		1,027,015,247	531,277,078 (51.73)	495,738,169 (48.27)	23.86	21.34	927	933	267	324
Madhya Pradesh	23	60,385,118 (5.87)	31,456,873 (52.1)	28,928,245 (47.9)	27.24	24.34	912	920	158	196
Sheopur	01	559,715 (0.92)	295,630 (52.81)	264,085 (47.19)	33.32	29.72	880	893	65	85
Morena	02	1,587,264 (2.62)	871,243 (54.88)	716,021 (45.12)	30.58	24.09	808	822	256	318
Bhind	03	1,426,951 (2.36)	780,122 (54.67)	646,829 (45.33)	25.18	17.06	816	829	273	320
Gwalior	04	1,629,881 (2.69)	882,258 (54.13)	747,620 (45.87)	27.97	26.00	831	847	284	357
Datia	05	627,818 (1.039)	337,842 (53.81)	289,976 (46.19)	26.01	21.82	847	858	192	233
Gwalior Region		5831619	3166825	2664301	28.62	23.738	836	850	214	263

Figures mentioned in brackets are indicatives of per cent of Total population Persons, Males & females

Source: Population Census 2001.

Table 2
Forest Cover in the Study Area of Gwalior Region

Stae/ region	*Geographical area (In Sq. KM.)*	*Forest Cover (In Sq. Km)* Very Dense	Moderate Dense	Open Forest	*Total Forest*	*Per cent*	*Change*	*Per capita (in Sq. Km)*
Madhya Pradesh	308245	4000	37843	34586	76429	24.79	-836	0.14 (hect.)
Sheopur	6606	13	1876	1743	3632	54.98	-117	0.0064
Morena	4989	0	254	523	777	15.57	-97	0.0048
Bhind	4459	0	40	81	121	2.71	25	0.00084
Gwalior	4560	5	558	760	1323	29.01	-17	0.000811
Datia	2691	0	81	83	164	6.09	-2	0.000261
Gwalior Region	23305	18	2809	3190	6017	19.6	-208	0.001031

Source: JFM-Cell M.P.

committee in the Gwalior region. It is clear from the Table 3 that 91.1% of the JFM Committee comes under the VFC; 4.8% FPC and 4.1% as EDC. It could be concluded that 3.1% of the JFM committee of Madhya Pradesh comes under the Gwalior Region.

Table 3
Details of Committee in the Gwalior Region

Circle / Region	*District*	*VFC*	*FPC*	*EDC*	*Total*
Gwalior	Gwalior	90	0	18	108
	Morena	121	3	0	124
	Sheopur	117	15	0	132
	Datia	45	0	0	45
	Bhind	25	3	0	28
	Total	398	21	18	437
	Madhya Pradesh	9035	4201	785	14073

Source: Forest Department-JFM Cell, Govt. of M.P.

Table 4
Details of Selected Forest Ranges

District	*No. of VFCs/ FPCs*	*Area in Ha*	*Forest ranges*	*Number of villages Surveyed*
Datia	52	24119.749	a. Datia	5
			b. Goraghat	
			c. Senwada	
Bhind	52	8119.02	a. Bhind	5
			b. Mehgaon	
			c. Ater	
Gwalior	1815	11069.805	a. Ghati gaon-North	
		3340.0	b. Ghatigaon-South (Mohana)	4
Morena	112	34915.540	Ambha Sub–Division	5
Sheopur	*145	90312.715	Birpur Sub Division	5

Source : DFO Office and from the MP. Forest Department; JFM- Cell, MP.
DFO Office Sheopur Latest information (as on March 2008).

Table 4 shows the description of selected forest ranges from Gwalior region. Ten Forest ranges were selected for in-depth study. The highest forest was recorded in the Sheopur district followed by Gwalior, Morena, Datia and Bhind respectively.

Table 5 shows the details of selected VFCs from the selected Forest Ranges. It also shows the details of the compartment number, area allotted to the VFCs, number of households Group discussion

Table 5
Details of Selected VFCs

Name of Forest division	*Name of VFCs*	*Year of formation*	*Compartment No*	*Area in Ha*	** Number of House holds*	*Group discussions organized*	*Number of House holds surveyed*
Datia	Hanotia	1997	P- 199, 200, 201	739.444	175	1	10
	Lariata	2001	P- 169, 170	109.625	200	1	10
	Dangara	1997	P, 197, 198	507.073	60	1	10
	Dangar ka Kuan	1997	P, 197, 198	507.073	50	1	10
	Raori	1998	P.190, 191	54.503	275	1	10
Gwalior	Berkheda	2000	597,598,599, 605	1038.291	58	1	10
	Dursedi	2000	P – 580, 582, 583, 592,593	1062.090	109	1	10
	Sahsari	1999	533	535	650	1	10
	Dadori	1999	P 352	310	135	1	10
Bhind	Bilaw	2002	P 72, 73, 74	539.690	672	1	10
	Sitaram ka Pura	2000	RF 70, 71 P 68, 69	467.625	125	1	10
	Soi	2000	P40, 41. 39, 37	372.00	350	1	10
	Sapad	2001	RF 37, 38, 40 P 39, 41, 42	258.621	190	1	10
	Kadura	2001	RF- 13 P 11, 14, 15	338.747	150	1	10

Contd...

Name of Forest division	Name of VFCs	Year of formation	Compartment No	Area in Ha	* Number of House holds	Group discussions organized	Number of House holds surveyed
Sheopur	Ranagwad	2001	RF 975-	157.50	45	1	10
			976	210.30			
	Bangraud	2000	PF 980	250.88	300	1	10
			PF- 981	249.55			
	Itwai	2000	PF 980	280.88	90	1	10
			981	249.55			
	Gurja	2002	RF- 978	87.08	20	1	10
			RF -977	202.25			
	Gohra	2000	PF-989	159.75	250	1	10
Morena	Nand ka Pura	1999	P 08	187.900	150	1	10
	Usad	2000	P-01	270.250	30	1	10
	Gaudhupara	2000	P- 03	258.400	56	1	10
	Dimni Khurd	1995	P-14	168.200	150	1	10
	Nayapura (New Samiti)	2007	not	-	70	1	10
Total	24 villages					24	240
Average						1	10

Source : Survey in VFCs of Gwalior Division; From DFO Office / range office.

organized and number of respondents surveyed. The village profile of the study area is detailed as follows.

ANALYSIS OF ECOLOGICAL INDICATORS OF DESERTIFICATION

Under the category of Ecological Indicators the following variables are very important to judge the Spread or the extent of crawling desertification or the conversion of the fertile land into waste and barren lands. Based on survey and focal group discussion, the availability status or the changes observed by the people in the specific area over the period of more than 50 years back from the present status, and the changes occurred in the vegetation status is a very good indicator to judge the spread of or extent of desertification in the region or area. The following Table 6 shows the availability status of Tree herbs and shrubs in the study area of Gwalior Division. The Three-dimensional data collected from the field shows the changes occurred in the vegetation from Fifty Years before as compared to present time.

The table shows the availability status of the various trees, shrubs and Herbs species found in the study area. It could be concluded that the species that were found in abundance Fifty Years before has gradually and simultaneously been changed, and started disappearing 25 years before and at present time. The temporal changes in the vegetation also indicate that at the present time the thorny and xerophytes vegetation has spread over in the study area.

Shankar (1977) found that the plants are very important indicator by which the desertification could be measured.

The spreading of Thorny herbs shrubs and tree species indicates that the desertification has started in the pre-stage of advancement in the study area. The continuous loss of soil fertility and declining moisture contents in the soil has resulted in not carrying out the species which earlier was surviving on the same soil in the study area. This is because of the changes in the rainfall, temperature, and raising demand of the people living in the area. (Singh, *et.al* 2006).

The present status of availability of species in the study area was also assessed by quadratic method to know the Density per hectare. The following Table 7 shows the vegetation density of different species per hectare.

Table 6
Availability Status of Vegetation in the Study Area

Species	*Fifty years Before*	*25 years before*	*At Present Time*
Related to changes in vegetation/plant species			
TREES			
Neem (*Azadirachta indica*)	√	–	–
Aam (*Mangifera indica*)	√	–	–
Babul (*Acacia nilotica*)	√	√	–
Bariya (*Zizyphus moriciana*)	√	√	√
Imli (*Tamarindus indica*)	√	–	–
Jamun (*Eugenia jambolana*)	√	–	–
Ghot (*Zizyphus xylopyra*)	√	√	√
Eucalyptus (*Eucalyptus spp.*)	–	√	√
Rinjha (*Acacia leucophloea*)	–	–	√
Palash (*Bueta monosperma*)	–	–	√
Mahua (*Madhuca latifolia*)	√	–	–
Pipal (*Ficus relegiosa*)	√	–	–
Bargad (*Ficus benghalensis*)	√	√	√
Khair (*Acacia catechu*)	–	–	–
Sagoun (*Tectona grandis*)	√	√	–
Bamboo (*Dendrocalamus strictus*)			
SHRUBS	√	√	√
Nagfani (*Opuntia monacantha*)	–	–	√
Pilua(*Salvadora oleodes*)	–	–	√
Dakhani(*Antidesma diandrum*)	√	√	√
Guggal (*Commiphora wightii*)	√	√	–
Satawar (*Asparagus racemosus*)	–	√	–
Hingote(*Balanites rouxburghii*)	–	–	√
Nimboo (*Citrus medica*)	√	√	√
Karil(*Gymnosporia royleana*)			
HERBS	√	√	–
Dab ghas (*Cynadon dactylon*)	√	√	√
Makoi (*Zizyphus Oenoplia*)	√	–	√
Bhatakatar (*Solanum indicum*)	–	√	√

Note: Based on the Group discussion with the Key Informant and Forest Department officials the availability status of species.

√ Shows–High, in the three dimension temporal Changes.

Source: Survey.

Table 7
Density of Species Found in the Study Area. (Per hectare)

Tree species	*Gawalior*	*Morena*	*Datia*	*Sheopur*	*Bhind*
Neem (*Azadirachta indica*)	1/Ha.	>1/Ha	Nil	1/Ha.	>1/Ha.
Babul (*Acacia nilotica*)	4/Ha	6/Ha	4/Ha.	5/Ha.	3/Ha.
Imli (*Tamarindus indica*)	1/Ha.	.>1/Ha.	>1/Ha.	Nil	Nil
Ghont (*Zizyphus xylopyra*)	5/ha.	Nil	2/Ha.	4/Ha.	2/Ha.
Eucalyptus (*Eucalyptus spp.*)	2/Ha.	3/Ha.	2/Ha.	>1/Ha.	Nil
Rinjha (*Acacia leucophloea*)	3/Ha.	2/Ha.	1/Ha.	>1/Ha.	>1/Ha.
Palash (*Bueta monosperma*)	2/Ha.	Nil.	Nil	2/Ha.	>1/Ha.
Mahua (*Madhuca latifolia*)	1/Ha.	>1/Ha.	>1/Ha.	2/Ha.	Nil
Khair (*Acacia catechu*)	6/Ha.	7/Ha.	2/Ha.	1/Ha.	2/Ha.
Bamboo (*Dendrocalamus strictus*)	2/ha.	2/Ha.	>1/Ha.	1/Ha.	Nil
Bel (*Aegle marrmelos*)	>1/Ha.	2/Ha.	>1/Ha.	Nil	Nil
SHRUBS					
Nagfani (*Opuntia monacantha*)	1/Ha.	Nil	>1/Ha.	4/Ha.	1/Ha.
Pilua (*Salvadora oleodes*)	3/Ha.	>1/Ha.	>1/Ha.	3/Ha.	>1/Ha.
Dakhani (*Prosopis juliflora*)	2/Ha.	5/Ha.	6/Ha.	2/Ha.	4/Ha.
Guggal (*Commiphora wightii*)	1/Ha.	>1/Ha.	2/Ha.	3/Ha.	>1/Ha.
Satawar (*Asparagus racemosus*)	5/Ha.	>1/Ha.	2/Ha.	5/Ha.	>1/Ha.
Hingote (*Balanites rouxburghii*)	4/Ha.	2/Ha.	Nil	3/Ha.	1/Ha.
Nimboo (*Citrus medica*)	3/Ha.	2/Ha.	Nil	Nil	Nil
Karil (*Gymnosporia royleana*)	Nil	>1/Ha.	>1/Ha.	Nil	Nil
HERBS					
Dab ghas (*Cynadon dactylon*)	25/Ha.	16/Ha.	10/Ha.	30/Ha.	22/Ha.
Makoi (*Zizyphus oenoplia*)	10/Ha.	7/Ha.	4/Ha.	17/Ha.	7/Ha.

Source: Survey.

The ecological data of tree species depicted in Table 7, indicates that population density of broad leaved species like Palash, Neem, Mahua, Bel was observed very less in all the districts studied (varied from less than 1/Ha. to 2/Ha.), except in Gwalior district where density was more in almost all species occurred in the quadrate. Species like Bel, Bamboo, were slightly seen in the Sheopur and Bhind area. Palash was completely absent in the Morena and Datia districts. However, poor density of Imli, Bel, Mahua (1/Ha.) was also observed in the study area. On the other hand population density of thorny trees species were observed very high as compared to other tree species in the study area, like Babul (4 to 6/Ha.),Ghont (2 to 5/ha.), Khair (1to 7/Ha.), Reonjha (>1 to 3/Ha.).

The population density of various shrub species like Dakhani (2 to 6 /Ha.), Hingote (1 to 4/Ha.), Pilua (1 to 3/Ha.) was found more among other species in the study area. Karil and Nimbu species were sparsely seen in Bhind and Sheopur districts. Poor density was observed in case of Karil (>1/Ha.) and Nagfani (>1 to 4 Ha.). On the other hand Satawar and Pilua, density varies from 1 to 5 plants per hectare.

Density of herbs i.e. grasses was found more in all the study area. Dab is the common most grass in the whole Gwalior circle including three selected districts. Dab ghas was found as much as 10 to 25/Ha, whereas Makoi was found less (4 to 17/Ha.) in all the selected districts.

Due to the changes occurred in the availability status of the different species, the wild life was also associated with the density of trees, shrubs and herbs species in forest area. The table 8 shows that how the wild life species has disappeared from the adjoining forest areas if compared from Fifty Years before with 25 years and up to present time.

Table 8
Status of Wildlife in the Study Area

Disappearance of wildlife (Disappeared-Yes. Not disappeared-No)	*Fifty Years before*	*25 years before*	*At present time*
Tiger (*Panthera tigris*)	No	Yes	Yes
Tendua (*Panthera pardus fusca*)	No	No	Yes
Fox (*Vulpes bengalensis*)	No	No	Yes
Python (*Python molurus*)	No	No	Yes
Snake (Kobra)	No	No	No
Rabbit (Hare)	No	No	No
Rat (Mouse)	No	No	No
Deer (Cheetal)	No	No	Yes
Goh (Monitor lizard)	Yes	Yes	No
Porcupine	Yes	No	No

Source: Survey.

It is evident from the table 8 that the wild life population was not disappeared 50 years before in case of Tiger (*Panthera tigris*), Tendua (*Panthera pardus fusca*), Fox (*Vulpes bengalensis*) Python (***Python** molurus*), Snake (Kobra), Rabbit (Hare), Rat (Mouse), Deer(Cheetal) were concerned. The disappearance of the wild life has been observed by the people of the region that now the big animals like, Tiger,

Tendua, Fox, Python are not seen now. While at present time the reptile animals are seen which are having the living characteristics of dry-zone or found in desert areas has now been often seen in the region.

It could be concluded from the table that the changes in wild life habitat over the spatial and temporal variation has been replaced with the crawling creatures and animals of the dry zone, which were found in the desert area. The appearance of the dry zone animals and reptiles are the good indicators by which the extent /spread of desert advancement could be judged. The increase in the population of such reptiles and animals found in desert area is the indicator of crawling desertification, which is now seen in the study area of Gwalior region.

Table 9 shows the Indicators related to water resources in the study area of Gwalior region. It is evident from the table that the changes have been occurred in the nature and pattern of rainfall. Based on the secondary and primary data as collected from the area shows that the continuous rainfall was observed 50 years before by the people and *JHAR were seen for the duration 10-15 days and the sunlight was not seen by the old people,. However the nature of rainfall has been disturbed totally as the continuous rainfall now has taken the shape of very erratic and it was only for the duration of 4-5 hours.*

It could be concluded from the secondary and primary data the rainfall received by the region is facing the problem of water resources because of the prime source of water means rainfall is not seen or received by the region as what region was receiving fifty years before. The cumulative impact of the same was also observed by the people on the availability of water in surface as well as ground water.

The over flooding condition was seen by the old people in the main rivers in the region which latter was converted in low flood areas. The water logging and the hindrance in the flow of current of water in the river is the major cause of flooding (Singh *et. al*, 2007).

This could be judged by the spread river water on the either side of the main rivers in the region Like Chambal, Quari, Pahuj, sen. It was reported by the people in the region that the spread of above rivers was seen 2-3 kms 50 years back while the spread of flood was seen up 1 km in the study area. This also proves that the precipitation as received by the region is continuously declining.

The variable of availability of water in the main rivers of the region indicates that the current of water has reduced while availability

Table 9
Indicators Related to Water Resources

Indicators related to water resources	*Fifty Years Before*	*25 years*	*At Present*
Pattern of Rainfall in the region	Continuous rainfall for 10-15 days	Continuous rainfall for 2-5 days	Erratic rainfall, not more than 4-5 hrs.
	Over Flooding condition near by Chambal, Kuar, Sind, Pahuj river (High)	Flooding condition near by Chambal Kuar, Sind Pahuj river (Medium)	Flooding condition near by Chambal quari, sen, Pahuj river (Low)
Spread of river water on either side due to rains (In Km)	2-3 Km	1.5-2 Km	1 km
Availability of water in No. of days			
(a) Surface water resource			
1. River (main River)	365	365	365
2. Tributary rivers	365	300	180
3. Nallah	300-350	250-320	70-90
4. Ponds	365	300	90-120 or dries up
5. Stop dams	–	–	150
6. Reservoir etc	–	–	150-180

Contd...

Indicators related to water resources	*Fifty Years Before*	*25 years*	*At Present*
(b) Underground water resources (Duration- availability of water No. of days.)			
7. Hand-Pump	–	365	180-250
8. Tube-Well	–	365	120-150
9. Well	365	365	120
10. Jhiri	365	300	120
(c) Biota in ponds	High	Medium	Low
Drinking Water Availability (Distance traveled in Km.)	2 k.m.	1 k.m.	200 mts to 500 mts..
Ground Water Resource			
(1) Well, (Rope Length)	5 mts	10-15 mts	20-25 mts or
	–		up to 30mts
(2) Tube-well (Electric / Diesel	–	50-100 feet	200-300feets

Source: Survey in the Study area 2006-07.

of water in the river continues throughout the year. While the availability of water in the tributaries of theses rivers were found throughout the years if we go 50 years back, but at present it continue upto 6 months and latter converts in the bed of small pond in the tributaries... or dries up.

The availability of water in *NALLAHS* at present was recoded for not more than 90 days. The other activities in the region is based on the availability of water in the pond is related with the drinking water for bovine or non bovine animals and performing the activities of bathing cleaning clothes or attaining sustainability through pisi-culture etc. (Singh, 1994).

It is also evident that the stops dams and reservoirs were not there 50 years before have emerged out at present time and the availability of water remains not more than for 6 months. This is also very important indicator to charge the ground water resources through the watershed or the government/specific department has introduced the micro-watershed development in the area. (Prakash and Singh 2006).

The hand pumps and tube wells were not seen by the people 50 years back while this has been seen by the people 25 years before. In many of the villages the installation of the tube well and hand pump has attracted the villagers attention a great crowd was seen during installation. The Motors or hand pumps, which were working through out the years, now have been dried up due to multiplier installment of more than by 10-20 folds. At present the tube-wells and hand pumps gives out the water for not more than 6-7 months in the study area. This is a very important indicator of which affects the moisture containment in soil and affects the agricultural productivity per hectare in the study area. The loss in moisture retainment is a very good indicator to judge the extent of increasing waste land which may have a trend to convert in barren land or desert area.

The drinking water source was the Jhiri well and river water in the study area which last throughout the year Fifty Years Before now these resources last for 120 days in area or dries up, till coming up of monsoons. The declining biota in the ponds is also important from the point of view of Aquatic animals. It is also clear from the table that the distance traveled by the people in the region to bring drinking water has reduced from 2 km up to 200-500 mts. in the studied villages.

The impact of water resources has also been recorded on the depletion of the ground water in the form of increase in the length of drawing water from the well. While the depth of digging or boring of tube wells has increased by 200-300 feet. The excess draining of ground water is also an indicator to judge the depletion of water resource in the region. (Singh, 1992, Singh 2007).

It could be concluded that the surface water and ground water resource in the region is depleting very fast as compared to the recharge of this resource. This very important indicator to judge the moisture , fertility and productivity of land in the region as its have a very serious impact on the sustainable livelihood (Singh, 1989, 2003, 2006, and 2007). The social impact of depleting water resources in the region has increased the domestic violence and hike in the crime graph. (Singh and Biswas, 2008; Singh 2007).

From, the profile of the study area and based on the primary data Table 10, furnishes the information related to Permanent pastures and grazing land, Occurrence of Dust Storms, Typhoons Hurricane, Andhi; Temperature; soil erosion and Moisture retainment in the soil. It is evident from the table that the status of Permanent pastures and grazing land has decreased as compared to 50 years before and 25 years before respectively. The contracting permanent pastures and grazing land has a direct impact on the feeding capacity of livestock in the region. (Singh, 1994, 2004 and 2006; MOEF 2006; Swift, 1996).

The increasing trends in the barren land and waste land formation have been seen at the present time. This trend is an indicator of crawling desertification in the study area.

The another indicator related to occurrence of dust Storms, Typhoons Hurricane , Andhi, etc. was also documented during the intensive survey in the study area. The five variables as tested in the study area, Related to Intensity, Velocity, frequency, duration and impact was changes drastically as compared to the condition of Fifty Years Before and at present time. The changing nature of storms, hurricane, Andhi, Typhoons, etc. has the impact o the The flying away of Flying away of Thatch roof (*chhapar),* Falling of trees *(Pedon ka Ukhadana),* Falling of Immature fruits and flowers from the branches of trees, Birds stops flying and Population was not seen outside of the houses all sit inside the house till the *andhi* gets over.

Table 10
Other Indicators of Desertification–related to Land Resource, Temperature, Wind erosion

Other Indicators of desertification	*Fifty Years Before*	*Before 30 years*	*At Present*
Pasture/grazing land			
1. Present Status	More	Medium	Less (decreased)
2. Barren Land	More	Less	More
3. Waste land Formation	More	Less	Increasing trend
Occurrence of Dust Storms, Typhoons Hurricane, Andhi			
1. Type (Intensity)	High	High	Moderate/Low
2. Velocity (Speed Per Hours)	100 Kms	90-100 Kms	50-70 Kms
3. Frequency	4-6	3-5	1-2
4. Duration	2-3 Hrs.	upto 2 hrs	1-2 Hrs
5. Impact			
(a) Flying away of Thatch roof (*chhapar*)	Yes-High ratio	Yes-Moderate rate	Yes-Low ratio
(b) Falling of trees (*Pedon ka Ukhadana*)	Yes-High ratio	Yes-Moderate ratio	Yes-Low ratio
(c) Falling of Immature fruits and flowers from the branches of trees	Yes-High ratio	Yes-Moderate ratio	Yes-Low ratio
(d) Birds stops flying.	Yes-95% stops flying	Yes-80% stops flying	Yes- 75% stops flying
(e) Population was not seen outside of the houses all sit inside the house till the *andhi* got over.	Yes-95%	Yes-90%	Yes-75%
Temperature			
1. Low	Yes	Yes	No
2. High	No	No	Yes

Contd...

Other Indicators of desertification	*Fifty Years Before*	*Before 30 years*	*At Present*
Traditional Indicators of Rise in Temperature			
1. Clothing condition changes.	Timely	Before Time	Before Time
2. Sowing of crops.	Timely	10-15 days before	20-25 days before
3. Flowering on trees	Timely	15-20 days before	30 days before
4. Increasing swatting	Timely		Yes before 30-35 days
5. Observing physical indicators of other season.	Timely	Yes before 20-30 days	
6. Early harvesting of crops.	Timely	Not in Time	20-30 days before time
7. disappearance of vegetation and survival of tree and plant species.	Not seen	Not seen	Seen, many shady trees now can not be grown. Now thorny vegetation has spread up
Soil Erosion			
1. Water becomes muddy with heavy water current	Higher level	Medium level	Higher level
2. Wind erosion (carrying sandy/dust particles.	High	Medium	Medium
Moisture			
1. High	Yes	No	No
2. Medium	Yes	Yes	No
3. Low	No	Yes	Yes
4. Poor	No	No	Yes

Source: Survey 2006-07.

The variable related to temperature has also registered a change over the 50 years of period. At present the average temperature was recorded more than 43^0. The rise in temperature in the study area was documented through changes in Clothing condition, Sowing of crops, earlier coming of flowering on trees, increasing swatting before 30 days, Observing physical indicators of other season before the coming of season and Early harvesting of crops followed by disappearance of vegetation and survival of tree and plant species.

The variable related to erosion was also documented at higher level as compared to 30 years before, the Water becomes muddy with heavy water current. While the wind erosion (carrying sandy/dust particles) was recorded medium at present time in the study area. The control over the flying of sandy or dust particles by the wind erosion also indicates the government measures to check the further spread of sandy particles in the study area by creating row plantation against the direction of wind to reduce the velocity. (Mann, *et. al.* 1974).

The variable related to moisture containment in the soil has reduced from high medium to low or very low due to climate change at present time. The conversion of High and medium moisture in the soil has a direct impact on the agricultural production and changing cropping pattern in the study area. As per the estimate of (Shekar, 2008) the agricultural production affected by 17% decline in the production which may latter on creates the condition of Domestic violence, and increase in the crime graph due to less food grain production (Singh and Biswas, 2008). The impact of above variables was not only seen on the agricultural production but also on the forest productivity in the deficit water zones (Singh, 2006).

CONCLUSION

The above indicators are verified through was field-testing during intensive study in the 24 selected villages in the study area of Gwalior region. The testing of the indicators was also based on the secondary data.

The Ecological Indicators could be judged, as it is important indicators related to the spread of desertification.

1. Under the category of Ecological Indicators the following variables are very important to judge the Spread or the extent of crawling desertification or the conversion of the fertile

land into waste and barren lands. Based on survey and focal group discussion, the availability status or the changes observed by the people in the specific area over the period of more than 50 years before from the present status, and the changes occurred in the vegetation status is a very good indicator to judge the spread of or extent of desertification in the region or area. The Table 4, Shows the availability status of Tree herbs and shrubs in the study area of Gwalior Division. The Three-dimensional data collected from the field shows the changes occurred in the vegetation from Fifty Years before as compared to present time.

2. The table shows the availability status of the various trees, shrubs and Herbs species found in the study area. It could be concluded that the species that were found in abundance Fifty Years before has gradually and simultaneously been changed, and started disappearing 25 years before and at present time. The temporal changes in the vegetation also indicate that at the present time the thorny and xerophytes vegetation has spread over in the study area.

3. The spreading of Thorny herbs shrubs and tree species indicates that the desertification has started in the pre-stage of advancement in the study area. The continuous loss of soil fertility and declining moisture contents in the soil has resulted in not carrying out the species, which earlier was surviving on the same soil in the study area. This is because of the changes in the rainfall, temperature, and raising demand of the people living in the area.

4. The present status of availability of species in the study area was also assessed by quadratic method to know the Density per hectare. The Table 5 shows the vegetation density of different species per hectare.

5. The ecological data of tree species depicted in Table 5 indicates that population density of broad leaved species like Palash,Neem, Mahua, Bel was observed very less in all the districts studied (varied from less than 1/Ha. to 2/Ha.), except in Gwalior district where density was more in almost all species occurred in the quadrate. Species like Bel, Bamboo, were

slightly seen in the Sheopur and Bhind area. Palash was completely absent in the Morena and Datia districts. However, poor density of Imli, Bel, Mahua (1/Ha.) was also observed in the study area. On the other hand population density of thorny trees species were observed very high as compared to other tree species in the study area, like Babul (4 to 6/Ha.), Ghont (2 to 5/ha.),Khair (1to 7/Ha.), Reonjha (>1 to 3/Ha.).

6. The population density of various shrub species like Dakhani (2 to 6 /Ha.), Hingote (1 to 4/Ha.), Pilua (1 to 3/Ha.) was found more among other species in the study area. Karil and Nimbu species were sparsely seen in Bhind and Sheopur districts. Poor density was observed in case of Karil (>1/Ha.) and Nagfani (>1 to 4 Ha.). On the other hand Satawar and Pilua, density varies from 1 to 5 plants per hectare.

7. Density of herbs i.e. grasses was found more in all the study area. Dab is the common most grass in the whole Gwalior circle including three selected districts. Dab ghas was found as much as 10 to 25/Ha, whereas Makoi was found less (4 to 17/Ha.) in all the selected districts.

8. Due to the changes occurred in the availability status of the different species, the wild life was also associated with the density of trees, shrubs and herbs species in forest area. The table 6 shows that how the wild life species has disappeared from the adjoining forest areas if compared from Fifty Years before with 25 years and up to present time.

9. Table 8 reveals that the wild life population was not disappeared 50 years before in case of Tiger (*Panthera tigris*), Tendua (*Panthera pardus fusca*), Fox (*Vulpes bengalensis*) Python (*Python molurus*), Snake (Kobra), Rabbit (Hare), Rat (Mouse), Deer(Cheetal) were concerned study conducted by Singh and Chandra (2001) shows the sustainable wild-life management of Canids and Felids is essential to maintain the ecological balance so far the case of Van Vihar National park is concerned. The disappearance of the wild life has been observed by the people of the region that now the big animals like, Tiger, Tendua, Fox, Python are not seen now. While at present time the reptile animals are seen which are

having the living characteristics of dry- zone or found in desert areas has now been often seen in the region. It could be concluded from the table that the changes in wild life habitat over the spatial and temporal variation has been replaced with the crawling creatures and animals of the dry zone, which were found in the desert area. The appearance of the dry zone animals and reptiles are the good indicators by which the extent /spread of desert advancement could be judged. The increase in the population of such reptiles and animals found in desert area is the indicator of crawling desertification, which is now seen in the study area of Gwalior region.

10. Table 9 shows the Indicators related to water resources in the study area of Gwalior region. It is evident from the table that the changes have been occurred in the nature and pattern of rainfall. Based on the secondary and primary data as collected from the area shows that the continuous rainfall was observed 50 years before by the people and *JHAR were seen for the duration 10-15 days and the sunlight was not seen by the old people,. However the nature of rainfall has been disturbed totally as the continuous rainfall now has taken the shape of very erratic and it was only for the duration of 4-5 hours.*

11. It could be concluded from the secondary and primary data the rainfall received by the region is facing the problem of water resources because of the prime source of water means rainfall is not seen or received by the region as what region was receiving fifty years before. The cumulative impact of the same was also observed by the people on the availability of water in surface as well as ground water.

12. The over flooding condition was seen by the old people in the main rivers in the region which latter was converted in low flood areas. The water logging and the hindrance in the flow of current of water in the river is the major cause of flooding (Singh *et. al*, 2007).

13. This could be judged by the spread river water on the either side of the main rivers in the region Like Chambal, kuari, Pahuj, sen. It was reported by the people in the region that

the spread of above rivers was seen 2-3 kms 50 years back while the spread of flood was seen up 1 km in the study area. This also proves that the precipitation as received by the region is continuously declining.

14. The variable of availability of water in the main rivers of the region indicates that the current of water has reduced while availability of water in the river continues throughout the year. While the availability of water in the tributaries of theses rivers were found throughout the years if we go 50 years back, but at present it continue upto 6 months and latter converts in the bed of small pond in the tributaries or dries up.
15. The availability of water in *NALLAHS* at present was recoded for not more than 90 days. The other activities in the region is based on the availability of water in the pond is related with the drinking water for bovine or non bovine animals and performing the activities of bathing cleaning clothes or attaining sustainability through pisi-culture etc. (Singh, 1994).
16. It is also evident that the stops dams and reservoirs were not there 50 year before, but the stops dams has now emerged out at present time and the availability of water remains not more than for 6 months. This is also very important indicator to charge the ground water resources through the watershed or micro-watershed development in the area has been introduced by the government or specific department. (Prakash and Singh 2006).
17. The hand pumps and tube wells were not seen by the people 50 years before while this has been seen by the people 25 years before. In many of the villages the installation of the tube well and hand pump has attracted the villagers attention a great crowd was seen during installation. The Motors or hand pumps, which were working through out the years, now have been dried up due to multiplier installment of more than by 10-20 folds. At present the tube-wells and hand pumps gives out the water for not more than 6-7 months in the study area. This is a very important indicator of which affects the moisture containment in soil and affects the agricultural

productivity per hectare in the study area. The loss in moisture retainment is a very good indicator to judge the extent of increasing waste land which may have a trend to convert in barren land or desert area.

18. The drinking water source was the Jhiri well and river water in the study area which last throughout the year Fifty Years Before now these resources last for 120 days in area or dries up, till coming up of monsoons. The declining biota in the ponds is also important from the point of view of Aquatic animals. It is also clear from the table that the distance traveled by the people in the region to bring drinking water has reduced from 2 km up to 200- 500 mts. in the studied villages.
19. The impact of water resources has also been recorded on the depletion of the ground water in the form of increase in the length of drawing water from the well. While the depth of digging or boring of tube wells has increased by 200-300 feet. The excess draining of ground water is also an indicator to judge the depletion of water resource in the region. (Singh, 1992).
20. It could be concluded that the surface water and ground water resource in the region is depleting very fast as compared to the recharge of this resource. This very important indicator to judge the moisture, fertility and productivity of land in the region as its have a very serious impact on the sustainable livelihood (Singh, 1989, 2003, 2006, and 2007). The social impact of depleting water resources in the region has increased the domestic violence and hike in the crime graph. (Singh, 2008).
21. From, the profile of the study area and based on the primary data Table 10, furnishes the information related to Permanent pastures and grazing land, Occurrence of Dust Storms, Typhoons Hurricane, Andhi; Temperature; soil erosion and Moisture retainment in the soil. It is evident from the table that the status of Permanent pastures and grazing land has decreased as compared to 50 years before and 25 years before respectively. The contracting permanent pastures and grazing

land has a direct impact on the feeding capacity of livestock in the region. (Singh, 1994, 2004 and 2006).

22. The increasing trends in the barren land and waste land formation have been seen at the present time. This trend is an indicator of crawling desertification in the study area.
23. The another indicator related to occurrence of dust Storms, Typhoons Hurricane, Andhi, etc. was also documented during the intensive survey in the study area. The five variables as tested in the study area, Related to Intensity, Velocity, frequency, duration and impact was changes drastically as compared to the condition of Fifty Years Before and at present time. The changing nature of storms, hurricane, Andhi, Typhoons, etc. has the impact o the The flying away of Flying away of Thatch roof *(chhapar),* Falling of trees *(Pedon ka Ukhadana),* Falling of Immature fruits and flowers from the branches of trees, Birds stops flying and Population was not seen outside of the houses all sit inside the house till the *andhi* gets over.
24. The variable related to temperature has also registered a change over the 50 years of period. At present the average temperature was recorded more than 43^0. The rise in temperature in the study area was documented through changes in Clothing condition, Sowing of crops, earlier coming of flowering on trees, increasing swatting before 30 days, Observing physical indicators of other season before the coming of season and Early harvesting of crops followed by disappearance of vegetation and survival of tree and plant species.
25. The variable related to erosion was also documented at higher level as compared to 25 years before, the Water becomes muddy with heavy water current. While the wind erosion (carrying sandy/dust particles) was recorded medium at present time in the study area. The control over the flying of sandy or dust particles by the wind erosion also indicates the government measures to check the further spread of sandy particles in the study area by creating row plantation against the direction of wind to reduce the velocity.

26. The variable related to moisture containment in the soil has reduced from high medium to low or very low due to climate change at present time. The conversion of High and medium moisture in the soil has a direct impact on the agricultural production and changing cropping pattern in the study area. As per the estimate of (Shekar, 2008) the agricultural production affected by 17% decline in the production which may latter on creates the condition of Domestic violence, and increase in the crime graph due to less food grain production. The impact of above variables was not only seen on the agricultural production but also on the forest productivity in the deficit water zones (Singh, 2006).
27. The earlier finding based on the three dimensional data gathered from the study area. Also reveals and suggests.
    - The spread of Thorny and xerophytes plants and tree species has been seen in the study area which namely *Acacia nilotica, Zizyphus xylopyra,* Kareel, Pilua.
    - The three dimensional data gathered for assessing the vegetation tree species etc. shows that the upper canopy tree or shadow providing trees like Mango, Neem, Ficus spe. these specie shave now been replaced by xerophytes plants. The wildlife which appears at the time of grandparent's like-Tiger, Tendua, Deer, Neelgai, Hare, Cats etc. Now at present time were not seen and reptile family like lizard, Goha, *vishkhanpar* (snake), camel, sheep's etc. seen in the adjoining area of the villages.
    - The water resources surface/ground water has depleted with an alarming rate. Due to installation of tube-wells, pumps and the availability of water in different resources has shown a negative trend. The increase in bringing water from the distant place has evolved heavy government expenditure to restore it to its past condition. The variation in rainfall receipt in the region has declined due to increasing temperature climate change, which was raised up to 47 degree in summer is now have become a new menace to the agriculture production and changes occurred in the cropping pattern in the area.

- The status of permanent pastures and grazing land is declining while barren and waste land s are increasing due to loss of moisture retainment in the soil. The frequency and duration of dust storms has reduced in the study area.
- It is Suggested that some of the tree species are very important from the point of view of soil conservation and slowing down the process of desertification There have been several species which grows in hostiles soil in arid region are Jatrpha curcus *Prosopis juliflora, Tribulus teristris and the next identified species which could help in combating desertification is Balanitis and Aegyptiaca.*
- *During group discussion the villagers informed that the fruit, nut wood is very important from economic medicinal and ecological point of view which helps in eradicating poverty in the area.*
- *The awareness generation programme related to desertification control, drought mitigation etc. should be conducted at the regular interval in the affected area. Especially in rural area, in collaboration with forest department.*
- The initial process of desertification could be combated through effective community participation by developing micro-watershed, stop-dams and check dams in the area.

RECOMMENDATIONS

Based on the conclusion it strongly recommended that:

- The ecological indicators related to desertification have a significant role to play in formulation and implementation of plan in the region related to desertification control.
- The developed and identified indicators of desertification related to Ecological Indicators of desertification, indicates the present status of spreading and the management strategies may be formed in tune with the measurement of above broadly categorized indicator of desertification so as to combat it in the pre-stage.

- There is an urgent and immediate attention of Planner, administrator, community and all those NGOs who concerns about the issue of spreading desertification or environmental degradation in the study area or other area to look into the causes and to find out the remedial measures by incorporating peoples plan and their priority in the study area.
- The indicator as developed for measuring the status of desertification viz. Ecological Indicators of desertification, may be replicated in other areas where the symptom of land degradation or desertification is seen.
- It is highly recommended that the responses as related to combating of desertification is concerned should be in a tune with the peoples plans those who are living in the study area of Gwalior region or in other region. Therefore, *their responses should be given high weight age with priority and must be incorporated while formulation of Plans.*
- For the ecological sustainability the control on spreading barren and increasing wasteland is very important indicator to enhance livelihood of the rural people forest productivity. The committee members have perceived that spread of wasteland and desert or barren land not only affects the ecology and natural habitat of their area but also affects the socio-psychological and economic condition of the people. The increased income may help the people to come up from the clutches of vicious cycle of poverty in the region.
- Some of the findings related to identification of Indicators during the intensive study in the Gwalior region must have to be taken into consideration to combat the desertification in the pre or initial stage rather than for waiting for further advancement.

ACKNOWLEDGEMENT

This paper is an outcome of RCNAEB Sponsored Research project "Titled" Planning Management and Developmental strategies for Crawling desertification in North West Region of Gwalior Division. Author sincerely acknowledge the NAEB, MOEF, New Delhi for the sponsoring this special study. *There is no word to express sincere gratitude to Prof. B. P. Pethiya, Director (In-charge, Coordinator RCNAEB, IIFM, Bhopal for their support and continuousinspiration to bring out this paper. This study would not have been completed unless we express our sincere thanks to the entire Villagers of 24 villages, and CF Gwlaior Circle and DFO of all five selected districts and Forest officials.*

References

Aubréville, A. (1949), Climats, forêts et désertification de l'Afrique tropicale. Société d'Edition de Géographie Maritime et Coloniale, Paris.

Anglo-French Commission (1973), Rapport de la Mission Forestière Anglofrançaise Nigeria-Niger (Decembre 1936-Fevrier 1937). Bois et Forêts des Tropiques 148:3-26.

Census of India (1991), M.P. Directorate of Population Census, GOI, Madhya Pradesh

Census of India (2001), M.P. Directorate of Population Census, GOI, Madhya Pradesh.

Chazdon, R. L. (1998), Tropical forests-log'em or leave 'em? *Science,* 281:1295-1296.

Condit, R., N. Pitam, E. G. Leigh Jr., J.Chave, J.Terborgh, R.B. Foster, P.Nunez, S.Aguilar, R.Valencia, G.Villa, H.C. Muller- Landau, E.Losos, and S. P. Hubbell (2002), Beta –diversity in tropical forest trees. *Science,* 295: 666-669.

Danjani, S. and L.Ortolano [eds.] (1979), Methods of forecasting the Reciprocals Impacts of Infrastructure Development and Land use. Report IPM –11 Stanford, C.A: Department of Engineering, Stanford University.

Elmqvist, T., M.Wall, A. L. Berggren, L. Blix, A. Fritioff, and U. Rinman (2001), Tropical Reorganization After Cyclone and Fire Disturbance in Samoa: Remant Trees as Biological Legacies. Conservation Ecology 5(2): 10 (on line, URL : *http://www.consecol.org/vol5/iss2/art 10.*

Forest, C. E., P. H. Stone, A. P. Sokolov, M. R. Allen, and M. D. Webster (2002), Quantifying uncertainties in climate system properties with the use of recent climate observations, *Science,* 295:113-117.

Helldén, U. (1991), Desertification: Time for an Assessment? Ambio, 20:372-383.

Holzel, N., Haub, C., Ingelfinger, M. P., Otte, A., and Pilipenko, V. N. (2002), The Return of the Steppe-largescale Restoration of Degraded Land in

Southern Russia during the Post-Soviet Era. *Journal for Nature Conservation,* 10:75-85.

Horstmann, B. (2002), Desertification-A Worldwide Problem. Entwicklung + Landlicher Raum 9:46-48.

Hoven, I. G. (2002), The Convention to Combat Desertification-Aims and Implementation. Entwicklung + Landlicher Raum, 9:49-53.

Jain, Hans. K. (1988), "Desert: At the Door Step of Malwa Plateau", Vol. 6, No. 3. (July-Sept. 1988) *ESCAP Environment News,* 29.

Jain, Hans. K. (1988), "Desertification in Western Madhya Pradesh", *Desertification Bulletin, No.* 19.

Krishnan, M. S. (1952), "Geological History of Rajasthan and to Present Day Conditions", *Bull, natn. Inst. India.* 1: 19-31.

K. N. Krishna Kumar, Singh, S. P. Gautam Ashok (2005), A Methodological Frame Work for Gender Participation in Livestock Resource Management. *Wasteland News, SPWD,* New Delhi. November 2004-January 2005, Vol. XX, No. 2, pp. 15-19.

Loreau, M., S. Naeem, P. Inchausti, J. Bengtsson, J. P. Grime, A. Hector, D. U. Hooper, M. A. Huston, D. Raffaelli, B. Schmid, D. Tilman, and D. A. Wardle (2001), Biodiversity and Ecosystem Functioning: Current Knowledge and Future Challenges, *Science,* 294:804-808.

Lukose, N. C. (1972), "Palynology of the Syb-surface Sediment of Manfera. Tibba Structure, Jaisalmer, Western Rajasthan." The Palaeobotanist 21 (3) 285-297.

Mann, H. S., Malhotra, S. P. and Kalla, J. C. (1974), "Desert Spread: A Quantitative Analysis in the Arid Zone of Rajasthan". *Anals of Arid Zone,* 13 (2): 103-113.

Meher-Homji (1971), "Bio-clımatic Variability with Special Reference to India", *Trop. Ecol.* 12 (2) 155-176.

M. D. OmPrakash, S. P. Singh (2006), "Micro-Watershed Approach in Rainwater Harvesting: A Case of Semi-Arid Region of Central India.", "Natural Resource Management in the Catchments area of Big Dams", Organized on 28 November 2006, by School of Economics, at Devi Ahilya University, Indore. *Paper presented as Key Resource Person.*

Mortimore, M. (1989), Adapting to Drought: Farmers, Famines and Desertification in West Africa. Cambridge: Cambridge University Press, pp. 299.

MoEF (1990), Involvement of Village Communities and Voluntary Agencies for Regeneration of Degraded Forest Lands. No. 6-21/89-F.P. Ministry of Environment and Forests Government of India, New Delhi Dated June 1, 1990.

MoEF. (2006), Combating Desertification.

Pandey, D. N. (2002), Sustainability Science for Tropical Forests, Conservation Ecology 6(1):r13.[online]URL: *http://www.consecol.org/vol6/iss1/resp13*

Phillips, O. L., Y. Malhi, N. Higuchi, W. F. Laurance, P. V. Nunez, R. M.Vasquez, S. G. Laurance, L. V. Ferreira, M. Stern, S. Brown, and J.Grace (1998), Changes in the Carbon Balance of Tropical Forests: Evidence from Long Term Plots. *Science,* 282: 439-442

Saiko, T. A. and Zonn, I. S. (2000), Irrigation Expansion and Dynamics of Desertification in the Circum-Aral Region of Central Asia. *Applied Geography*, 20:349-367.

Sala,O. E., F. S. Chapin III, J. J. Armestro, E. Berlow, J. Bloomfield, R. Dirzo, E. Huber-Sanwald, L. F. Huenneke, R. B. Jackson, A. Kinzig, R. Leemans, D. M. Lodge, H. A. Mooney, M. Oesterheld, N. L. Poff, M. T. Sykes, B. H. Walker, M. Walker, and D. H. Wall (2000), Global Biodiversity Scenarios for the Year 2100, *Science,* 287:1770-1774

Sankar, S., P. C. Anil and Amurth in collaboration with Ram Prasad, S. Raghavan, Abey George, S. P. Singh, Jyothi Krishnan. D. Duggaya, M. Mishra, B. Sreekumar and S. C. Prasad (2000), Testing and Developing Criteria and Indicators for Sustainable Management of Tropical Forests in India (Results of the Test Conducted in Kerala and Madhya Pradesh) Kerala Forest Research Institute (KFRI) Externally Funded Project. Published by KFRI.

Sankar, S., P. C. Anil and Amurth in Collaboration with Ram Prasad, S. Raghavan, Abey George, S. P. Singh, Jyothi Krishnan. D. Duggaya, M. Mishra, B. Sreekumar and S. C. Prasad (2000), Criteria and Indicators for Sustainable Plantation Forestry in India Centre for International Forestry Research,(CIFOR) Bogor, Indonesia with support from Australian Centre for International Agricultural Research (ACIAR).

Schimel, D. S., J. I. House, K. A. Hibbard, P. Bousquet, P. Ciais, P. Peylin, B. H. Baraswell, M. J. Apps, D. Baker, A. Bondeau, J. Canadell, G. Churkina, W. Carmer, A. S. Denning, C. B. Field, P. Friedlingstein, C. Goodale, M. Heimann, R. A. Houghton, J. M. Melillo, B. Moore III, D. Murdiyarso, I. Noble, S. W. Pacala, I.C. Prentice, M. R. Raupach, P. J. Rayner, R. J. Scholes, W. L. Steffen, and C. Wirth (2001), Recent Patterns and Mechanisms of Carbon Exchange by Terrestrial Ecosystems. *Nature*, 414: 169-172

Singh, Gambhir (1952), "The Rajputana Desert, Geography", Proc. Rajputana Desert. Bull. Natn. Inst. Sci. India, 151-152.

Singh, S. P. (1989), Impact of Drought: A Study of Ratlam District of M. P., M.Phil Dissertation, Department of R.P.E.G. Barkatullah Bhopal M.P. , pp. 73-76.

Singh, S. P. (1990), "How to conserve Diesel Electric Power and Under Ground Water Resource : A case study of some cluster villages of Bhopal district, Madhya Pradesh and Etawah district of Uttar Pradesh." Proceedings of 24th Annual Regional Science Conference, Organised by the Institute of Development Studies, Lucknow, U. P . Findings Implemented.

Singh, S. P. (1992), "Why we are not able to check the rapidly increasing population ? A search of some authentic cases: A case study of Etawah district, U.P." Proceedings of *25th Silver Jubilee International Regional Science Conference*, Indian Institute of Technology, Kharagpur on 17-19 December, 1992. page 3. 17. Paper referred in Project by Centre for Future Study at Pondicherry University.

Singh, S. P. (1993), "How Individual Decisions are Affected by Social and Institutional Values in Drought Affected Areas? A Case Study of Sailana Block of Ratlam district" in International Symposium on Modelling and Simulation, Organized by Dr. Tony Jackman, at National University of Australia,22 Dec. to 26 Dec. 1993. Vide acceptance letter of Dr. A.J. Jackman, President, MSSA, National University of Australia.

Singh, S. P. (1993), "Planning, Management and Developmental Strategies to combat Crawling Desertification: A case study of North-Western Region Madhya Pradesh", Paper Accepted in International Conference on Regional Development Challenge of Frontier, Org. Deptt. of Geography. Ben-Gurion University. Bheer Sheeba ISRAEL, held on 28th December to 31st December, 1993. Time: 28 December 1993 at 13:05–13:30. As Panelist.

Singh, S. P. and Singh Dharam (1993), "Drinking Water Crisis: A Study of Chaturvedi Nagar of Bhind City, M.P.", Proceedings of *National Seminar on Ground Water Management*, Organised by: Deptt. of Geography, Govt. P. G. College, Tikam Garh, M.P. February 1993.

Singh, S. P. (1994), "Will the Drought be Occurring this Year? A Search of Some Traditional and Cultural Indicators: A Case of Etawah Proceedings of 26th Annual Regional Science Conference, Organized by Prof. Nagalingachar at K.E.L.S.'s College of Engg. and Tech., Balgaum 29 and 30 April, 1994.

Singh, S. P. and Alok Devidi (1994), "Impact of Drought on Fish Production: A Case Study of Some Ponds in Mahewa Block of Etawah District of U.P." in Proceedings of International Seminar on Disaster's, Environment and Development, held on 9-12 December 1994, Organised by: Deptt. of Geography, Delhi School of Economics, Delhi University, page 26.

Singh, S.P. (1994), "Impact of Drought on Eco-system: A Case Study of Ratlam District. Communicated for Publication by the Editor Prof. C. R. Pathak, Secretary, *Indian Journal of Regional Sciences.*

Singh, S. P. (1996), Why Our Permanent Pastures and Grazing Lands are Contracting? A Search of Some Responsible Factors in Balaghat and Mandla Region. (pp. 31) *Proceedings of National Workshop* (2-3 Feb. 1996) on Environmental Impact on Human Health, Organised by Maharaja Autonomous College Chhattarpur. M.P.

Singh, S. P. and Chandra, Jagadish (2001), *Application of Cartographic Techniques in Wild life Management with Special Reference to Canids and Fields of Van Vihar National Park*, Bhopal M. P. in XX INCA International Congress: Cartographic Challenges at the Dawn of the New Millennium. Replicated In Assam.

Singh, S. P. (2004), Socio-Economic Issues in Sustainability of Joint Forest Management in Madhya Pradesh, Ph.D. Thesis, Department of Regional Planning and Economic Growth, Barkatullah University, Bhopal.

Singh, S. P., Phukan, B. R., Manish M, Mishra Apurva (2005), Application of Cartographic Techniques at Grass Root Level for Sustainable Fire Management: A Case Study of Betul District in Indian Cartographer Silver Jubilee Volume, Published in 2006 Oct. (Proceedings of 25 International Cartographic Congress–Bridging the Digital Divide and Taking Cartography to Grass Root Level), *Journal of Indian National Cartographic Association*, Vol. 25, pp. 143-149.

Singh S. P., Phukan B. R, Mishra Manish, Mishra Apurva (2005), Application of Cartographic Techniques at Grass Root Level for Sustainable Fire Management: A Case Study Betul District. Souvenir & Abstract of XXV International Cartographic Congress 'Bridging the Digital Device and taking cartography to grass root level held at H. S. Gour University Sagar, M.P. During 28 Nov. to 1st December, 2005. PP. 46-47. One copy of Paper is requested by the chairperson of the technical session for the benefit of Geographers Association of India.

Singh, S. P., Phukan B. R., Mishra Manish, Mishra Apurva (2006), Impact of Forest Fire on NTFPs: A Case Study of Betul Forest Division. M.P. Souvenir & Abstract of XIIth Silviculture Conference (February 1-3, 2006) Organized by Forest Research Institute, Dehradun. Two Conclusions of the paper are accepted as recommendation of the conference.

Singh, S. P., Phukan B. R., Mishra Manish, Mishra Apurva (2006), Mapping of Forest Fire Damages and Fire Induced Disease Management Through Cartographic Techniques: A Study of Betul District, Madhya Pradesh. Souvenir & Abstract of National Seminar on Environmental Conservation and Mapping) held at National Atlas and Thematic Mapping, Kolkata, Organized during 2-4 March 2006.

Singh, S. P., Phukan B. R., Mishra Manish, Mishra Apurva (2006), Regional Planning for Fire Prone Zones of Betul Forest Division through Community Participation, *Proceedings* of National Seminar on Role of Urban Local Government in Disaster Management , during 23-24 March 2007,Organized by Regional Centre for Urban & Environmental Studies, Ministry of Urban Development, GoI, Lucknow, U. P., pp. 6-7.

Singh, S. P. (2006), A Quest for Sustainable Development and Management of Natural Resources: A Future Road Map. *Indian Journal of Development, Research and Social Sction (An International Journal,* Jan-June-2006) Serials Publication New Delhi, 2 (1) 31-52.

Singh, S. P. (2006), A Quest for Sustainable Development and Management of Natural Resources: A Future Road Map. Paper presented in National Seminar on Sustainable Development and Land Resources: Opportunities and Challenges held at Armapore P.G. College Kanpur, during 27-28, January, 2006. Implemented in Land use Planning Board by Govt. of Uttar Pradesh.

Singh, S. P., (2006), "Forest Productivity in Surplus and Deficit Water Resource Regions: A Comparative Study of Jhabua and Mandla Districts of Madhya Pradesh" In one day Panel discussion on "Natural Resource Management in the Catchments area of Big Dams", Organized on 28 November 2006, by School of Economics, at Devi Ahilya University, Indore.

Singh R. D. and Singh S. P. (2006), Involving and Evolving: Impact on Ecological Sustainability and Related Issues, pp. 34-37, Vol. XXI, No. 2., *Wastelands News*, November 2005-January 2006, SPWD, New Delhi, India.

Singh, R. D. Singh S. P. (2006), Impact of Joint Forest management on Ecological Sustainability and Related Issues: A Comparative Study of

Jhabua and Mandla Districts of Madhya Pradesh, pp. 145-152, *Indian Journal of Millenium Studies: An International Journal,* Vol. 1 (1), March 2006, Serials Publications, New Delhi.

Singh, S. P. (2006), A Quest for Sustainable Development and Management of Natural Resources: A Future Road Map. *Indian Journal of Development, Research and Social Action (An International Journal,* Jan-June-2006): 2 (1) 31-52.

Singh R. D. and Singh S. P. (2006), *Involving and Evolving: Impact on Ecological Sustainability and Related Issues.* Silver Jubilee Publication, Selected Readings from Wastelands News on Forests, SPWD's, New Delhi, India, Vol. (1), pp. 07-11.

Singh, S. P. and Mishra, Apurva (2007), Impact of Population Growth on Economic Development and Environment: A Comparative Study of Uttar Pradesh and Madhya Pradesh. Proceedings of National Workshop on "Trends in Population: Its Impact on Economic Development and Environment", during 9-11 February 2007, Organized by Department of Economics, Govt. P. G. College, Khargone, M. P. pp. 15-45 Paper Presented as Key resource Person.

S. P. Singh, M. Mishra, Phukan, B. R., Mishra Apurva (2007), Impact of Forest Fire on Ecological Sustainability and Fire Induced Disease Management: A Case Study of Betul District of M.P. Paper Presented in Special Technical Session-3 on Natural Resource Management and Sustainable Livelihood in Mountains on 3rd December 2007, in International-Tropical Ecology Congress 2007 to be Organized by HNB Garwal University, Srinagar (Garwal), Uttarakhand at FRI Dehradun during 2-5 December 2007. As Resource person.

Singh, S. P., Manish M, Phukan, B. R., Mishra Apurva (2007), 'Economics of Forest Fire Management: A Study of South Betul Forest Division of Madhya Pradesh' Published in Krishnamoorthy G.R., Awadesh Kumar Singh (2007) India in Global Economy-In Association with Ananya Institute of Development & Social Action, Lucknow, Chapter 23 , pp. 359-374 , Serial Publications, New Delhi.

Singh, S. P. and Biswas, P. K. (2008), "Impact of Domestic Violence against women on Forest Conservation and Sustainable Livelihoods: A study of Sheopur District of Madhya Pradesh paper presented as Key resource person In the National Seminar on " Domestic Violence Against Women and Role of Domestic Violence Act. 2006 Jointly organised by Pt. G.B.Pant Institute of Studies in Rural Development and ANANYA-Institute For Development Research and Social Action at Lucknow

During 19-20 July 2008, Sponsored by Planning Commission Government of India New Delhi.

Singh, S. P. and Hota D. K. (2008), "Ecological and Socio-Economic Impacts of Caution Diversion of Road ways Network on Forests Land Cover : A Concept paper presented and also Published in the souvenir of International Seminar of IGU Commission on Land Use Land Cover Change and Agro- Bio-diversity, pp. 74 , Organised by National P.G. College, Lucknow U. P., March 7-8, 2008.

Singh, S. P. (2008), Participated in One day Seminar on "Global Warming and Climate Change", Organised by Asian Education Society in Collaboration with IIFM, M.P. Forest Department at IIFM, Bhopal March 15, 2008.

Singh, Shekar (2008), "Climate Change and Development", Paper Presented in One day Seminar on "Global Warming and Climate Change' Organised by Asian Education Society in Collaboration with IIFM, M.P Forest Department at IIFM, Bhopal March 15, 2008.

Swift, J. (1996), Desertification: Narratives, Winners & Losers, p. 73-90 in Leach, M. and Mearns, R. (eds.), The Lie of the Land: Challenging Received Wisdom on the African Environment. London: James Currey/ International African Institute.

UNCCD (1995), Down to Earth: A Simplified Guide to the Convention to Combat Desertification, why it is Necessary and what is Important and Different About it. Bonn, Germany: Secretariat for the United Nations Convention to Combat Desertification.

(see also Facts Sheet, FAQ and Explanatory Leaflet at *http://www.unccd.int/knowledge/menu.php)*

UNCED, or the Earth Summit) in Rio de Janeiro in 1992.

UNEP/CBD/COP/7/21 Pp. 186-191, ref. Decisions V/6 and VII/11. On web at http://www.biodiv.org/decisions/default.aspx?lg=0&dec=V/6 and at

http://www.biodiv.org/decisions/default.aspx?m=COP-07&id=7748&lg=0

UNDP (1999), Innovating with the Internet, p. 64 in UNDP Human Development Report 1999. New York: United Nations Development Programme.

UNEP (1999), UNEP Initiative on Success Stories in Land Degradation-desertification Control: Summaries of 'Saving the Drylands' Award-winning-projects, 1995-1998. Nairobi: United Nations Environment Programme (UNEP), Land Unit, Dryland Ecosystem and Desertification

Control/PAC. 21 pp. Also available on *website at http://www.unep.org/unep/envpolimp/techcoop/1.htm*

UN (2000), United Nations Millennium Declaration. Section IV Para. 23. General Assembly Resolution 55/2 of 8 September 2000. New York: The United Nations.

UN (2001), Road Map Towards the Implementation of the United Nations Millennium Declaration. Report of the Secretary General. General Assembly document A/56/326, 6 September 2001. New York: The United Nations.

UNCBD (2004), Decisions Adopted by the Conference of the Parties to the Convention on Biological Diversity at its Seventh Meeting, Kuala Lumpur, Malaysia 9-20 February. UNEP 1997. World Atlas of Desertification. London: Arnold.

UNEP (2003), State of the Environment. UNEP/GCSS.VIII/2. Nairobi: United Nations Environment Programme.

Vinod, Shankar (1977), "Measuring Desertification Through Plant Indicators" Desertification Control, ICAR PUE 1977. 20: 193-195.

Vishnu–Mittre (1977), "Origin and History of the Rajasthan Desert–Paleobotanical Evidence", Desertification Control, ICAR PUB. 1977. 2: 6-9.

Wadia, D. N. (1960), "The Past Glacial Desiccation of Central Asia.", Monogramme. Natn. Inst. Sci. India, 10: 1-25.

Winslow, M., Shapiro, B. I., Thomas, R. and Shetty, S. V. R. (2004), Desertification, Drought, Poverty and Agriculture: Research Lessons and Opportunities. Aleppo, Syria; Patancheru, India; and Rome, Italy: Joint Publication of the International Center for Agricultural Research in the Dry Areas (ICARDA), the International Crops Research Institute for the Semi-Arid Tropics (ICRISAT), and the UNCCD Global Mechanism (GM). 52 pp.

6

COMMUNITY PARTICIPATION FOR RURAL DEVELOPMENT IN INDIA

D. Pulla Rao

INTRODUCTION

It has been the constant endeavor of the "planners" to give adequate thrust to rural development as the sector is directly related to agriculture –still the mainstay for the majority of India's population. The focus has never shifted from developing the country's vast tracts of rural lands where the majority of the population exists. And as far as planning goes, it dates way back to the 1930s. Even before Independence, the colonial government had created a planning board that lasted from 1944 to 1946 where private industrialists and economists published three development plans in1944 where there were several references to agriculture and allied areas.

Though India has gained vast experience in the implementation of rural development programme over the last several decades, it has been ranked as low as 135th in the development ranking among a total of 174 countries by the United Nations Development Programme (UNDP). The approaches to rural development have changed over a period of time. In the light of the experience gained by following a particular approach, a new approach has been evolved. The shift in the emphasis is intended to accelerate the pace of growth. Right from the beginning of planning it was rightly thought that rural development planning could not be effective without substantial participation of the people.

MEANING OF COMMUNITY DEVELOPMENT

Community Development has been variously described as a process of change from old ways of life of rural communities to new and progressive one, as method by which people can be helped to develop their own capacity and resources, as a programme for accomplishing certain activities in certain fields and as movement with certain ideological background.

COMMUNITY DEVELOPMENT: AN HISTORICAL PERSPECTIVE

The Community Development Programme, in its present shape, had its beginning early in1952 when the Ford Foundation established a dozen or more "Projects" in different parts of the country. It was closely associated with the Bhadson Project in erstwhile PEPSU state. The concept of the community projects is based on the faith that "gram Kalyan" can be brought about by the joint efforts of the services and the people if they are properly co-ordinated and directed. The Community Development Programme envisages a very ideal state of village development and is in this respect closely related to Gandhiji's concept of Ramarajya. The community development programme in India is aiming at the all-round development of the rural people.

During the pre-Independence era, various scattered and short lived efforts were made towards rural development in various parts of the country by individual or some organizations. Notable among these were Mahatma Gandhi's work at "sevagram." Tagore's work at "shantiniketan," Spencer Hatch's efforts at "Marthandam," F.L. Brayne's work at "Gurgaon", Firka Development Scheme in Tamil Nadu, India village service, etc.

It was during this period that the Department of Agriculture came into being in June, 1871 under the Government of India, and by 1882, agricultural departments in most of the provinces started functioning in skeleton form. Recognising the need for new and improved method of cultivation based on agricultural research, the then Government of India also set-up an Institute of Agricultural Research at Pusa in Bihar in 1905. The village continued to remain neglected and disorganised. The yield of crops were low, the animals remain underfed with very low productivity. The villager's lot, on the whole presented a gloomy picture. Before independence,

Government efforts to bring about improvement in rural areas were directed though fairly well organised Development Departments, such as agriculture, irrigation, animal husbandry, cooperation, health, education, etc. These, however, worked independently of one another, following their own programme and without a sense of common objective.

Thus, the process of Community Development is made up of two elements: the participation of the people themselves in efforts to improve their lives with as much reliance as possible on their own initiative; and the provision of technical and other services in ways which encourage initiative, self help and make these more effective. It is expressed in programmes designed to achieve a wide variety of specific improvements.

ROLE OF GOVERNMENT IN RURAL DEVELOPMENT

A strong commitment to rural development policies at the national level is required if the impact on the problems of rural poverty is to be effective and broad-based. The present policies and institutional structures have been so far from favorable to rural development that a policy shift can emerge only after a major political change. This is a key problem in situations demanding extensive land reform; it applies even more where the Government itself is dominated by special interests, which are unsympathetic to the objectives of rural development. In most other countries, governments are prepared to experiment at the project level. But some hold the view that rural development is technically difficult or economically unsound, for it may lead to slower growth in output and exports. Whatever the reasons, unless more governments commit themselves firmly to devising strategies and policies to raise the standards of living of the rural poor, the lot of millions of people will not improve significantly. Rural development objectives can be sought in various ways once there is firm commitment on price policy, fiscal policy, land policy, regional policy, technology policy, etc.

VOLUNTARY AGENCIES IN RURAL DEVELOPMENT

The voluntary agencies working for the uplift of rural people have had a long history in this country. The earliest to take up this work were missionaries and religious organizations. The impact of their work may be seen in the fields of education and health and the general uplift of the people in backward and remote areas of the country.

It has been recognised that voluntary agencies can play a very creative role motivating the people and supervising the distribution of the resources with a view to ensuring their proper utilisation. They can also play a very useful role in matching projects to the local conditions and supplying local know-how about the various factors affecting productivity marketing.

The experience of some of the voluntary agencies shows that where they have sought to tackle the social problems related to traditions and religious values, they have had to face problems of acceptance by the villagers. This factor has been recognized by the newer voluntary organizations, which avoid areas of confrontrations and plan their programmes specifically for the purpose of raising productivity and providing employment. They feel that other social changes and changes in outlook and attitudes will follow, however slowly.

Individuals or a group of individuals have generally started voluntary agencies, often motivated by the sprit of charity or social work. Some of these agencies have had people working on a part-time/honorary basis. But the situation appears to be changing now, as evidenced by such agencies as the Maliwada Human Development Project (Aurangabad, Maharashtra), Kishore Bharati (Hoshangabad, Madhya Pradesh), Social Work and Research Centre (Tilonia, Rajasthan), Land Research Institute (Shedgewadi, Maharashtra), and Rural University (Jawaja, Rajasthan). Professional people have formed these organisations, and they have been able to attract others with similar interests.

Although voluntary agencies have, by and large, adopted the integrated development approach, they initially concentrated on the provision of such basic services as medicine, education etc. The rapport with local leadership and the acceptance by the local community are easier to establish in this manner. It is only after this has been achieved- and it may sometimes take as long as five to six years- that they have sought to take up more comprehensive programmes of village improvement covering such aspects as agriculture extension, construction of roads and minor irrigation projects and, at times, even social problems. The emphasis given to each of these activities depends on the needs of the particular area and the specialization of the agencies. For example, the Yusuf Meherally Centre (Bombay) places greater emphasis on medical services; Kishore Bharati on agricultural extension and education; and the Social Work and Rese arch Centre on groundwater surveys and the promotion of handicrafts.

Voluntary agencies have an important role in informing and motivating people and in carrying out supplemental action for improving incomes by promoting silf-employment activity, helping in the identification of eligible households, organising them for group action, informing them about schemes and official procedures, preparing applications, and offering follow-up and liaison services etc. The main responsibility for resources transfer has to remain with official and financial institutions. They can help in guiding and project formulation processes. Universities and professional institutions, for example, can help in block and village planning exercises. The voluntary agencies may bring supplementary funds to oil and lubricate the movements of projects, which often get blocked because of the rigidities inherent in official progtammes and procedures.

RURAL DEVELOPMENT STRATEGIES AFTER INDEPENDENCE

The initial post-independent rural development strategy was developed with the approach of rural reconstruction and much emphasis was laid on village centred movement based on principles of voluntary effort. The first massive rural development strategy called the Community Development Programme (CDP) was launched with the beginning of the First Five Year Plan. In this approach, a lot of importance was given to rural development based on ideas of motivation, self-help and self-reliance. This programme was a cooperative partnership between the Government and the people for the all-round development of the people in a particular area. By the Third Five Year Plan, the entire country was covered with community development blocks numbering over 5,000. The community development blocks became the units of administration, planning, coordination and development for rural people with focus on integrated rural development.

The integrated approach to the rural development however, got gradually diluted with the work relating to village industries were being handed over to the Khadi and Village Industries Commission (KVIC). The greater emphasis on food production resulted in the launching of Intensive Agriculture Development Programme (IADP) in selected districts followed by the Intensive Agriculture Area Programme (IAAP) and the High Yielding Varieties Programme (HYVP). All these programmes or strategies of Rural Development were formulated with the target sector approach, which had its emphasis on the intensive development of a selected sector or sectors of activity with emphasis on concentrating in areas of comparative advantages.

By the late 1960s and the early 1970s it was perceived that even though the intensive effort in agriculture had led to the green revolution, the benefits of this largely confined to the big farmers and areas, which were better placed to receive the benefits of HYV technology. This resulted in inter-regional and intra-regional disparities. Therefore, the need to take special measures for the benefit of the poorer sections of the population and for the development of backward and disadvantaged areas was felt. In view of this, the next phase of rural development strategies focused on target groups, growth centres, backward area development and catering to the minimum needs of the poorer sections. The emphasis was given to growth with social justice, (the weaker sections of population) special planning and development, the reduction of regional imbalances like Small Farmers Development Agency (SFDA), Marginal Farmers and Agricultural Labourers (MFAL), cash schemes for rural employment, pilot intensive rural development programme, Food for Work programme, Drought Prone Areas and Desert Development Programmes and the minimum needs programme were launched.

With the launching of the Sixth Plan the attempt to tackle the problems of the deprived sections of the population and geographical areas were further consolidated, rationalised and expanded. The SFDA and MFAL were replaced by the Integrated Rural Development Programme (IRDP), which was extended to cover the entire country and its scope expanded to all activities in the primary, secondary and tertiary sectors. Under this programme, income base criteria for identification of the target group were prescribed and household approach was adopted. The IRDP strategy was gradually transmitted with an approach of area planning with full employment while laying emphasis on rural development in an area for removal of unemployment and poverty as an important aim. In this direction IRDP also aimed to provide skills through Training of Rural Youth for Self-Employment (TRYSEM) and assist through a mix of subsidy and credit with the ultimate objective of raising the people above the poverty line. A special programme for economic Development of Women and Children in Rural Areas (DWCRA) was also developed and linked to the self-employment programme. The food for Work Programme was restructured in the form of National Rural Employment Programme (NREP). Another special employment programme of Rural Landless Employment Guarantee Programme (RLEGP) was launched in 1983-84 with the specific objective of providing up to 100 days of employment per year to at least one member of each rural landless household.

The programmes of the Sixth Plan were continued with a sharper focus and higher outlays during the Seventh and Eighth Plan periods. The aforesaid wage employment programmes (NREP) and (RLEGP) were merged into Jawahar Rozgar Yojana (JRY), and Indira Awaas Yojana (IAY), and the concept of JRY was strengthened both qualitatively and quantitatively. Subsequently, Employment Assurance Scheme (EAS) was introduced for assured employment up to 100 days in the lean agricultural season. Though the choice of interventions in planning rural development process has shifted from the target sector to the target areas and target groups, and employment generation approaches and their combinations, all the economic indicators relating to Indian rural economy explain very clearly that it was not possible to meet most of the basic needs of the rural people. In this context to provide basic needs to the common rural population, the Government of India changed the direction of rural development planning towards micro or grass root level planning in a phased manner.

THE SHORTFALLS OF THE COMMUNITY DEVELOPMENT PROGRAMMES

- A large chunk of the benefits went to the rich farmers only.
- Small farmers and marginal farmers are left behind.
- Rich farmers became more rich and small farmers and marginal farmers lagged behind and became more poor and thus the gap widened further.

- The rich farmers, the major beneficiaries did not contribute any thing for the development plans as was contemplated in the original community development programme.
- Faulty plan implementation.
- No balanced development.
- It is very ambitious programme with limited funds.
- Lack of adequate training to the personnel involved.
- Grass root level participation was lacking.

THE NEED FOR A NOVEL METHOD OF RURAL DEVELOPMENT AT GRASS ROOT LEVEL

Peoples participation occupies a central place in development thinking and practice. Governments, funding agencies, donors, and civil society actors including NGOs and multi-lateral agencies like the World Bank and the International Monetary Fund (IMF) have all arrived at a near consensus that development cannot be sustainable and long-lasting unless people's participation is made central to the development process. While there is a virtual unanimity about the need for people's participation in development, there is a wide spectrum of views on the concept of participation and the ways of ensuring it. This paper makes a rudimentary attempt at summarizing some of the contemporary thinking on participatory development.

What is Participation?

Participation means doing things together, exchanging ideas and experiences, consulting and considering all views, sharing in decision making, co-implementing, co-operation, sharing and learning, empowerment, democratic, risk sharing, collective ideas and efforts, getting involved, sharing ideas, opinions and experiences, doing things together in work, analysis and decision making and consulting together all views in survey or interview and other activities. Examples of participation are workshops, farmers group meetings or group training, on-the-job training including on-farm training, networking with other institutions, and monitoring and evaluation such as self-evaluation. Participation is also the sensitization of people to increase their reception and ability to respond. Participation is also the fostering of a dialogue between the local people and project preparation, implementation, monitoring and evaluation in order to obtain information on the local context and on social impacts.

The participatory approach involves face-to-face relationships and this leads to better understanding to a pooling of diverse talents and a greater willingness to carry through the decisions once they are made. Participation leads to the development of individuals for positions of higher responsibility. There is nothing like exposing people to PRA for improving their skill and knowledge about local situation and making them more amenable to change.

Participation in Participatory Rural Appraisal (PRA) process is communication between development and research workers and local people, where local people take the leading role to analyze the current situation and plan to implement and evaluate agricultural development activities. So all the stakeholders directly or indirectly gain in a given activity.

Basic Elements of Participatory Approaches

White (1982) wrote that community participation has three main elements:

(a) the involvement of the community in deciding what should be done and how it should be carried out; (b) a mass contribution to the development effort; (c) a sharing of the benefits a given program may bring. A fourth element may be the involvement of the community in the evaluation process.

White gave the following ten arguments for community participation in local development projects in various fields:

1. More will be accomplished.
2. Services can be provided at a lower cost.
3. Participation has intrinsic value for participants, alleviating feelings of alienation and powerlessness.
4. Participation is a catalyst for further development efforts.
5. Participation leads to a sense of responsibility for the project.
6. Participation guarantees that a felt need is involved.
7. Participation ensures that things are done the right way.

8. Participation ensures the use of indigenous knowledge and expertise.
9. Participation brings freedom from dependence on professionals; and
10. Participation brings about 'conscientization', i.e., it helps people understand the nature of the constraints, which are hindering their escape from poverty (pp. 20-34).

Advantages of PRA in Rural Development

Participation in development is now being sought the world over, not because it is a fad but because there has been a consensus on the usefulness of participation in development projects. The major advantages of participation as enumerated by Oakley *et. al.* (1991) are:

Efficiency: Participation can ensure effective utilisation of available resources. The people and other agents work in tandem towards achieving their objectives. The local people take responsibility for various activities. Alt these improve efficiency and make the project more cost-effective.

There is the danger, however, that the government and other agencies, in the name of people's participation, may assign fewer resources and transfer the burden of project costs onto the local people.

Effectiveness: Lack of people's involvement has been seen as one of the major causes of the failure of most projects to be effective. People's participation can make the projects more effective by granting them a say in deciding the objectives and strategies, and by participating in implementation, thereby ensuring effective utilization of resources.

Self-reliance: Many development interventions have been seen to create a kind of dependence syn-drome. For instance, in India, because of widespread government development programmes, people have started looking to the government for solutions to every problem that they face. If the local resources however—both human and material—are utilised on the basis of decisions taken by the people themselves, the realisation grows that many problems faced by the people have local solutions at their levels. With active involvement of the local people, it is possible not only to break the mentality of dependence but also to increase their awareness, self-confidence, and control of the development process. In fact, the involvement in decision-making, implementation, and monitoring helps in developing local human resources.

Coverage: Development interventions are directed towards the upliftment of the weaker sections of society. Despite professed target groups and attempts to cover the weaker sections, however, most projects have been at best only partially successful. The benefits are cornered off by the non-poor, the elite, and the powerful. People's participation can be a potent way of ensuring the flow of the benefits to the target groups. Furthermore, the cost-effective operations can ensure that resources are available for wider coverage of the weaker sections of society than would otherwise be possible.

Sustainability: Generally, development interventions are funded either by governments or by donor agencies. Experience has shown that development interventions from the externally assisted projects fail to sustain the required level of development activity once support or inputs are diminished or withdrawn by the funding agencies. People's participation is regarded as an essential prerequisite for the continuity of the activities. The involvement of local people and the utilization of local resources generates a sense of ownership over the development interventions to the people. This sense of ownership is essential for the sustainability of the interventions even after external funds cease to flow.

ROLE OF UNIVERSITIES IN RURAL DEVELOPMENT

Universities can play an important role in the community development especially in the developing countries like India.

In our country H.N.Bahuguna Garhwal University, Srinagar, is participating in a large number of extension activities such as Adult Education Population Education, Continuing Education Courses, AIDS Awareness, Consumer Education, Environmental Education, Women Empowerment, Science for the Masses, Mobile Library, Legal Literacy etc. are being organized by the department for the benefit of rural/ urban communities and university/colleges students. These programmes are being organized with the help of students and teachers of the university and colleges.

The University of Delhi is also playing an important role in community development. The impact study of educational interventions in north-east Delhi has been a study of prolonged interventions in the urban cluster 'Jagatpur' just 10 kms away from the University of Delhi. The educational interventions are done in two phases adopting integrated approach of development.

The University of North Bengal is also doing extension, outreach and consultancy services. The university of North Bengal is aware of its responsibilities for knowledge dissemination in transforming the social base, in particular, in backward districts on North Bengal. The social dynamics of North Bengal is a complex one having multi-ethnic cultures in social milieu. The society-university interaction may ease social tension and strife in rendering valuable services for developmental programmes. The Centre of Adult and Continuing Education plays significant role in human resource development through various training programmes on mushroom culture, fisheries, medicinal plants and health awareness.

The Karnataka University, which is a pioneer university in this regard even, went out to establish a position of an educational counselor in its centre to guide and direct the students in the bureau, where information regarding higher education and job opportunities was available in abundance.

Besides, several Agricultural Universities and Universities with rural development extension departments are playing a very important role in rural development designing, implementation and evaluation programmes.

THE INVOLVEMENT OF THE DEPARTMENT OF COOPERATION AND APPLIED ECONOMICS IN COMMUNITY DEVELOPMENT THROUGH PRA

The Department of Cooperation and Applied Economics, Andhra University is offering a course on Participatory Rural Appraisal (PRA) for M.A. Final year students. The paper constitutes both theory and fieldwork. Every year, batch after batch of 40 students are being taken into rural areas and are involved in assessment of the various rural development programmes being planned and implemented at the village level in Visakhapatnam District of Andhra Pradesh.

Village Study

As a part of fieldwork in 2003 we had visited Tadi village of Paravada Mandal, Visakhapatnam District and conducted a survey on social, economic, educational, health and infrastructural facilities in the village through participatory methods. This is a dry village with scanty of rainfall.

Our study revealed that the status of education is very low in Tadi Village. About 46 per cent of people are illiterates. This suggests enhancement of educational facilities. In the village 40 per cent are main workers and remaining 60 per cent are non-workers. Among workers only 5.7 per cent are cultivators and 22.8 per cent are agricultural labourers. So Government should provide food for work programme to increase the wage employment opportunities in this village. About 97 per cent of the villagers are suffering from common diseases like cold, cough and fever, and 14 per cent people are suffering from chronic diseases. Some medical facilities need to be improved.

Medical and Health Programmes

Some of the staff members of our department are actively involved in a voluntary organization i.e., Sri Gayatri Welfare & Cultural Youth Academy. And through this organization we are conducting many community development activities like legal awareness programmes, eye camps, dental camps, blood donation camps, AIDS awareness programmes, medical and health programmes etc., in various slums and schools in Visakhapatnam city with the help of the medical and para medical personnel from King George Hospital and Regional Eye Hospital etc. We collect the medicines from various doctors and medical representatives etc., and distribute them to the poor free of cost. We also assist in admitting the patients in the local government hospitals as per need.

So far the Sri Gayatri Welfare & Cultural Youth Academy had organized more than 300 medical and health camps in slums and municipal schools in Visakhapatnam Corporation and also in some tribal areas of the district. This organization was awarded the National Youth Award and also received a cash prize for the year 2002-2003.

Survey on the Outbreak of Fevers in Paderu Tribal Belt

In response to the media reports and the declaration of 'Medical Emergency' by the Government of Andhra Pradesh, The School of Economics and Department of social work jointly undertook Rapid survey of outbreak of fevers in Paderu area in Visakhapatnam District in the month of August, 2005. The study covers 80 affected households in four Mandals (Paderu, Hukkumpeta, Dumbriguda and Araku) covering 140 illness episodes.

Our vice-chancellor had released the report and handed over a copy of it to the Chief Minister of Andhra Pradesh. We received a word of appreciation from the Chief Minister of Andhra Pradesh.

The department also participated in collaboration with the State Bank of Hyderabad in the survey of fever-affected households at Valasi village in Anantagiri Mandal of Visakhaptnam District in the month of September, 2005. We surveyed all the households in the village and assessed their health status and distributed blankets, mosquito nets, rice, Ayden salt and red grams etc., to the deserving poor.

SUMMARY AND CONCLUSIONS

The Community Development Programme in India is aiming at the all-round development of the rural people. Before Independence, private individual/ organizations made some efforts towards rural development in various parts of the country. But, after Independence, India has started implementation of various rural development programmes. And the approaches to rural development have been changing over a period of time in tune with the changing needs of the people. Right from the beginning of planning it was rightly thought that rural development in India could be more effective with peoples' participation.

The Government plays an important role in rural development. A strong commitment to rural development policies at the national level is required if rural poverty is to be eradicated on a time bound frame.

The voluntary agencies are also working for the uplift of rural people. The NGOs play a very creative role in motivating the people and supervising the distribution of the resources with a view to ensuring their proper utilization. Most of the shortfalls in community development programmes could be overcome with people's participation in the community development programme at the grass root level. In the participatory approach the main principle is that all people come together, work together and share together right from decision-making stage through implementation stage. Making the villagers to participate in decision making, project design, execution and monitoring is essentials for participatory approach. Local people know the best about their own problems and solutions. Universities are also playing an important role in community development programmes in conducting various surveys on social, economic, educational, health and infrastructural facilities in the villages through participatory methods. Our department is also participating in collaboration with some NGOs and governmental organizations in the community development programmes in urban slums, municipal schools and also in some tribal areas in and around Visakhapatnam District.

All these efforts, from all sides, need to be intensified for achieving higher rates of growth and development with in the given time frame.

References

Dhillon and B. S. Hanssa. (1995), "People's Participation in Rural Development Programme", *Kurukshetra,* January.

Dwarakanath. (1995), "Rural Development Policy and Programme Implementation: An Evaluation", *Social Action,* October-December, Vol. 45, No. 4.

Khurana, I. R. (1988), "Strategy for Rural Development", *Khadi Gram Udyog.* 34 (8). pp. 335-344.

Maheswari, S. R. (1995), Rural Development in India-A Public Policy Approach, Sage Publications, New Delhi.

Neela Mukherjee (1998), Participatory Rural Appraisal-Methodology and Applications, Concept Publishing Company, New Delhi.

Okley, P. *et. al.* (1991), Projects with People–The Practice of Participation in Rural Development, pp 2-10. International Labour Office, Geneva.

Tyagi, B. P. (1990), Agricultural Economics and Rural Development, Jai Prakash Nath & Co., Meerut.

Udaya Bhaskara Reddy (1987), "Role of Voluntary Agencies in Rural Development", *The Indian Journal of Public Administration,* July-September, Vol. XXXIII. No. 3, New Delhi.

Vasant Desai (1988), Rural Development-Programmes and Strategies, Himalaya Publishing House, New Delhi.

White, A. T. (1982), "Why Community Participation? A Discussion of the Arguments". Assessment Children, 59/60, UNICEF, Geneva.

7

FINANCIAL RESOURCE MOBILIZATION STRATEGIES IN INDIA

V. Gnaneshwar

URBAN FINANCIAL CRISIS IN INDIA

With the prolonged neglect of the urban local bodies in the face of urban growth and metropolitaniztion in India, the urban financial crisis was immanent. The Urban Local Bodies (ULBs) revenue base is very weak due to structural constraints of Indian federalism. For instance, the size of the municipal fiscal sector in India is very small compared to that in many developed and developing countries and in relation to the public services that the urban local bodies are mandated to deliver. It is reported that the total municipal revenue in India account for about 0.75 per cent of the country's GDP as against a figure of 4.5 per cent for Poland, 5 per cent for Brazil and 6 per cent for South Africa. In terms of revenue as well as expenditure, the urban local bodies account for little above 2 per cent of the combined revenue and expenditure of Central Government, State Governments and ULBs. This is in contrast to the situation obtaining in advanced countries, where local bodies normally account for 20-35 per cent of the total government expenditure.[1]

The basic factor of the urban financial crisis is the widening gap between the available revenues and expenditure commitments of the ULBs. Though the exact data is not available due to inadequate database in India, calculations are made based on certain norms to workout the gap. For instance, an USAID report on Indian Urban Infrastructure estimated that the expenditure required on O&M itself mass transit included, was to the tune of Rs. 28/- to Rs. 40/- billion per annum whereas the available sources including institutional lending could provide only about Rs.5/- billion leaving a gap of Rs. 23/- billion on the lower side. Further, Rakesh Mohan Committee Report, which is popularly quoted in India, estimated a gap of Rs. 185/- billion on O&M and Rs. 1250/- billion or 1.25 trillion on O&M and capital investment for a five-year period of 2000-05. The annual gap then works out to Rs. 37/- billion on O&M and Rs. 250/- billion on capital investment plus O&M.[2] The Ministries of Urban Development and Housing & Urban Poverty Alleviation have estimated a huge financial requirement of Rs. 76,896 crore for all States during the period 2005–10 for O&M of various civic services in urban areas.[3] Further, it was brought-out that the annual expenditure of the ULBs on core civic services like water supply, sewerage, sanitation, roads, street lighting, etc. was 130% less than the Zakaria Committee's norm updated to 2001-02 prices indicating the level of under spending.[4] These estimations may look mind-boggling but, they broadly indicate the magnitude of the financial need confronting the urban India.

Looking at the aspect of financial transfers from the central and state governments, these governments operate under their own fiscal constraints, pressures and demands. In view of competing demands from different sectors, urban sector normally receives lesser priority in India. It is also argued that urban areas are economically stronger with more revenue potential. They, therefore, need lesser central and state assistance compared to the backward rural areas. From the population point of view too, the government assistance tilts toward rural areas.

If the spending on urban services and infrastructure is very low, it will adversely affect a country's development in multiple ways. The urban areas can not attract the necessary investments thereby causing retardation in their economic growth over a period. Lesser urban spending will deteriorate the urban environment and quality of life. The urban poverty cannot be tackled as the employment opportunities and living conditions of the poor in urban continue to decline leading to several social and political problems. Realization of these consequences in public domain is taking place only in recent years.

The institution of the State Finance Commissions and international funding opened new vistas and innovative thinking on municipal finance in India. The Government of India and the state governments have also followed this and are initiating several financial reforms to strengthen the fiscal base and financial management capabilities across the urban local bodies. This calls for galvanizing the ULBs to marshal concerted efforts for mobilizing financial resources by all possible means-traditional and innovative.

RESOURCE MOBILIZATION INITIATIVES

Resource mobilization has become central to the urban reform agenda being pursued in India. Resource mobilization initiatives are discussed broadly in two streams, internal and external. If the taxes and non-taxes levied by the ULBs constitute the internal stream, the external sources comprise of state transfers, central assistance, borrowings, capital market and international assistance.

Internal Resource Mobilization

The financial strength of ULBs depends to a large extent on the internally raised revenues as they are independent sources giving freedom to initiate and plan the expenditure commitments in advance. The internal revenues have become more significant in view of increasing uncertainties of state devolutions to ULBs and flow of plan funds from the central and state governments. This apart, ULBs must rely more on the internal resources to function as self-governing institutions. There is vast scope for mobilizing additional revenues from the existing sources by adopting innovative methods and performance improvement. Exploiting the urban land tax, optimizing property tax yield, user charges and taping the private and voluntary sectors are some of the several mechanisms available at the local level. New sources could be exploited based on the local potential. Several resource mobilization measures are taken-up by the ULBs as part of the reform exercise underway. The initiatives presented here provide an insight into these exercises.

Initiatives of Bangalore Mahanagara Palike (BMP)

Ever since octroi was abolished in 1979, the BMP has been facing resource crunch to meet the increasing demand on municipal services.

At the other end, the Bangalore Metro Region has been growing very fast especially, during the last decade or so. The fast deterioration in the civic service status in the city compelled the State Government to think on innovative lines and it resulted in the setting-up of the Bangalore Agenda Task Force (BATF). The BMP could mobilize funds to the tune of Rs.43/- crores by involving the private sector under the BATF. Though the initiative could not sustain, the experiment of BATF has indirectly contributed for reforming the financial system of the BMP in the areas of accounts, revenue mobilization and computerization. The focus has been shifted to financial management and performance improvement. It is interesting that the BMP has entered into an MOU with the State Government for performance based grants/loans for urban infrastructure development in Bangalore.

On the revenue mobilization front, certain steps were taken to mobilize additional funds. Property tax assessment was standardized and self-assessment scheme was introduced to improve tax compliance. Additional properties are being identified and assessed for taxation on a continuing basis through application of GIS technology. For instance, the BMP could add over 87,000 new assessments during the last three years from 2003-04 to 2005-06 with additional revenue of Rs. 63/- crore-form property tax. The property tax system was computerized totally. New avenues are also created by way of infrastructure cess, solid waste management cess and service charges on exempted properties.[5] Collection of the infrastructure cess has been pending Government's approval while the solid waste management cess came into effect from 01-01-2006. The levy of service charges on exempted properties was introduced on 1-4-2005. But, discussions with the BMP officials reveal that these decisions are yet to be implemented. The BMP, however, could generate considerable income from pay and park scheme. Under this, user charges are collected for parking. The BMP collected over Rs.86/- lakhs in 2000-01 under this scheme, which increased to Rs. 405/- lakhs by 2004-05. But, this scheme was withdrawn from 1-4-2005 onwards at the behest of the public requests.[6]

Transfer of Development Rights (TDR) is a method adopted in BMP to acquire lands for public purpose free of cost on the lines of Hyderabad. It makes available certain amount of additional built-up area in lieu of the area relinquished or surrendered by the owner of the land, so that he can use extra built-up area either himself or transfer it to another in need of the extra built-up area for an agreed sum of money. This is provided to facilitate land acquisition for purposes like road widening, parks, playgrounds, and schools etc. which is otherwise a complicated process. The Karnataka Town & Country Planning Act 1961 was amended by a new section 148 which empowers corporations and planning authorities to permit additional FAR for land handed over free of cost whenever such lands are acquired for the above purposes. For implementing the TDR, the city is divided into intensively developed, moderately developed and sparsely developed zones. The TDR shall be from intensively developed zone to other zones but not vice versa. The TDRs shall be valid for five years extendable to another five more years maximum. The BMP has identified 45 roads where TDR facility is available.

Efforts are also being made in BMP to raise revenues from privatization on a smaller scale. For instance, bus shelters are being built on BOT system. The BMP could generate Rs. 62/- lakhs in 2000-01 under this component. The income steadily increased to Rs. 149/- lakhs by 2005-06. Action is being taken to construct 455 bus shelters and 14 road medians on BOT basis.

Chennai Municipal Corporation-Focusing on Property Tax

The property tax reforms were introduced in Chennai Corporation and self-assessment method was introduced as an optional facility. It is reported that the self-assessment scheme did not yield the desired results. However, the tax administration was streamlined linking it with building permission unit. The collection drives are being adopted to improve the collection performance and to review the entire process of collection, teams of officials comprising of Jt. Commissioner, ROs, assessors and other revenue staff were constituted. The entire property tax system was computerized and online payment facility was introduced to improve tax compliance. With these streamlining measures implemented over a period of ten years, it is reported that there has been considerable increase in the property tax revenues from about Rs. 62 crore to Rs. 220 crore at present. As a result, the tax revenue position was quite strong during

2000-01 and 2001-02. However, there has been a slow-down later a trend similar to that observed in Bangalore.

Initiatives of Greater Hyderabad Municipal Corporation (GHMC)

The GHMC had initiated several measures to increase the internal revenues from taxes and non-taxes. On the tax front, self-assessment scheme was introduced in December 1999 for property tax and it was extended to the advertisement tax/fee also in the subsequent years. In the non-tax sphere, several measures were introduced to streamline the tax administration and also to raise additional revenues. Some of the important measures are explained below.

Use of FSI as a Resource

Keeping in view the need for road widening, the State Government has permitted the Municipal Corporation of Hyderabad to undertake widening of roads by using Floor Space Index (FSI) as a resource. The Commissioner is authorized to grant building permissions for additional construction area over and above that permitted by the Zoning /Building Regulations. Land surrendered horizontally is compensated by additional construction vertically. The Corporation rebuilds the demolished compound walls/other structures and grants permission to go vertically. The extent to which vertical construction is to be permitted depends on the extent of land surrendered by parties and the prevailing FSI in the area. If there is no scope for going vertical, the landowner can avail Transferable Development Rights for using the same elsewhere or selling to others. In some cases, even the construction of buildings for non-residential use (commercial/ institutional) is permitted to induce landowners to part with valuable residential land for road widening.

Impact Fees

The Government of Andhra Pradesh has permitted the GHMC to levy Impact Fees to mitigate the impacts of construction of commercial buildings by change of land use that lead to increased traffic and necessitate decongestion measures. The fee is being levied since 2002. Distinction is made between on-site and off-site (local area) development cost and citywide impact. The Impact Fees are meant to address citywide problems emanating from high-density commercial development. These fees-levied at Rs. 50 per square feet for ground floor and Rs. 25/- per sft. for others are to be deposited in a separate account of the Municipal Corporation and utilized for implementation of the Capital Improvement and Decongestion Plan i.e., for works such as road widening, link roads, slip roads, parallel roads, junction improvements including traffic signals, flyovers, rail over-bridges, rail under-bridges, etc. Under no circumstances, the amount is to be spent for salaries and maintenance works. It is proposed to extend impact fee to all major commercial constructions (more than 1000 square feet) in the city to create resources for decongestion activities. The GHMC could collect Rs.589/- lakhs in 2003-04, Rs. 846.63/- lakhs in 2004-05 and Rs.586/- lakhs during 2005-06 totaling a sum of Rs. 20/- crore in three years so far. The trend shows that there is lot of scope for exploiting this source further.

Other Non-Tax Measures

The GHMC has been focusing on generating revenues from several non-tax sources within the existing legal provisions. Some of these are:

- Levy of external betterment charges of 30% of the regular betterment charges.
- Bulk garbage collection charges in respect of properties generating huge waste viz., agricultural markets, commercial complexes, hospitals, clinics, hostels, hotels, functional halls, cinema theatres, workshops, etc.
- Levy of administration charges for certain offences like littering, debris dumping, garbage throwing, roadside dung depositing, etc.
- Storm-water drainage charges for those who connect their sewers to the storm-water drains as a temporary measure.
- Installation of parking lots and collection of parking charges.
- Projection charges
- Demolition charges
- Levy of user charges in respect of parks and public conveniences.
- Auctioning the rights for development and maintenance of traffic islands, central media/dividers, etc. to private sector/ corporate bodies.

- Conversion of leasehold land to freehold lands.
- Bringing all advertisements viz., hoardings, glow-signs/cable TV, etc. under one tax net. A survey was done to identify all the advertisements while giving unique code numbers and the entire data was computerized.
- Facility to pay taxes through e-Seva centers was provided to the taxpayers for bringing-out more tax compliance.

As a result of these initiatives, it is reported that revenues have gone up considerably. Property tax increased by more than 70 per cent during 1999-2000. The period 1998-2000 witnessed an unprecedented rise in advertisement fee collection by more than 230 per cent. Trade licensing fee went up by 63 per cent during 1999-2000. Town planning-related charges registered more than 100 per cent growth during 1999-2000. The trend during the period 2000-01 and 2004-05 shows that the share of property tax in total revenue increased from 30% in 2000-01 to 37% by 2004-05. The non-tax revenues also registered increased during 2003-04 and 2004-05 reflecting in the overall share of the internal revenues in total revenues.

Revenue Improvement Action Planning (RIAP)-The Initiative Under APUSP in Andhra Pradesh

Preparation of a Revenue Improvement Action Plan (RIAP) is made an integral part of the APUSP project towards municipal revenue improvement, especially, from the internal sources. Every municipality selected under APUSP has to prepare a RIAP for the town. The objectives of the RIAP are to:

- Analyze various sources of revenue of the municipality.
- Identify constraints and problems relating to municipal revenues.
- Identify innovative measures and sources for improving revenue of the municipality
- Prepare an action plan for revenue improvement including details like budget, time frame, costs, roles, etc. and focus on practical and effective measures for improving assessment and collection of taxes and non-taxes.

The RIAP adopts an integrated perspective as against the existing peace meal approach. Scientific analysis of the problems/constraints to identify appropriate solutions that are within the reach of the municipalities and participatory approach involving the stakeholders are the key components of this perspective. In order to facilitate the process, a working group is constituted at the town level. The APUSP project team prepared a detailed module on RIAP to train and guide the functionaries involved in the preparation The action areas identified for revenue improvement are:

- Up dating and reconciliation of revenue-arrear-demand registers.
- Special drives for identification of new and under-assessed properties.
- Up-dating pending accounts.
- Introduction of self-assessment system in property tax.
- Painting of property tax demand on the buildings.
- Levy of user charges on hospitals and commercial establishments.
- Introduction of 'Tatkal' services with additional charges.
- Outsourcing of service of bills.
- Survey of unauthorized layouts.
- Identification and regularization of unauthorized water taps.
- Introduction of paid parking.
- Protection of open spaces, vacant lands and burial grounds.

It is observed that the measures initiated under the project yielded good results in terms of increased revenues from taxes and non-taxes, improved accounts and audit pendency, introduction of double entry accrual system, GIS applications and vigorous capacity building through training at the ULB level. Following are the perceived benefits as per the APUSP project assessment:

- Significant improvement in the property tax administration in terms of registering new assessments, enhancement of under-assessments and plugging of loopholes in the levy and collection process. All this resulted in considerable revenue improvement under property tax. It is estimated that property tax which was Rs. 7189.97/-lakhs before commencement of the project in March, 2000 increased to Rs. 23500.05/- lakh by March, 2004 registering 226% increase in the 32 project towns. As against this, it was only 114% in the entire state during that period. Similar increase was noticed in case of total taxes also (Table 1).

- It is observed that the APUSP towns are ahead in increasing the water charges and moving towards cost recovery compared to the other towns in the state.
- The betterment charges and town planning permission fees are also increased in the towns like Chittor and Qutubullapur Municipalities.

Table 1
Growth of Tax Revenues in APUSP Towns

(Rs. in Lakh)

	Status in 2000–01 (Before APUSP Project launch)		*Status in 2003-04*		*% Increase*	
Tax	*APUSP Towns*	*Entire State*	*APUSP Towns*	*Entire State*	*APUSP Towns*	*Entire State*
Property Tax	7189.97	9782.46	23500.05	20938.27	226.84	114.04
Advertise-ment Tax	137.86	108.82	364.86	357.08	164.66	228.14
Total Tax	7540.69	9922.65	24715.45	21371.24	227.76	115.38

The concept of RIAP is a very useful tool for planning municipal revenue improvements. An integrated perspective, which was visualized, is, however, lacking at the municipal level. Discussions at the municipal officials reveal that they prepared plans in the initial years of scheme under the guidance of the consultants and some enthused commissioners. RIAP is not a one-time affair. It has to become an annual process built into a town level financial plan. Revenue improvement plan has no meaning unless a financial operating plan and an investment plan are prepared and implemented.

IMPACT OF REFORMS ON INTERNAL REVENUES

Property Tax Collection Performance

The collection performance of the property tax has been given top priority in the urban financial reforms sector. The JNNURM &

UIDSSMT schemes of the Government of India accorded top priority to the internal revenue mobilization efforts of the ULBs in its financing scheme. Especially, they stipulate that 85% of property tax collection as one of the ULB level reform to be targeted. The collection of property tax is generally reflected in the Demand-Collection-Balance (DCB) statements of the ULBs, which are to be prepared annually and monitored continuously. The actual collection percentage was better in the municipalities than corporations. In Hyderabad, it ranged between 66% and 74% and in Chennai the percentage was between 51% and 75%. In Tenali, in (Andhra Pradesh) and Erode (Tamil Nadu), the percentage was well above the stipulated 85%. In Nedumangad, Kerala the percentage appears to be very poor compared to other municipalities (Table 2). In Tamil Nadu municipalities, the collection percentage was reported as 78% on average during the years 2003-04 and 2004-05. Karnataka has introduced self-assessment system. In this system, the taxpayer has to submit annual returns along with the payment of tax. In this situation, the ULBs are not maintaining any DCB in traditional sense since introduction of self-assessment in 2002-03. The Byatarayanapura figures are therefore, available only for 2001-02 when the percentage was 74%. The existing DCB format here shows only the number of returns received and the amount collected. The GIS surveys have identified un-assessed properties, which are being brought under tax net. The traditional DCB is not being maintained. It is explained that the annual self-assessment returns as also collection are taken as demand. If at all a DCB is to be maintained, it has to be in terms of assessments received each year. In Bangalore Corporation also, there is self-assessment system but not as an annual affair like the other ULBs. The self-assessment is made only once and every year the tax payers have to pay the same tax until it is revised either by the tax payers themselves due to extensions or by the Corporation. In this situation, there is scope for maintaining DCB. Discussions with the corporation officials revealed that they are simply going by budget proposals. The estimate made in the budget based on last year's performance is being considered as the target. The officials feel that DCB could be another performance indicator. But, unfortunately, it is not being maintained. The overall collection performance of property tax was thus, poor compared to the target of 85% set in the national urban reform agenda.

Table 2
Property Tax Collection in ULBs

(In % of demand)

Year	Hyderabad	Chennai	Tenali	Erode	Byatarayan apura	Nedumangad
2001-02	-	51	94	93	74	37
2002-03	-	71	90	90	-	48
2003-04	71	68	90	87	-	-
2004-05	66	75	93	100	-	52
2005-06	74	-	94	87	-	-

Source: Official records of ULBs

Other Revenue Parameters

A comparison of the per capita and average growth rates has been made in respect of the property tax, total tax income and non-tax income between the ULBs discussed above with the respective state level figures to assess the impact of the reform initiatives on the revenues generation during 2000-01 and 2004-05. The comparative perspective brought-out that all the ULBs registered higher per capita's in respect of property tax and total taxes compared to the state averages (Table 3). In respect of the non-tax revenues, however, Bangalore maintained its superiority while Chennai and Hyderabad registered lower per capita compared to the state level picture despite consistent increase over the period under report.

The dimension of average growth rate in respect of property tax reveals that Bangalore and Hyderabad registered lesser growth rate compared to the state level figures while Chennai and Tenali had higher growth rates. It is interesting to note that despite increased emphasis on property tax reform in Bangalore and Hyderabad, they still under-perform compared to the state level figures. The total tax angle brings-out that all the ULBs under performed compared to the state level averages. It is a surprising and disturbing trend indeed. The non-tax angle appears to be better. Except Bangalore, all other ULBs recorded higher average growth rates compared to the state level picture. The over all growth rate perspective reveals a very dismal status in Bangalore as it under–performed in all categories of internal revenues. At the other end, Chennai position appears to be better as it fared well compared to the state level performance. Hyderabad could show its

Table 3
Growth of Internal Revenues-ULB and State Level Comparison

Year	*State Level*	*Bangalore*	*State Level*	*Chennai*	*State Level*	*Hyderabad*	*State Level*	*Tenali*
				Per Capita in Rs.				
Property Tax								
2000-01	250.82	365.78	290.23	299.38	211.21	251.27	93.92	101.20
2001-02	243.15	350.47	285.63	390.23	280.58	354.19	103.18	142.33
2002-03	300.27	443.76	354.15	377.01	342.00	440.51	166.90	196.40
2003-04	398.27	582.45	302.87	475.66	381.20	476.92	201.03	256.15
2004-05	NA	528.74	NA	507.75	NA	433.19	NA	266.95
Avg.	292.23	445.35	307.08	403.06	296.47	381.67	134.28	180.85
Total Tax Income								
2000-01	268.41	368.52	306.10	370.68	223.21	268.89	95.27	111.17
2001-02	262.08	352.14	345.37	456.25	294.66	377.20	105.10	154.73
2002-03	320.73	447.21	357.79	447.90	356.23	457.77	169.50	214.26
2003-04	421.40	586.13	441.73	545.37	397.45	497.14	207.63	277.28
2004-05	NA	535.98	533.19	615.66	432.18	456.61	277.52	287.28
Avg.	312.26	448.92	389.01	479.82	331.85	402.31	157.78	196.58

Contd...

Year	*State Level*	*Bangalore*	*State Level*	*Chennai*	*State Level*	*Hyderabad*	*State Level*	*Tenali*
				Per Capita in Rs.				
Non-Tax Income								
2000-01	344.01	461.49	179.87	98.44	310.32	184.14	137.06	91.52
2001-02	255.19	331.78	181.79	97.78	335.52	159.07	145.19	109.34
2002-03	318.02	407.51	200.15	112.81	344.31	145.11	165.39	166.17
2003-04	371.70	493.82	219.70	123.01	201.42	198.98	120.57	218.22
2004-05	NA	437.76	258.13	162.33	218.13	243.96	122.97	199.06
Avg.	319.17	422.66	206.02	116.74	275.08	183.19	137.30	148.51
% Average Growth Rates								
Property Tax	16.66	9.65	1.43	14.12	21.75	14.59	28.87	27.44
Total Tax	16.22	9.82	14.88	13.52	17.96	14.15	30.64	26.79
Non-Tax	2.61	-1.31	9.45	13.32	-8.44	7.29	-2.68	21.44

superiority only in case of non-tax income growth. Tenali, an APUSP town and considered very progressive on reforms area, had shown, fairly good performance with respect of growth rate. Better performance from the per capita angle and under-performance from the point of growth rate, brings-out the critical issue of sustainability of the reform momentum.

EXTERNAL RESOURCE MOBILIZATION

In a historical perspective, the post Constitution 74th Amendment Act period coincided with the economic reform era in India has witnessed several public policy changes that not only impacted the institutional framework of urban governance, but also created more congenial investment opportunities, particularly in the urban infrastructure sector. It is true that the post-reform era has opened-up municipal finances to market forces more than ever before. There have been some innovative initiatives in mobilizing funds through market instruments such as municipal bonds, institutional borrowing, infrastructure bonds, pooled financing, etc., in recent times. The achievements in these areas are discussed below.

Municipal Bonds

Municipal bonds are debt instruments issued by ULBs and parastatals like urban development authorities and water supply and drainage boards to raise funds from the capital market to finance urban infrastructure. The concept of municipal bonds as an additional source of raising funds was first introduced in India by the USAID. The Rakesh Mohan Committee also recommended municipal bonds as a strategy to finance urban infrastructure in India.

Despite the allegation of commercialization of urban infrastructure, municipal bonds have good potential to mobilize the resources for meeting increasing urban sector demands on sustainable basis through cost recovery. As accessing the capital market demands better financial management, ULBs will be under some compulsion to improve their accounting, budgeting and asset management practices.

Municipal Bonds were successfully issued by several corporations viz., Bangalore, Chennai, Ahmedabad, Ludhiana, Nagpur, Nasik, Madurai, Visakhapatnam, Indore and Hyderabad mobilizing over

Rs.700/- crore to finance urban infrastructure. This apart, bonds were also issued by several water supply and sewerage boards and under pooled finance schemes (Table 4). As a promotional measure, the Central Government had announced tax exemptions for bonds issued by Municipal/Local Authorities. Section 10(15) (vii) of the Income Tax Act 1961 provides that the income earned through the interest on notified bonds issued by a local authority is exempt from tax. This provision, which came into effect from the assessment year 2001-02, could be applied to all ULBs too. Further, section 10(23G) also provides tax exemption from incomes generated out of investments made by the companies/funds which are solely engaged in developing, maintaining and operating infrastructure including urban infrastructure like roads, water supply, sewerage, sanitation, waste management, etc. The income could be interest, dividends or long-term capital gains. The deduction in respect of profit and gains for enterprises engaged in the development of urban infrastructure are also permitted under section 80-1A. The enterprise or company, however, should enter into concession agreement with state or local authorities under BOT, BOOT or any such method. The individuals who invest in infrastructure bonds or debentures are also eligible for tax deduction under 80L. The Income Tax exemptions provided have much scope for attracting investments in the urban sector.

The Ministry of Urban Development issued guidelines on 8.2.2001 for regulating the issue of tax-free municipal bonds. The guidelines state that such bonds will be issued for raising resources for capital investment in creation of new infrastructure as well as augmentation of existing systems. Further, the ULBs should create Escrow account for debt servicing with earmarked revenue and all state government grants or transfers. The Escrow account and project account will have to be audited by Chartered Accountants appointed by the state governments. The ULB concerned should also maintain a Debt Servicing Coverage Ratio of at least 1.25 throughout the tenor of the bond (DSCR is a ratio of net income of the entire entity as against the project financed). The periodicity of the bonds should be for a minimum period of five years. Income by way of interest (rate upto10.5%) is exempt from Income Tax without limits. The ULB should get credit rating for floating bonds. A ceiling of about Rs.50/- crore is put for floating tax-free bonds. Taking advantage of the tax exemption provisions, Ahmedabad, Chennai, Hyderabad and Visakhapatnam Corporations have issued tax-free bonds.

MUNICIPAL BONDS BY CORPORATIONS

The corporations being larger and financially sound could venture into bond market in India. Details of some of these bonds issued by the corporations in south India are explained in the following.

Bangalore Mahanagara Palike Bonds

The Bangalore Mahanagara Palike of Karnataka issued municipal bonds for Rs 125/- crore with 7 years maturity and a coupon of 13 per cent per annum in December 1997. The purpose was to raise resources for the development of roads, side drains and street lighting in Bangalore City. The bond issuance was made through private placement mode, and was guaranteed by the Government of Karnataka. CRISIL rated the bonds at A (SO), indicating adequate safety. The principal as well as interest payments were secured by way of structured payments mechanisms i.e., collection and deposit of property tax and government grants to a designated Escrow account, which were used for payments to the bondholders. The entire process was supervised by a trustee viz., The Karnataka State Financial Corporation. The State Bank of India Capital Markets Limited managed the issue. The bonds were issued to undertake road works in Bangalore.

Hyderabad City Development Bonds by GHMC

The GHMC floated unsecured and non-convertible tax-free municipal bonds in the nature of debentures with a face value of Rs 1,00,000/- per bond in March 2002 amounting to Rs. 82.5/- crore. One important factor was that both, CRISIL and ICRA rated these bonds at AA+ (S0) and LAA+ (S0) respectively, which is considered highest in the municipal bond market in India. The interest rate is 8.5% p.a. payable semi-annually with redemption period of 7 years. The lucrative sources of income like non-residential property tax, profession tax, advertisement tax, entertainment tax, surcharge on stamp duty and town-planning charges are escrowed. The proceeds were used mainly on city-wide development works relating to traffic and transportation sector including road widening, junction improvement, parallel roads,

Table 4
Municipal Bonds in India

City	*Amount (In Rs. million)*	*Placement*	*Guarantee*	*Interest Rate*	*Escrow*	*Purpose*	*Rating*
Ahmedabad	1000	Public & Private	No	14%	Octroi from 100 collection points	WS&S project	AA-(SO)
Bangalore Mahanagara Palike	1250	Private	State Govt.	13%	State Government grants and property tax	City roads / street drains	A-(SO)
Ludhiana	100	Private	No	13.5% to 14%	Water & Sewerage taxes and charges	WS&S Project	LAA-(SO)
Nagpur	500	Private	No	13%	Property tax and water charges	WS Project	LAA-(SO)
Nasik	1000	Private	No	14.75%	Octroi from four collection points	WS&S project	AA-(SO)
Indore	100	Private	Yes	NA		Improvement of City roads	A(SO)
Madurai	300	Private	No	12.25%	Toll tax collection	City road project	LA+(SO)
Ahmedabad (Tax Free)	1000	Private	No	9%	Property taxes of two zones	WS & S Project	AA(SO)
Hyderabad (Tax Free)	825	Private	No	8.5%	Non-residential PT, Advt. Tax, Prof tax etc.	Road construction and widening	LAA+(SO) AA+(SO)
Tamil Nadu (Pooled Financing)	304	Private	-	9.20%	Monthly payments equal to one-ninth of their annual payments	WS&S projects in 14 ULBs	LAA(SO) AA(SO) by FITCH
Chennai (Tax Free)	448	Private	-	5.45%	Property Tax collections	Road infrastructure	AA (SO)
Visakhapatnam (Taxable Bonds).	150	NA	-	7.75	By way of deposit of Rs. 50/- lakhs into MODS Account every month.	Godavari Water Supply Scheme	CARE AA (SO)
Visakhapatnam (Tax Free Bonds).	500	NA	-	7.25	By way of deposit of Rs. 50/- lakhs into MODS Account every month.	Godavari Water Supply Scheme	CARE AA (SO)

Source: Urban Finance News Letter, NIUA, New Delhi, Municipal Corporation of Hyderabad, Visakhapatnam Municipal Corporation Chennai Corporation and Bangalore Mahanagara Palike.

slip roads, link roads, signaling, etc. A sinking fund is created in the budget to repay the interest amount and for redemption of bonds.

Visakhapatnam Municipal Corporation Bonds

The Visakhapatnam Municipal Corporation (VMC) is the second city in Andhra Pradesh to float municipal bonds. The VMC floated both, tax-free and taxable bonds amounting to Rs. 65/- crores. The rate of interest was 7.5% p.a. The purpose was for implementing the Godavari Water Supply Scheme. The CARE had given AA (S0) rating for the bonds.

Chennai Tax-Free Municipal Bonds

The Chennai Corporation issued tax-free municipal bonds on 15-05-2005. Though the Corporation was permitted to float 44.8/-crore, it was restricted to only Rs.30.1/-crore later. The issue price was Rs10/- lakh per security with an interest rate of as low as 5.45% p.a. The tenure is 10 years with a call option at the end of 5th year. The redemption is 30% each on 15.05.2013 and 15.05.2014 and 40% on 15.05.2015. Bulk of the total 301 bonds was allotted to Indian Overseas Bank (250) followed by Tamil Nadu Urban Development Fund (30), United India Insurance Corporation Ltd. (20) and Bimetal Bearing Ltd (1). The Chennai Corporation opened an escrow account mainly of property tax to repay the interest and bond redemption. The money is used for works relating to road network.

POOLED FINANCING FOR MUNICIPAL INFRASTRUCTURE

In view of the huge resource gap, direct access to capital market would now be an accepted viable option. However, access to capital market requires financial discipline and enhanced credit rating. It has been the experience that only bigger municipal corporations are in a position to take the advantage of the resources available in capital market. Medium and smaller municipalities are unable to do so due to their weak financial position and lack of capacity to prepare viable project proposals. A State level pooled financing mechanism is being proposed for smaller and medium municipalities. The objective of a State level pooled finance mechanism is to provide a cost effective and efficient approach for smaller and medium sized ULBs to access the domestic capital markets for urban infrastructure. Two Pooled Financing schemes from Tamil Nadu and Karnataka are presented in the following.

The Tamil Nadu Water and Sanitation Pooled Fund-The First Pooled Urban Development Fund in India

The Tamil Nadu Water and Sanitation Pooled Fund (TNWSPF) is an institutionalized mechanism to raise low cost funds for water and sanitation needs and it is designed on the lines of US Bond Bank with assistance from the USAID-FIRE (D). The objective is to provide a cost-effective and sustainable method for small and medium sized ULBs to access the capital market for investments on core urban infrastructure in a resource constraint context. To be specific, it aims to mobilize resources from the capital markets, facilitate the participation of private sector through joint delivery mechanism of Public-Private Partnerships, improve financial status of local bodies by enabling their access to low cost debt finance from markets and to reduce their effective cost of borrowings by making them market sensitive.

The TNWSPF was incorporated as a trust in August, 2002 and is registered under the Indian Trust Act 1882. The TNWSPF is managed by the Tamil Nadu Urban Infrastructure Financial Services Ltd (TNUIFSL), the fund manager of the successful Tamil Nadu Urban Development Fund (TNUDF), a financial intermediary. Besides the trust manager, the Board of Trustees of the fund comprises the officials of Government of Tamil Nadu and MD&CEO and TNUIFSL.

This fund pooled credit risks of participating entities and made capital market access feasible for 13 small and medium sized Urban Local Bodies around Chennai. The first bond issue of Rs. 30.41 crore saved a sizable amount in debt servicing by Urban Local Bodies, thereby freeing up their resources for further augmentation of civic amenities. USAID extended guarantee to the extent of 50% of the principal for this bond issue. The credit rating awarded was LAA (SO) by ICRA and Ind AA (SO) by Fitch. The first level of credit enhancement is the escrow of the property tax and other collections of the ULBs. This is covered under a tripartite agreement among WSPF, ULB and ULB's banker. The second level of credit enhancement is covered by a Debt Service Reserve Fund in the name of Bond Service Reserve Fund (BSF) set up by the Government of Tamil Nadu with liquid investments of Rs.6.90 crore. This is regardless of ULBs cash flows. The next level is the guarantee issued by USAID to the extent of 50% of the principal. The balance is covered by an undertaking by Government of Tamil Nadu in the form of a Government order that the shortfall would be replenished to the BSF by deducting their respective share of State Finance Commission (SFC) devolution accruing to the ULBs. The WSPF represented by TNUIFSL would monitor the escrow account of the ULBs, coordinate with the State Government in case of a shortfall and ensure the repayment amount payable to the investors in the bank account of the WSPF, before 30 days from the due date of bond annuity. This pooled financing structure is the first of its kind in India and it thus established a major link between city civic need and capital market. The bonds amounting to Rs 30.41/-crore were allotted on private placement to the Karnataka Bank (Rs 20/0 crore), ICICI Bank (Rs 10/- crore), City Union Bank (0.25/- crore), Gujarat Industries Power Co limited (Rs 0.11/- crore) and Met life Insurance (Rs. 0.5/-crore).

The WSPF trust identifies viable projects and fund them on a commercial mode. The projects have been selected after careful consideration of their financial viability and commitment towards development. The TNWSPF lends to ULBs at the rate of 9.2% per annum. The loan has to be repaid in 15 years in 15 equal installments with annual payment of coupon on a diminishing balance method. The repayment mechanism is such that each ULB sets apart 1/9th of the annuity due in a Fixed Deposit as escrow account every month for a period of 9 months. At the beginning of 10th month, the amounts so placed in Fixed Deposits are transferred to the escrow account of WSPF. In case, there is a short fall in the amounts to be serviced, the same would be met either out of SFC devolution or other municipal tax sources. The State Government creates a Bond Service Fund of Rs. 6.9/ crore- reserve fund, an amount equal to about one and half times annual debt service before the bond issue. Whenever there is a shortfall, this fund would be tapped. Further, USAID's guarantee of 50% of the bond's principal would replenish the BSF, if need arises. This USAID's guarantee money appears to be a strong factor for the success of this bond scheme. Further, it is reported that all the projects pooled demonstrated collection of user charges and other fee.[7]

The TNWSPF is considered first successful bond issue outside the US using a pooled financing structure for water supply and sanitation projects of small and medium size towns. Majority of the ULBs got loans in January 2003 itself with amount ranging from Rs 16/- lakh to Rs. 547/- lakh and many of these ULBs used these loans to refinance the other loans of the TNUDF at lower interest rates for projects underway. Of these, eight projects are in the Chennai Region relating to the new Krishna Water Supply Scheme. Various works like laying of new water mains, construction of tanks and pumps were taken-up which are expected to increase the water supply significantly. This apart, three other water supply projects in the Chennai Region and an underground drainage project in Coimbatore and a solid waste management project in Madurai were also taken-up under the scheme.[8]

Pooled Financing Scheme of Greater Bangalore Water Supply and Sanitation Project

The Government of Karnataka also initiated such an innovative scheme of pooling funds for the implementation of the Greater Bangalore Water Supply and Sanitation Project. The Project being implemented by the Bangalore Water Supply and Sanitation Board (BWSSB), will provide a piped water supply system as well as services on par with Bangalore to the above seven City Municipal Councils and one Town Municipal Council viz., Bommanahalli, Byatarayanapura, Dasarahalli, Krishnarajapuram, Mahadevapura, Rajarajeshwarinagar, Yelahanka (CMCs) and Kengeri (TMC). The concept of Pooled Finance Mechanism is introduced to raise debt from investors through a Bond Issue. A debt fund called the "Karnataka Water and Sanitation Pooled Fund (KWSPF)" under the Indian Trust Act, 1882, was established to access the capital market through a bond issue on behalf of the participating ULBs. The KWSPF will borrow from the market and on-lend to the ULBs at terms determined by the KWSPF. The Karnataka Urban Infrastructure Development & Finance Corporation (KUIDFC) will be the Asset Management Company (AMC) for KWSPF.

The main security for the debt to be mobilized for the project will be a charge on receivables of the participating ULBs, to be escrowed in a Water Project Account (WPA) at the city level, with structured payment mechanisms to be monitored by a trustee. Each participating ULB will maintain a dedicated WPA. An amount equal to 1.5 times the annual debt service payments of market borrowing will be transferred to this account from the ULBs' general and annual operating grants form the State Government for the debt servicing. The necessary amount will be transferred to the KWSPF from WPA for debt servicing prior to the due date of payment.

A Bond Service Fund (BSF) has been set up for the pool of participating ULBs with Rs. 25.5 crore. This Fund will be administered by the Asset Management Company, i.e., KUIDFC. USAID under its Development Credit Authority (DCA) Program provided a Guarantee of up to 50 per cent of the principal amount of market borrowing, so as to enhance the borrowing capacity of the ULBs.[9] The total cost of the project is Rs. 658/- crore of which water supply component is estimated to cost Rs. 340.55/- crore which will be implemented in the first stage. Funding Structure of the Water Supply Component is as follows:

	Rs. in crore
Beneficiary Capital Contribution	119.44
Mega City Loan	46.82
Grants form GOI and GOK	74.28
Market Borrowing	100.00
Total	340.54

The market borrowing of Rs. 100/- was mobilized through secured non-convertible redeemable tax-free bonds of Rs. 1-/- face value each by private placement. The bonds were issued at the rate of 5.95%. ICRA has rated the bonds at LAA (SO). The Government of India permitted the bond issue in the tax-free category.[10]

Inspired by the success of the TNWSPF, the Government of India too launched a Pooled Finance Development Fund on 29th September 2006 to provide credit enhancement to the ULBs to access market borrowings based on their credit worthiness through State-level Pooled Finance mechanism. During 2006–07, Rs. 50/- crore was provided by the Ministry of Urban Development for scheme which was doubled to Rs 100 crore in the year 2007–08. For the Eleventh Plan period, a provision of Rs. 2500 crore has been made. The broad objectives of PFDF are to:

- Facilitate implementation of bankable urban infrastructure projects through appropriate capacity building measures and financial structuring of projects.
- Facilitate the ULBs to access capital and financial markets for investment in critical urban infrastructure by providing credit enhancement grants to State-pooled Finance Entities for accessing capital markets through Pooled Financing Bonds on behalf of one or more identified ULBs for investment in the urban infrastructure projects.
- Reduce the cost of borrowing to local bodies with appropriate credit enhancement measures and through restructuring of existing costly debts.
- Facilitate development of Municipal Bond Market.[11]

Municipal Bonds-Emerging Issues

It may look discouraging that only about ten corporations could go for issuing municipal bonds in India in spite of tax concessions and decreased interest rates. This calls for some introspection. The municipal bond market requires efficient legal and administrative framework to monitor municipal borrowing. Often the municipal acts impose ceilings on borrowing of the ULBs. But, it is brought–out that Chennai Corporation borrowed money beyond its legally permitted ceiling. In this context, it is commented that the municipal legislation in India either does not incorporate ceilings on local borrowing or they are not followed rigorously when such ceilings exist.[12] It is apt to mention here that in Kerala Municipality Act (Sec. 299), there was a ceiling for municipal borrowing that is, the total repayment (interest and principal) including charges for maintaining a sinking fund shall not exceed 12½ per cent of the annual value of the buildings and lands. This provision was amended in 1999 and the Government now provided that the limitation for borrowing should be related to the total annual receipts of the municipality as prescribed in this regard. Provision is also made to float municipal bonds and debentures. Though such changes are being made, there is need to evolve a comprehensive policy to deal with insolvency problems.

Another problem identified in municipal bond market is abnormal delay in the procedures often taking one to two years time before actually going for bonds. The formalities like municipal council resolution, rating by the rating agencies, sanctions by the Municipal Administration and Finance Departments, conforming with the SEBI guidelines-all these procedures consume lot of time.

The most threatening danger identified is that there are no specific statutes in India to deal with insolvency problems of the local bodies. It is argued that insolvency procedures applicable to corporate sector do not apply in case of the local bodies, which make the municipal bonds less attractive. The only remedy lies in the relief under Article 226 of the Constitution, which is more complicated.[13] The courts would be reluctant to enforce any security offered by a local body as these are protected by the principle of sovereign immunity. Alternate remedies must be provided to overcome this problem. It is put-forth that a separate law need to be promulgated laying down the insolvency process and special insolvency courts also must be constituted to try matters pertaining to local government borrowings and their insolvency issues on a fast-track recovery process.[14] This will improve confidence of the private sector to invest in the municipal bonds. Further, other regulatory issues also must be sorted-out. There is need to amend the Local Authority Loans Act, 1914 or enacting a new Act which comprehensively deals with the borrowing powers, security, insolvency and other local borrowing issues.

Effective linkages with the stock exchanges and conformity with the SEBI Act 1992 for private placement issues also need to be developed. The state governments should come out with effective debt management policy, debt service indicators and risk management measures for ULBs. Ultimately, it is the capacity building at the ULB level that matters for successful municipal bonds in India. Introduction of accrual based accounting, financial discipline and commercial approach for capital works especially, the works financed by debt instruments like bonds. Finally, an enabling environment with broadening of the issuers and investor base and institutional support system like credit enhancement, guarantees, underwriters, merchant bankers, etc., are essential to develop municipal bond market.

Comparisons are generally made between the bank loans and bonds to finance infrastructure by the ULBs. The ULB concerned has to take a conscious decision before choosing an alternative. Both, bank loans and bonds have certain advantages and disadvantages.

The basic difference relates to the size of borrowing. Bank loans are considered better for smaller borrowings compared to bonds. In this situation, bank loans are better for smaller ULBs and bonds more suitable to the corporations, which have larger fund requirements. Repayment options are also more flexible in case of bank loans compared to bonds. The situation may change in case of the pooled financing as smaller ULBs come together to borrow thus raising economics of scale.[15] Further, bonds are generally for longer tenors compared to bank loans. The other advantages of bonds are larger investor base, transferability, liquidity, lesser restrictions on use of funds and standardized credit rating by professional rating agencies. The most attracting feature is that bonds are considered cheaper compared to loans on total cost basis.[16]

CONCLUSION AND WAY AHEAD

Rakesh Mohan feels that life would be easy if financing sources were such that civic authorities could raise resources in such a manner that the repayment schedule matched the benefit schedule.[17] The Government polices and an effective incentive system play significant role in motivating the ULBs to raise more resources internally. In fact, the Eleventh Plan strategy reiterates this aspect. The Plan recognizes the need to create a conducive environment for efficient tax administration, increasing use of non-tax sources, efficient pricing of services, PPPs in provision and maintenance of urban services, adopting alternative sources of finance including access to capital markets, involvement of community and private sector in raising revenue. The Plan also suggests that the States need to ensure rating of municipalities for facilitating access to capital markets.[18]

The resource mobilization initiatives met limited success in India confined to few progressive corporations and ULBs. The property tax reforms and user charges have become more popular instruments for internal resource mobilization in India. One common trend noticed in India has been lack of commitment to the resource mobilization initiatives at the local and state government levels. That is why, the ULBs are favoring external financial assistance that come in the form of grants and loans from Government sponsored schemes and programmes.

Another trend noticed was ad hoc nature of initiatives, which are mostly short-lived providing certain short-term benefits. Sustenance of the reform initiatives demands long-term policy and administrative support systems based on competitive spirit and incentivization of urban infrastructure financing. In property tax reforms, it was observed that the Governments often succumb to local pressures by reducing incidence of tax, which affects the reform momentum adversely and also acts as a de-motivating factor to the local administration.

The municipal bond market and pooled–finance schemes are, no doubt, good fund raising instruments. The ESCROW accounts could enhance transparency of the cash flows and ensure sufficient balance for loan repayment. Municipal bond system was successful in countries like USA where incentive structures encourage the cities and towns to remain credit worthy and self-reliant. But in countries like India, the systems are not well designed and the meager incentives available are not adequate enough to motivate the ULBs to be essentially self–financing. The Government, therefore, should come-out with an apt policy backed with necessary legal and administrative changes which facilitate self-financing initiatives at the local levels. In fact, the SFC devolution itself could effectively be linked to the internal revenue mobilization performance of the ULBs as recommended by several SFCs. Unfortunately, the state governments prefer population as the basis. A combination of population, backwardness and ULB mobilization effort must be considered for state and even CFC devolutions to ULBs.

There is also a need to devise a strategy like demarcating the functional responsibilities of the ULBs into two main streams: one, consisting of functional responsibilities which should exclusively be financed by the internal revenues; and the other one could be financed either internally or externally depending on the financial status of the ULBs. Such a functional demarcation appears essential to fix financial responsibilities on the ULBs. Any incentive system cannot work unless functional responsibilities are clearly fixed. This, however, must be accompanied by an exclusive financial resource base consisting of taxes and non-taxes. Ultimately, it drives us to strive for the function-finance balance, which is central to make ULBs efficient, effective and self-governing institutions.

Notes

1. According to a study sponsored by the Reserve Bank of India, *http://rbidocs.rbi.org.in/rdocs/Content/PDFs/82508.pdf*
2. USAID, Assessment and Analysis of the Status of Urban Service Delivery and Urban Infrastructure Sector Reform in India-Draft Final Report, November 2, 2001 New Delhi, India.
3. Government of India, Eleventh Five Year Plan Document, pp. 417.
4. O. P. Mathur, Urban Finance, India Infrastructure Report (2006), 3i Network, Oxford University Press, New Delhi, p. 87.
5. G.O.Ms UDD/MNU/02, Government of Karnataka, dated 27-02-2004.
6. Bangalore Mahanagara Palike, Performance Budget 2006-07.
7. Lee Baker, Chief of Party Of the FIRE (D) Project, Project Note No. 31, May, 2003.
8. *Ibid.,*
9. Urban finance, Quarterly News Letter, Vol. 8, No. 2, April-June 2005 NIUA, New Delhi.
10. Letter No. K-14011/10/2004-(UD II), dated 25-08-2004, Government of India.
11. Government of India, Eleventh Five Year Plan, pp. 397.
12. Soumyadip Chattopadhyay, Municipal Bond Market for Financing Urban Infrastructure, *Economic and Political Weekly,* June 30, 2006, p. 2787.
13. *Ibid,* p. 2789.
14. H. K. Pradhan, Local Government Finance and Bond Market Financing: India, October 2002, ADB Report.
15. Manju Ghodke, Accessing Capital Market by Urban Local Bodies in India: An Assessment of Municipal Bonds, India Infrastructure Report–2004, 3i Network, pp. 142-143
16. *Ibid.*
17. Rakesh Mohan, Asia's Urban Century-Emerging Trends, Key Note Address, Conference on Land Policies and Urban Development organized by Lincoln Institute of Land Policy, Cambridge, Massachusetts, June 5, 2006.
18. Eleventh Five Year Plan, *op.cit.,* p. 419.

8

RURAL SOCIAL WORK PRACTICE: PROSPECTIVES AND IMPLICATIONS

Nanjunda D. C.

INTRODUCTION

A young Graduate/Post Graduate in Social Work begins his first job at a rural health center in Bangalore-Karnataka (India). The rural health center' is part of a State department that has its central offices in Bangalore City. At the state office there are many specialists, among whom are social workers, psychologists, psychiatrists, speech therapists, sex therapists, family planners, and alcohol specialists. In one of the sub-branch of the same health centre however, there is one psychologist, one social worker, and one secretary. The psychologist, an M A who had graduated the previous year from the University, is the director of the agency. He believes that his job is to see children who are referred from the Bangalore International Public Schools and other schools throughout the Bangalore distract. He usually does a battery of psychological tests for a thorough diagnosis and then observes the children in play therapy.

The secretary answers the phone for both the mental health center and the adjacent family planning and health clinics next door. She sees her job as a good receptionist and enjoys the time she spends talking with the mothers as they wait for their children in play therapy. Mr. Ramesh is the new MSW graduate-having just graduated-and is sitting at his desk. He rereads his job description for the fourth time, trying to figure out where to begin-after all, he's always had a supervisor to assign him cases before now. The job description reads: "Provide comprehensive services to low-income families in rural areas, primarily focused on strengthening family ties and roles; do preliminary screening of perspective state hospital patients; provide assistance in identifying and developing necessary community mental health oriented resources: plan with community agencies on behalf of the released patients, e.g., social and family adjustment, employment, finances; and provide consultation and education for interested groups, citizens, colleges, and community agency staff."

Mr. Rmaesh knows how to work with families because of the clinical courses on family therapy that he took at the university. He knows how to arrange the chairs to promote openness and how to use his training knowledge. Thus he talks to' the psychologist about working with the mothers while the children are in play therapy. The psychologist readily accepts this and before long Mr. Ramesh has a caseload of mothers, a few fathers, and some children. Mr. Ramesh is very happy; the secretary is upset but no one knows why; and the psychologist really wants to go to graduate school to learn more about diagnosis. Mr. Ramesh is very successful as a family therapist and before long he even has a waiting list.

SCEAN-2

Basically the same scene, but while Mr. X is reading his job description, his .attention goes to the parts on developing needed resources, providing consultation and education, and helping patients reenter their communities after being hospitalized 100 miles away. He decides that in order to do these he must get to know the community. Thus he sets informal meetings with the town's mayor, the city commissioners, the school principals, and even travels to Bangalore City to meet with the state senator and legislators from that area. He wants to meet them and let them know that he is living and working in their area, and that he's interested in human needs and. problems. He also meets with the psychologist to clarify what his expectations are of a social worker. He tries to plan his coffee breaks at the local drugstore when the town's two policemen and usually the county highway patrolman, also break for coffee. He drops. by the county welfare office, visits the visiting nurses association, shares a game of basketball with the juvenile services workers, and visits the American Indian boarding school at the edge of town. He even discovers two other MSWs in town one at the boarding school and one at the welfare office.

He soon hears about the local problems with alcoholism, about the teenage group that harasses the boarding school children, and about the drug problem at the boarding school. Several families tell him about the lack of summer employment for teenagers. He is asked by the visiting nurses association to visit some of the homes of their patients to help with understanding what's going on and several families call on him to get resources for a retarded child or an elderly parent.

Before long Mr. X finds that he is very busy-he conducts several groups a week on parenting skills; he provides consultation and gets referrals from the visiting nurses association; he is involved with the policy, city commissioners, and school officials in organizing a slimmer recreation and employment program for adolescents; he is called on by almost everyone in town when they want some information on mental health services 'available in Bangalore City; he has started a volunteer programme to assist patients who are returning from the state hospital; and he has begun a community wide alcoholism program with the assistance of an alcoholism specialist from the state office.

Scene One and Two portray two different professional approaches to social work in rural communities. The first one might be recognized as a family specialist and the second as a social work generalist. It is easy to see many differences between these two scenarios, but it becomes difficult as we try to define these differences and as we an attempt to decide how the specialist and the generalist relate to each other and to the overall objectives of the social work profession. It is the thesis of this paper that social work in small towns and rural areas requires a generalist social worker and that the generalist worker requires a distinct knowledge foundation that will allow him or her to cut across multiple levels of systems and work with individuals and their communities. It is agreed upon in the literature that rural areas demand as much of a focus on the community as on the individual. When this consideration is given, it changes the nature of all the subsequent professional roles of the social worker.

For example, although the clinical role remains an important one the generalist social worker must be aware that as the clinical role is applied, it affects the community involvement in problem resolution. Twenty, in her work with aging in rural areas, found that "*as persons in the community refer difficult situations to the social worker for solutions, local citizens' efforts are likely to decline...with decreased involvement. public understanding and concern wane.*" Thus social workers in rural areas not only must be able to work with both the individual and the community, but they also must understand the degree of interrelatedness of the individual and the community. It becomes increasingly evident that the rural social worker must focus on the delicate balance between the individual and the community and aim to improve that balance for' the benefit of both. I n the following sections of this paper. I would like to share some of my ideas about (I) the generalist approach to practice, (2) how an ecological-theoretical perspective may be useful as a knowledge foundation for generalist practice, and (3) how generalist practice based on an ecological perspective "fits" with the salient characteristics of rural communities.

GENERALIST–A PROSPECTIVE

Some people say that social workers have always focused on the person in the community-more commonly known as person-in-situation. It seems that some have emphasized both the individual and the community. Many others, however, make an assessment based on a person in situation configuration, then intervene with only the individual or, at best, with the family.

Others say a social worker must focus on either the person or the situation and thereby specialize in changing people or changing social institutions and society. This duality has characterized our profession for a long time. Historically, our profession has derived from many specialists who have emphasized one or the other part of the person-in-situation configuration.) In 1969 Gordon helped merge this problematic duality by defining the focus of social work as: Placed at the interface between or the meeting place of person and environment-at the point where there is or is not matching with all its good and bad consequences for the person and environment. The phenomenon of concern at this interface is the "transaction" between person and environment. Transaction is "exchange in the context of action or activity." This action or activity is a blend of person-activity and impinging environment-activity. The dual notion of person and situation is now tied together by the of transaction-which is not a person-variable or a situation-variable alone, but it blend of the two.

Schutz and Gordon (1969) have further elaborated on the concept of transaction. Man is unceasingly in transaction with his environment so long as he is alive and wherever he is. at whatever time. Thc quality and kind of transaction that he has with his environment determines very much what happens to both him and his environment. It is a universal principle that if there is a mismatch between his coping abilities and the demands of the impinging environments. both will suffer in a very practical sense. Every problem of individuals and society ultimately traces to some breakdown in or between man and his environment for whatever reason. Following the work of Schutz and Gordon, it is suggested that the generalist is one who focuses on the interface between the person and the environment and looks for transactions that may be the source, or the potential source, of problems.

Generalist practice may not be a good term for what is being conceptualized here. It is clear that we are not talking about a "jack-of-all-trades and master of none." In fact, we are suggesting a highly, killed social worker who knows about people and environments and the subsequent transactions. We are talking about a social worker who is expert in helping people who are experiencing transactional problems such as obtaining needed resources (money, food, housing, knowledge, skill, or love) or interacting with other social systems (spouses, families, schools, communities, or agencies).

It seems that we are advocating a new paradigm or way of thinking about the phenomena which social workers encounter daily. We are suggesting that social phenomena be viewed as interactive, with multiple connections and relationships within multiple environments. This implies that the individual can only be understood in terms of the whole interactional system.

Steven (2001) A systems theorist, illustrated this new way of thinking when he compared specialists and generalists: The specialist is motivated by a desire to achieve optimum adequacy to the phenomena in his constructs, and builds models and proposes theories with an eye solely on the accuracy of the match with nature. The generalist believes, on the other hand, that one does not adequately understand the phenomena unless one knows its interconnections \\'ith other phenomena. He seeks to produce those general concepts and frameworks which prove to be adequate for the understanding not only of isolated events, but of general patterns of relationships."

This view indicates an important difference between specialists and generalists-that is, the way of thinking about phenomena. I think this also is a critical distinction in defining the generalist in social work. Turning now to social work, Mermelstein and Sundet (2001) gave a definition of a social work generalist: *"The generalist social worker assesses, within the framework of the professional values, social phenomena in their various systemic ramifications and, based upon that assessment, identifies and intervenes at whatever systemic levels are efficient and effective within the internal and external resources of the action system to bring about the desired social change."*

It becomes clear that the generalist practitioner must possess a distinctive way of thinking about social phenomena. He or she must be able to see the interconnections and patterns of relationships within and between social systems and make interventions according to that assessment. Schutz and Gordon said that any true professional generalist must start from a thorough grounding in that profession's total frame of reference and an understanding of the broad perspective which gives the profession its distinctiveness. This distinctiveness for social work is the focus on the interface of social systems and the transactional nature of social problems. Thus, in accordance with Schutz and Gordon, the 'heart and core of the social work generalist lies in the knowledge and value realm'.

FOUNDATION FOR GENERALIST PRACTICE

What then is the necessary knowledge foundation for the generalist practitioner? I suggest that we explore an ecological-theoretical perspective for the foundation. Many features of an ecological perspective fit well with the generalist focus. First, using the concepts and terms from the work of Hartman and Busby (2002)," the ecological perspective is a biological orientation. It deals with living systems and how these systems interact with their multiple physical, social, emotional, and political environments. It has a holistic emphasis as opposed to an elementaristic one. That is, meaning is established by the general system and all part analyses proceed in the context of the general system. It emphasizes the interrelatedness and interdependence of all of life. It emphasizes the reciprocal nature of interactional processes whereby people affect their environments, and in turn, the environments affect people. It views this process as an adaptational one that is ongoing and evolutionary. It emphasizes the "fit" between the person's needs and capacities and the demands and nutriments from the environment. It recognizes the possibility of mismatches between the person's needs and capacities, and the environmental demands and supports. When this fit or match is poor, this disjunction is viewed as stress. When the fit is good, it is beneficial for both the person and the environment.

If an ecological perspective is accepted, the generalist social worker will focus on improving the fit between person and environment. Problems will be reconceptualized as transactional problems-that is, a blend of person variables and environmental variables. Clinical pathology will be viewed as mismatch phenomena and will then become a problem of balancing the person's needs and capacities with environmental demands and supports. This is not denying that there are intra psychic factors such as human attitudes, expectations, fears, and hopes, and that these have their origins in the past. Watzlawick (1999) has stated that regard-less of the causes or origin of a problem, it is maintained only by the interactional connection. And finally, if the ecological perspective is accepted, it offers hope for social work's dream of playing a preventive role rather than a therapeutic one.

RELATION TO RURAL COMMUNITIES

What does this knowledge base and generalist approach have to offer the rural generalist practitioner? It seems to offer a way of understanding and explaining what is already going on in his or her work with individuals and communities. This understanding is necessary for an effective practice in a rural area. Rural problems cannot be separated into neat packages of individual problems, family problems, and community problems. When compartmentalization occurs it reduces the effectiveness of social work. Hartman (2002) has aptly criticized this packaging mentality when she expressed astonishment that practice often is conceptualized in some programs as "social action for the poor and psychotherapy for the middle class." Each group, she said, is poorly served by such a reductionist response. This is most evident in small towns and rural communities. The whole community is poorly served by a reductionist approach.

It is useful to consider the characteristics of rural communities and how they fit with the ecological perspective and generalist practice. First, rural communities often are clearly identified and boundaries easily can be established. For example, it is fairly easy to see where Bangalore begins and ends, whereas a neighborhood in Bangalore City is more difficult to define. Thus the notion of a social ecosystem is easy to apply.

Likewise, relationships and interaction within rural communities are more visible and open for public scrutiny. Thus the processes and structures of system transactions are available to the alert and knowledgeable social worker. Another notion often cited in rural literature is the rural community's reliance on informal networks for social service delivery. We know that networks exist as semi-permanent social structures in all communities-cities as well as rural communities. These networks are one of the most vital bridges between the individual and the environment. In rural areas, it is mandatory to be aware of. to understand, and to be able to work with the various types of networks. Research is increasingly showing the importance of natural helping networks and that building on these may be a reasonable way to enhance the quality of life for all.

Another characteristic of rural communities is their "sense of community." The citizens are very aware of their community and consider it theirs. A quotation from a recent issue of Mother Earth News illustrates a young woman's experience in a rural community: Most rural communities are made up of a few large families that have lived in the area for generations. Their ancestors were probably among the first local sellers and these people feel close to (and often protective) the land maybe even of your land. Sure. There will be a few other 'outsiders' here and there', but the ones who've 'stuck' are the ones who, understand the people around them and strive to be accepted into the community family. If you choose to keep yourself detached, your chances of 'making it' in a rural environment can be pretty slim. This advice also illustrates the interrelatedness and interdependence of the people and their community. The charắcteristic of inter relatedness and interdependence also affects the social worker's position in the community. Nowhere is a social worker more affected by the client system than in the rural areas. For example, in urban areas the worker often lives in an entirely different neighborhood than most of his or her clients; but in a rural area, the worker lives, shops, and lives his or her private life within the same community in which he or she practices. The ecological notion of reciprocity certainly becomes evident here.

Finally, the relationship between the past and the present is another rural characteristic that needs consideration. Rural communities have a historical continuity of long standing that influences present events and interactions. For example, little-remembered family conflicts, church schisms, and migration of newcomers may be influential-it may even influence who sits by whom at the town's meetings. The ecological concept of social and historical evolution is relevant here. These are only a few of the characteristics of rural areas. It is clear that they must be considered by the rural social worker. When they are considered in an ecological framework, the entire community becomes an ecosystem and the individual and the community no longer can be considered as separate and independent variables.

CONCLUSION

In conclusion rural areas could be viewed as distinct communities in which individuals and the processes and structures of the community are intricately interrelated. The social worker must be able to understand and intervene on the basis of this knowledge. Thus a generalist is suggested for rural areas. A generalist is not a jack-of-all-trades but rather a specialist who has expertise in working with transactions between the person and the environment. In order to have an understanding of these transactions, an ecological perspective is suggested as the knowledge foundation for the worker.

References

Ann Lert (1991), "Developing Planning in Practice-Leading Issues in Development Organisations", *Journal of Social Work,* Vol. 3, No. 2.

Brkman (2002), A Social Work Strategy on Health, *Journal of Health Work,* Vol. IIX, No. 23.

Datt (1996), 'Collective Bargaining on Rural Social work Indian', *Journal of Labour Economics,* Vol. 41, No. 11, pp. 14-24.

Guy Hunter (1991), "Indian Economics and Village Development", *Journal of Rural Development,* Vol. 13, No. 5, 23-34.

Guptha (2001), Rural Development in India, *Journal of Rural Developement,* Vol. 23, No. 5.

Hartman and Busby (2002), "Environment and Social Work: Two Antagonistic Prospectives", *Man and Ecology,* 23(3): 23-34

Mermelstein and Sundet (2001), "Rural Development; A Prospective from an Ecological Prospective", *South Asian Development Review,* Vol. 23, No. 11, 11-13

Mathur, H. M. (1996), Anthropology and Development in Rural Societies, New Delhi, Vikas Publishing.

Schutz and Gordon (1969), "Ecological Prospective of Developmental Orgisations", *Journal of Social Science Review,* Vol. 11, No 4., pp. 45-57.

Steven (2001), "Rural Health Care in India, Health and Social Work", Vol. 22, No. 9.

Suresh Rao (1997), "Rural Development in India", *Journal of Social Research,* Vol. 23, No. 1, pp. 12-23.

Watzlawick (1999), NGOs and Development,

Journal of Social Science, Vol. 11, No. 4, pp. 45-57.

9

SOCIO-ECONOMIC DIMENSION OF RETAILING IN INDIA

Awadhesh Kumar Singh & Satya Prakash Pandey

INRODUCTION

The world economic scenario has undergone a metamorphic change. There are several forces which are moving the world towards a single economy. Advances in transport, communication and the technological revolution have reshaped competition, helped reduce cost, improved production methods and make products available for worldwide distribution. With liberalization, privatization and globalisation competition has increased and it has changed the business environment, which now requires business process reengineering. The emergence of vast potential of rural markets in India has attracted the multinationals and other corporate houses for exploiting the emerging potential of the rural markets. Thus the supply chain management has become the significant dimension of distribution channel. However traditional markets such as haats and fairs have emerged as supermarkets in rural areas. A journey of organized retailing in India demonstrates that it started in year 2000 and the forthcoming year are likely to be the era of supply chain management technology and merger and acquisition.

OBJECTIVE OF THE STUDY

This study has following main objectives:

- To study the growth of retailing in India,
- To examine the socio-economic issues evolved in retailing.

METHODOLOGY

Present paper is empirical in nature and based on mainly primary data collected through field survey. The field survey was conducted in Eastern Uttar Pradesh, in the district of Allahabad, Varanasi, Ballia and Faizabad. Besides collection and analysis of primary data, the secondary data and pertinent literature has been compiled from published, documented and internet sources.

RETAILING IN INDIA

Growing integration of the Indian economy with the global markets, there has been a rapid transformation of the Indian retailing sector as reflected in the growth of organized retailing. Indian retailing sector is witnessing increasing investment from the corporate sector, development of various retail formats and shopping infrastructure. This is evident from the fact that India is emerging rapidly as sourcing hub for international retailers. In this context, opening up of the retailing sector to foreign retailers, has, of late, assumed great significance and has been engaging interest of various stakeholders. In spite of the introduction of economics liberalization in 1991, the bulk of the retail sector in this country is in the un-organized sector with the organized sector accounting for only 2% of the retailing in the country. (Sinha 2006).

Retailing is the largest private industry in India and second largest employer after agriculture. The sector contributes to around 10% of GDP and 6-7% of employment. With over 15 million retail outlets, India has the highest retail outlet density in the world. This sector witnessed significant developments in the past 10 years from small unorganized family owned retail formats to organized retailing. Liberalization of the economy, rise in per capita income and growing consumerism have encouraged large business houses and manufacturers to set up retail formats, retail estate companies and venture capitalist are investing in retail infrastructure. Retailing provides a crucial link between producers and consumers in a modern market economy. The performance of this sector has strong influence in consumer welfare. Retailers not only provide consumers with a wide variety of products, but also a wide range of complementary services (such as assurance of product delivery), which can lead to more informed choice and greater convenience in shopping. They also provide procedures with the much-needed information on consumers demand pattern. Productivity and efficiency in retail operations lower price levels and reduce distortions in the price structure, through backward and forward linkages. Performance of retailing services affects the performance of interlinked sectors such as tourism, recreational and cultural services, manufacturing of consumer goods, agro-foods processing industries, etc. (Mukherjee and Patel 2005).

Socio-economic and demographic factors also contributed towards the development of modern retail formats since the late 1980s, there have been noticeable changes in the family structure, especially in urban areas, with nuclear families gradually replacing joint families. In these nuclear families, women play an active role in decision-making. Education levels and labour market participation rates of women have increased overtime. Many consumer surveys show that Indian women are increasingly under time pressure to use convenience option such as supermarkets where they can purchase all their necessities under one roof. They have also become more demanding on stores ambiance and quality of products (Mckinsey 2000). There has been a noticeable increase in the demand for consumers goods in rural areas. Indian rural market accounts for over one-third of the demand for many durable and non-durable products, and is growth at a faster pace than the urban market. In order to cater to this growing demand, manufacturers have developed new products such as shampoo sachets (Mckinsey 2000).

The retailing sector in India has undergone significant transformation in the past 10 years. Traditionally, Indian retail sector has been characterized by the presence of a large number of small-unorganized retailers. However in the past decade there has been development of organized retailing, which has encouraged large private sector players to invest in this sector. Many foreign players have also entered India through different routes such as test marketing, franchising, wholesale cash-and–carry operation.

India is sometimes referred to as the nation of shopkeepers. This is because the country has the highest density of retail outlets-over 15 million (PWC 2004-05) in the world. Comparatively, the US has only 9 million catering to more than 13 times the total retail market of India. since most outlets in India are located in the unorganized sector, the average size of these in much smaller that that of other countries. Only 4% of Indian retail outlets are larger than 500 square feet (ASSOCHAM 2000). Retailing is the largest industry in India and second largest employer after agriculture. Presently, the sector contributes to around 10% of GDP and 6-7% of employment (Bajpai 2004). However, unlike most develop and developing countries, India retail sector is highly fragmented and bulk of the business in the unorganized sector. With the liberalization in the 1990s, modern distribution service sector started evolving. On the supply side, consumer goods industry saw significant growth with the reduction in custom duties and a shift from quota to tariff-based system. Entry barriers on multinationals were largely removed and many multinationals such as Sony, Kellogg's and Samsung entered the Indian market. With the increases in cost labor in their home market, many foreign retailers and manufacturers are sourcing products from developing countries. India, with its advantage of cheap labor and availability of raw material, has strengthened its position as a sourcing hub.

FUTURE GROWTH OF OORGANIZED RETAILING

The future growth of organized retailing would depend on the ability of retailers to widen their customer base. This has already started in a big way and large retailers have taken direct marketing initiatives such as loyalty programmes. The growth would also depend on the ablity of retailers to efficiently manage the supply chain and increase operational efficiency through economies of scale, optimal space management and serviceability. Government, through appropriate policy initiatives, would play a crucial role in the growth and development of this sector.

Domestic manufacturers have pointed out that India has raw material and cheap labour but the country needs machinery, designing, and latest technical know-how in areas such as tanning. Unlike the garment sector, consumers are not very brand conscious and foreign players would have to reorient their products and pricing to attract Indian growth of information technology and developments in marketing, various formats for selling goods and services are coming up, which do not confine themselves to the use of retail facilities.

DISTRIBUTION IN INDIA

Distribution sector provides the crucial link between producers and consumers and hence, the performance of this sector is vital to the functioning of a modern market economy. Since the distribution margin is a significant fraction of the price of final product, an efficient and competitive distribution system is likely to reduce distortions in the price structure. This sector plays an important role in providing consumers with a wide choice of goods and associated services and consequently, has a strong influence on consumer welfare. Distribution services also provide producers with the necessary information needed to cater to the pattern of consumer demand. Therefore, any inefficiency in this services sector is likely to lead to misallocation of resources and economic costs (Mukharjee 2000).

The structure of distribution sector in any country reflects its socio demographic characteristic. The size and density of retail outlets are determined by demand related phenomena such as population density, level of urbanisation, participation rate of women in the labour force, access to cars, taste, personal consumption expenditure, etc. The structure also varies with the level of development of the country and speed of adaptation of new technology such as use of credit cards. In the early stages of development, bulk of the retail enterprises consists of a single shop or sole proprietorships. As the economy diversifies and per capita income increases, these traditional small shops are gradually replaced by larger enterprises. This, in turn, results in concentration and currently more than fifty Fortune 500 companies and around twenty-five Asian Top 200 companies are retailers (Imges retail 2006). With increased sophistication of products, many smaller shops have re-emerged as a part of a larger chain of shops while others are cooperating in franchising agreements, often oriented towards more specialised segment of the market. With economic development there has been greater vertical integration of the distribution chain. This has reduced the role of traditional wholesalers since large retail chains are increasingly bypassing the wholesalers and dealing directly with the manufactures. This is particularly true in the case of food retailing. Improvements in information technology have contributed towards this trend by allowing the retailers to fine-tune their inventory needs and reducing the warehousing role of traditional wholesalers. Furthermore, large retail groups are presently integrating the wholesale and retail functions. Many large retailers have developed in-house product lines and brands and established their own regional distribution centers in order to improve the flow of goods (Patel 2005).

Indian distribution sector has traditionally been an employer of relatively low-skilled workers. Labour productivity in India ranges from a sixth to one half of the US average. The organized retailers are finding it difficult to recruit trained manpower. In order to overcome this difficulty, many of them have set-up in-house facilities.

The Indian unorganized retail sector made up of 4 crore. Small unorganized sector does not take any help from the government. The goods that are sold in these small retail shops reach the customer through a channel of c & F agents, distributors, wholesalers, and finally the retail shops. So in the terms of employment unorganized retail provides employment, direct and indirect to an estimated 35 cr. People. A single shopping mall means the livelihood of at least 5000 small shop owners is destroyed (*The Economic Times* 2006).

The most important argument against modern retailing and supply chain integration is that it displaces labour in a labour-surplus society. Till such time that we are in a position to create jobs on a large scale in manufacturing and construction, it would make eminent sense to keep on hold any policy that results in the elimination of jobs in the unorganised retail sector.

In a drive to consolidate the supply chain, the APMC (Agricultural Produce Market Committee) Act was enacted to consolidate buyers and sellers in a central place-market yards or mandis–which would reduce time, costs and efforts. Towards this end, market yards were set up at all major locations. It was expected that as volumes consolidate, truckers, buyers and sellers all could leverage the invested Rs. 40 cr. To build a plant in Bangalore that would manufacture 500,000 suits a year (Mukherji 2000).

With the growth in organized retailing and vertical integration of the distribution chain, retailers are now playing a crucial role in designing and branding new products, which would match consumer preferences. Consequently, manufacturers are loosing their predominated position and have to gear their products to meet the specific demand of retailers. In-house brands of many retailers such as pantaloon and shopper's stop are price competitive and offer significant competition to manufacturers. In order to increase efficiency in the supply chain, retailers are investing in supply chain management technologies and are sourcing products directly from the manufacturers, bypassing the wholesalers and middlemen (*www.theeconomictimes.com*). The growth of some retail chains is leading to mergers and acquisitions. For instance, Shopper's Stop has bought over crossroads while Viveks has acquired Jainsons. In cities where organized retailing is growing at a fast pace. Unorganized retailers are reinvesting their personal savings and consolidating their position to form stand-alone supermarkets. The small retailers are also becoming more organized in terms of merchandized sourcing and accounting. Growth of organized retailing is gradually eliminating the intermediaries and wholesalers from the market. International retail chains such as Wal-Mart and JC Penny as well as Indian organized players approach the manufacturers directly for sourcing their products. This is cost effective since they save on the commissions paid to wholesalers and middlemen (Tuli, Singh and Panday 2005).

Indian distribution services sector is characterised by the presence of a large number of intermediaries resulting in fragmented supply chain. The growth of organised sector would require new supply structures based on customised product and service offerings and a supply chain controlled through the Internet. A well-developed supply chain would reduce the role of intermediaries in the distribution chain. In the near future, Indian distribution services sector would have to adapt itself to fulfilling demands for increased services, consumer convenience and lend itself amenable to rapid consolidation across the supply chain.

DISCUSSION OF RESULTS

In all, 200 shop owners were surveyed in 4 districts. In the sample of shop owners, respondents were retailers who visited haats and fairs for marketing of consumer goods and services. Most of the respondents were belonging to upper-age group i.e. 35 and above years. Again, in Faizabad district, 46 per cent respondents were from 25-35 years. Only 21.50 per cent respondents were reported to be graduates. It was recorded as high as 42 per cent in Ballia and as low as 4 per cent in Faizabad. Thus, the educational levels among shop owners are low.

The main occupation of shop owners has been reported to be business (37 per cent) followed by agriculture (30 per cent). However, about half of the respondents in Allahabad district reported their main occupation as agriculture. Moreover, agricultural labourers, artisans and service class people also deal in retail business since during the festivities and periodic markets, they exploit opportunities for commercial purposes.Most of the respondents are males since carrying shop to different places of remote in rural areas is a difficult job, which may not be possible for females. However, 15 per cent respondents were found females. It was reported as high as 24 per cent in Allahabad and as low as 8 per cent in Faizabad. Again, the female respondents are mainly family members of the shop owners.

There is strong correlation between education and annual turnover of shop. The turnover has been reported higher among highly educated shop owners. Average annual turnover of shop has been reported to be Rs. 39800 in Varanasi and Rs. 90720 in Ballia. The retail business constitutes a large proportion in family income. It was reported as high as 86 per cent in Ballia and as low as 44 per cent in Faizabad.

The highest number of customers are being dealt by retailers dealing garments and clothes followed by agricultural inputs and equipments. It is because of the fact that customers negotiate on price and quality of the items before purchase. The retailers dealing in garments and clothes, cold drinks and sweets/chat and specific products attract a large number of customers. The retailers generally sell their products to local farmers, local male members, local service class workers, and local female members who visit to local haat and fair. In Allahabad, Ballia and even Faizabad, most of the customers are local wage earners.

The respondents were asked regarding use of transport to haat and fair. About 38 per cent retailers use their own motorcycle to reach haat and fair. It was reported very high in Allahabad (56 per cent). Even, less than half of the retailers use own cycle to reach and carry products to haat and fair. Less than one-fourth respondents said that they use public transport like bus to reach fair and haat. It was reported high in Ballia (60 per cent). About 36 per cent respondents in Varanasi use tempo to carry and reach haat and fair.

The retailers are also consumers and they purchase products for family consumption. The main products are vegetables, daily use items, fruits, agriculture produce, and artisan products from haat while fruits, daily use items, agriculture produce, and daily use products etc. from fair.

Advertising effect, low price small packed, price, innovative and new items, durability, brand image, gifts schemes and packaging etc are the important factors influencing customers preferences. With the help of principal component analysis (PCA) and factor analysis, there are 2 factors i.e. price and innovative items, which have all the positive factor loading. In the case of one negative factor loading, the highest arithmetic mean is of brand image i.e. 0.424. So, as per customer's preference, price, innovative items and brand image are the three most important factors.

Thus, the above analysis simply demonstrates that the retail business has increased significantly exploiting the opportunities in local fairs and haats. The retailers do their business in these traditional market centres which require a little bit of investment, infrastructure and facilities. Moreover, the retailers are mainly small and medium sized who face problems related to availability of consumer goods in the time of need and transporting them to market centres.

SOCIO-ECONOMIC DIMENSIONS OF ORGANISED RETAILING

The latest neo-liberal onslaught on the lives and livelihoods of working people in India is taking place in the retail sector. After agriculture, the retail sector employs the largest number of people in India. Of the 40 million people involved in retailing as an economic activity, 0.5 million are in organized retail whereas around 39.5 million people are employed in unorganized retail trade. This includes all sorts of small retailing operations ranging from neighbourhood "mom-and-pop" shops to street vendors to small farmers who travel to cities daily to sell their produce to the small- scale transporters who transport the retail goods. These 40 million adults in the retail sector roughly translates into 160 million dependents, making the retail sector the source of livelihood for approximately a sixth of India's population. The decade of liberalization, which has seen stagnation in the agrarian economy and large scale job losses in the manufacturing sector, has pushed more and more people into different aspects of retailing in absence of any other opportunities (Pradhan 2005).

On the other hand, the small but burgeoning middle class in India, with immense spending power compared to the vast majority of the poor people in the country, has been eyed for quite some time by both multinational corporations involved in the retail trade and by Indian corporations which want to enter the arena sensing it to be a source of huge profits. Walmart from USA, known for its hated business practices, Metro AG of Germany and Carrefour of France have all been trying to enter the Indian retail market. As the Indian government has still not allowed foreign direct investment (FDI) in the retail sector, Walmart is trying to enter the Indian market in a joint venture with Bharti, an Indian company. (P. S. Ray, Sanhati).

"If the Reliance does not wind up its shops then we will be left with no other option but to go for violent protests that happened in Ranchi," said Vinod Baitha, a member of Vegetable Sellers Association (VSA) of Dhanbad districts (Sanhati 2007).

Echoing his sentiment Kunti Mahto, another vegetable vendor, said: "The state government is helping Reliance and acting against the poor who earn daily livelihood by selling vegetables. If Reliance is not stopped from selling vegetables then we will starve to death" (Sanhati 2007).

In the name of hygiene and consumer consciousness, a vicious propaganda is on set by the State that people shouldn't buy products which are not sealed and not to buy goods without bill. What is the state of hygiene in MNC Products? Isn't the glossy covered Cadbuiy's chocolate was found with worms and got banned in Maharashtra? The Killer Coke bottles were found with cockroaches, lizards, nails and even condoms. (Arasu Balraj).

Indian Small-Scale Industry Association argues that global retailers have well organised sourcing channels and they would not source products out of Indian small-scale units. However, the available data shows that most existing foreign retailers/franchisees are sourcing products from Indian industries (imports constitute only 5-10 per cent). It is likely that in the long run the pattern of imports of foreign retailers would not be much different from that of the existing organised retailers. Moreover, competition from foreign brands would force the Indian SMEs (small and medium enterprises) to adapt global quality standards and product ideas. It would also enable them to showcase their products to foreign retailers. As the vendors' processes and sourcing standards of the larger retail chains becomes standardised throughout the world, Indian suppliers would gain an automatic share of global trade through an established presence and closer links forged with the global chains.

The Kirana practices customer relationship management (CRM) diligently. The shopkeeper knows about the customers' families, their purchase history, and their needs. Consumer familiarity runs down from generation to generation. There is no major dissatisfaction with these stores. They are open longer hours, stock most of the goods required by the residents in a given area, provide credit and home delivery, and in many cases, supply products that they do not stock without any extra cost. Consequently, a large number of customers are not willing to pay a premium for the shopping experience promised by large format retailers.

Many trading associations-both at the national and state levels (such as Federation of Association of small Industries of India, Federation of Association of Maharashtra, Bombay Small Scale Industries Association etc.), some political parties, chambers and other industry association have argued against organized retailing. They have pointed out that the existing retail scenario is characterized by the presence of a large number of highly fragmented family owned businesses, which would not be able to survive the competition from foreign players. Retailing contributes significantly to employment, especially self-employment. If the entry of foreign players drives the domestic unorganized retailers out of business, it would lead to widespread unemployment. They have alleged that after these Southeast Asian countries allowed foreign retailers, the domestic retailers were marginalized and this lead to unemployment.

Those who are against organized retailing have argued that large international retailers can upset the import balance by preferring to source majority of their products globally rather than investing in local production. In fact, FIPB receives far too many applications for trading, instead of investment proposals. Moreover, global retailers might resort to predatory pricing, due to their financial clout; they often sell below cost in the new markets. Once the domestic players are wiped out of the market, the foreign players have a monopoly position which allows them to increase prices and earn profits (Indian Management Jan-2007) The aggressive marketing techniques, including predatory pricing, allow the multinational retailers to capture large portion of the market in a short time span. In less than 10 years, organized retailers have acquired 40% of market share in Thailand, close to 30% in Poland and 19% in China. These increases in market shares have been at the cost of domestic unorganized players who are unable to fight the competition. The trading association have also pointed out that FDI in retail trade would not attract large inflows of foreign investment since very little investment is required to conduct retail business. Goods are bought on credit and sales are made on cash basis. Hence, the working capital requirement is negligible. On the contrary, after making initial investment on basic infrastructure, the multinational retailers may remit the profits earned in India to their own country. Since Indian retailing is growing towards an organized format on its own and the fixed capital requirement is small and can be financed by Indian business houses, there is no need to open up the sector for foreign investments. Some domestic retailers have argued that since lending rates are much higher in India, Indian retailers, especially small retailers, are at a disadvantageous position compared to the foreign retailers who have access to international funds at lower interest rates. High cost of borrowing forces the domestic players to charge higher prices for the products (Mukherji 2005, Mukherji 2000).

'HAATS' AND FAIRS: SUPER STORE IN RURAL INDIA

'Haats' and fairs held regularly, provide a unique opportunity for the marketers to access the rural consumers. Attendance here is very high. We will discuss these in two parts, viz., (a) the 'Haats' and (b) 'Melas' (fairs).

'Haats' are periodic (weekly) markets, offering very useful mechanism of reaching the interior rural markets. They have the capacity to reach a very large number of potential consumers. Kashyap (1998) estimated that there are 47,000 'haats' held periodically in rural India. According to another estimate Haats (village Bazaars) operate once a week or more often in a total of 41,888 villages (*Business Standard*-The Strategist, Tue., 27 April 1999, p. 2).

Rural folk assemble at a particular 'place', atleast once a week to buy or sell, which is called a 'haat'. Large haats are held at large 'places' whereas smaller ones at small places. The goods sold in these places vary from agricultural and forest produce, various village handicrafts, to anything having potential of being sold or purchased. In these 'haats space is rented out by paying nominal taxes for the stall.

People converge at specific places, on occasions or festivals or to commemorate other important events. These fairs can be held on occasions such Baisakhi, Holi, Dussehra, Durga Puja, or Deepawali, etc. These are connected to religious festivals that people attend as part of their deeply ingrained religious culture. Rural folk eagerly look forward to these fairs, which are often held when the farmers have reaped harvest, and can sell the excess produce. Villagers are in joyous mood and often are prepared to spend. Families take part in these fairs. Hence a good opportunity to the marketers. Marketers can launch new products in 'melas', and can carry out promotion of existing 'brands'.

The average number of stalls per mela is 854, the average sale per 'mela' day ranges from a low of Rs. 60,000 in Assam to Rs. 8.8 million in Haryana. The duration of a 'mela' varies from one to 45 days. A study indicated the average number of visitors as 0.76 million per 'mela'.

Unlike the 'haats', which cater primarily to the essential needs of the local people, 'melas' cater to a much larger population, both rural and urban, with more sophisticated factory-made products. Amost half the outlets in the 'melas' sell manufactured goods (Kashyap, 1998, quoted by Velayudhan, 2002, p. 162).

However, traditional markets such as *haats* and fairs may prove crucial commercial places in rural areas. These markets require a little bit of investment and infrastructure and provide enormous opportunities for marketing of products and services to the rural consumer. Even the fairs and *haats* attract millions of people across the regions, states and nations (Singh and Pandey 2005).

Liberalisation of the economy in the last decade initiated structural changes in the distribution services sector and led to the growth of organised formats. It is now widely debated whether organised retailing would benefit the Indian economy in the long run. It is often argued that the large organised retailers would squeeze out the small unorganised sector and since the unorganised sector is labour intensive this will have a negative impact on employment. Indian Small-Scale

Industry Association pointed out that organised retailing would have a negative impact on growth and employment in small- scale industries since organised retailers have well-established sourcing machineries and would not source products from small-scale units.

One of the principal reasons behind the explosion of retail and its fragmented nature in the country is the fact that retailing is probably the primary form of disguised unemployment/ underemployment in the country. Given the already over-crowded agriculture sector, and the stagnating manufacturing sector, and the hard nature and relatively low-wage jobs in both, many million Indians are virtually forced into the services sector. Here, given the lack of opportunities, it is almost a natural decision for an individual to set up a small shop or store, depending on his or her means and capital. And thus, a retailer is born, seemingly out of circumstance rather than choice. This phenomenon quite aptly explains the millions of 'kirana' shops and small stores. The explosion of retail outlets in the more busy streets of Indian villages and towns is a visible testimony of this. The presence of more than one retailer for every hundred persons is indicative of the lack of economic opportunities that is forcing people into this form of self-employment, even though much of it is marginal. Because of this fragmentation, the Indian retail sector typically suffers from limited access to capital, labour and real estate options.

Indian distribution sector is highly fragmented and is characterised by the presence of a large number of small players. Organised formats are slowly evolving and currently, only 2 per cent of the Indian retail trade is in the organised sector. In the recent years there has been a noticeable growth in franchising services. Organised formats enable the retailers and distributors to enjoy economies of scale; provide consumers with a wide range of choice, low prices, pleasant shopping environment and convenience; provide efficient after sales services; and improve productivity, working conditions and skill levels of the work force. It also increases government's revenue by reducing the possibilities of tax evasion. Competition from the organised retailers would force the local traditional stores to improve their service quality and store standards. In spite of the aforementioned benefits, the growth in organised formats in India has been much slower as compared to other countries and the develpopment of the sector is severely constrained by the presence of several infrastructural and regulatory constraints.

It may be concluded that India can not live in isolation. The adverse and negative effects of d retailing are likely to influence a large population of the country. Therefore strategies are to be evolved to regulate the organize retailing and setting norms standards and parameters for managing the organized retailing as well as empowering the small retailers. There may be two deferent approaches for strengthen the network of supply chain management, without effecting the deferent intermediaries engaged in unorganized retailing. Firstly, the organized retailers should involve small retailers in their retail business through providing capacity building. Secondly the retailers cooperatives and associations be formed, strengthen and be promoted for regulating the unfair practices in organized retailing.

References

ASSOCHAM 2000

Bajaj C. Tuli, Nidhi (2005), Retail Management, Oxford Press.

Bajpai N. and N. Das Gupta (2004)

Balraj A., Sanhati 2007, P. S. Ray, Sanhati, 2007.

Business Standard, 4 Apr. 1999.

Indian Management, Jan-2007.

Kashyap P. and Raut (2005), Rural Marketing book, Biztantra Publication.

Mckinsey 2000.

Mukherjee Arpita (2000), ICRIER New Delhi.

Mukherjee Arpita and Nitisha Patel, Acadmic Foundation-A Report on FDI in Retail Sector in India.

Pradhan S. (2004), TMH Publication Co. Ltd. New Delhi.

Price Waterhouse Coopers Report, 2004- 05.

Sanhati (2007),

Singh A. K. and S. P. Pandey (2005), Rural Marketing, New Age Publication, New Delhi.

Sinha Piyush Kumar (2006), Retailing in India, Oxford Press, New Delhi.

Velayudhan S. K. Rural Marketing, Sage Publication, New Delhi.

www.theeconomics.com

10

THE FUNCTION AND MANAGEMENT OF RAILSIDE PLANTATION: A CASE STUDY OF CENTRAL RAILWAY–BHOPAL DIVISION

S. P. Singh & S. Raghavan

INTRODUCTION

Indian railway while playing their vital function in connecting our villages and cities of our country has also contributed by creating green belts along the railway track in many parts of the country. Railways are considered as a lifeline of our economy on which the infrastuctural development is based. (Arya, 1990) stressed that how wastelands could be converted into greenery.

These green belts are now playing an important functions in conserving ecological, socio-cultural and economic values in the country. Many economist, Planners, geographers, ecologists, agricultural experts views that the land resource is a very important resource and the supply of land resource is inelastic and the supply of land cannot be increased. (Narayan, 1993) finds out the economic return of dry land farming v/s agroforestry on marginal unirrigated land in Khajriman District of Andhra Pradesh. (Rajesh Pon, 1990) attempts from the angle of management version, taking into account that the population being a dynamic resource, the per capita availability of the land resource is decreasing with an every increase in population, our efforts should be "optimisation" of that land resource which is available as "Vacant" or waste land of different Government departments. The optimum utilization of such available land from the point of view of enhancing income to the specific department will definitely be a source of income generation to manage other expenditure of the specific departments.

In many cases, forestry has been one of the last sectors to be affected by economic liberalisation. Concerns that the private sector would not take forest's environmental and social values into account when planning utilisation and management and would have a tendency to overexploit the resource, have caused government to think twice before reducing their control. A significant innovation in forest sector reform is new emphasis on Private sector participation in forest, conservation, and a renewed interest in forest environmental services as financially attractive alternative to timber. Traditionally forest conservation has been considered as a cost that only the public sector would bear as the benefit that results from protection, such as maintenance of bio-diversity do not generate income. The government have facilitated the growth in the PSP through three mechanisms. (Natasha & Ford, 1999).

1. To encourage forest protection, government has paid owners for forest conservation.
2. To help channel private finance for conservation activities, government has promoted the development of markets where private investors negotiate with forest owners to protect their forests.
3. To attract international or foreign finance for conservation. In many cases governments have spurred the development of markets for forest conservation by attracting multinational finance.

Wasteland News (1993) mentioned in its publication about the highly publicised scheme to commercially utilize the vacant land available with Railways announced by the then Railway Minister, Shri C.K. Jaffer Sharief, soon after the congress (I) Government assumed office in July 1991, has failed to take off. According to sources in the Ministry, the proposal, which was aimed to net an annual revenue of about Rs. 2500 crores for the railways has virtually been shelved.

The proposal which was sent to the Union Cabinet for the approval, is learnt to have been shot down and the government has favoured retention of the status quo in this regard. Official sources say the policy of the Government is that each piece of unutilised land will be considered as individual unit. Hence, a proposal to lease out railway land to private enterprise for commercial utilisation cannot take off unless the union cabinet puts its stamp of approval.

This will mean that the prevailing practice of leasing out railway land at considerable low rent will continue. The railways now lease out land for a meagre Rs. 410 crores which, as admitted by an expert committee of the Railway Board, is several times lower than the market value of the land. The Ministry has assessed on various occasions that the level of resource generation could be to the tune of Rs. 2,500 crores annually if the railway land put to optimal commercial exploitation.

Thus, this study aims at analysing the following as objectives of the study.

OBJECTIVES

- To identify and locate plantation sites at different railway stations in the study area.
- To find out how much of the available vacant land has been utilized by the railway authority.
- To study the function and management of railway plantation, and species planted.
- To assess the methods of conservation and protection of plantation.
- To evaluate the mechanism of revenue generation and future benefits from the existing plantation.
- To study perception, attitude and responses of the railway department, level of people's participation towards plantation.
- To suggest, in the light of above, future planning, management and developmental strategies.

METHODOLOGY

To meet with the above objectives the following methodology was adopted during study.

Selection of DRM Office/Controlling Centre

The Bhopal DRM Office is selected because of the less involvement of distance, time and cost factors and area is controlled by the DRM

Bhopal, which functions from Khandwa Junction to Bina Junction (407.56 Km) on Mumbai-Delhi Track via Bhopal-Bina- Jhansi and the universe of the present study and the selection of Railway track was done on the basis of number of trains plying per day.

Selection of Railway Track

Bhopal to Bina railway track was selected for the purpose of study as the total number of trains plying per day varies in the range of 120-140 trains per day and covers 34% of the total railway track. Moreover, Station Junction distance from one junction to other junction station is less than as compared to the other Junction station such as Itarsi (91.5Km) far from Bhopal where as Khandwa junction is far (177.54 Km). While the railway traffic on other track is comparatively low, In ITARSI it is near about 80- 100 Trains per day and on other track BINA-MAXI, 40-60 Trains per day (as per the information obtained from the different station masters/managers).

In the view of above reasons BHOPAL-BINA track was selected for the purpose of study.

This study is based on the primary and secondary source of data and information collected from the DRM office Bhopal.

Method of Collection of Primary Data and Information

Primary source of information was obtained through structured questionnaire, which deals with

(i) Discussion with Railway authority of DRM Bhopal, Station Masters/ Superintendents/ Managers, IOW Engineers, Railway staff, Passengers, Villagers.

(ii) Discussions with Economists, geographers, Ecologists, Planners and Defence Personnel's.

- Selection of sites
- Area planted in Sq mts/ Running Km
- Species planted
- Species survived
- Selection of old and new plantation
    1. Ecological quadrate Method-Quadrate size 10X10 mts.
    2. Cost-Benefit analysis method.

- Proposed plantation (1999-2000)
    1. Proposed species and its number
    2. Proposed area.
    3. Total number of plants to be planted number station wise
    4. Total area proposed for plantation station wise.

Method of Collection of Secondary Information

Secondary information has been collected with the help of records available with Bhopal DRM Office, a detailed list was prepared on stratified/ random sample ,which deals with the following.

- Total number of railway station which comes on the railway track "BHOPAL to BINA Junction", where plantation activities carried out.
- Selection of controlling stations on the railway track "Bhopal to Bina".
- Finalization of the list of stations where plantation are existing, consisting of old and new plantation, Old Plantation may be defined as sites where plantation was carried out before 5 or 10 years.
- Finding out vacant land in sq km on either side of Railway track.

Besides above information, the qualitative aspects related with perception, response and attitude of Railway department for plantation and how to utilize the vacant land of railways up to the optimum level has also been documented through structured schedule. The obtained responses were analyzed accordingly and attempted on graphs.

Simple statistical techniques were used in the study, viz average, graphs, comparative analysis to justify the proposed objectives of the study.

ABOUT THE STUDY AREA

Map 1, shows the study area selected for rail-side plantation. The Bhopal Division area comes under the Central railway commanded by Mumbai CST.

Area of Bhopal DRM starts from Khandwa Junction to Bina Junction, consisting of total 407.56 Km on the on railway track Mumbai (Via Itarsi, Bhopal, Bina) New Delhi. Another area starts from Sirolia to NayaGaon (Via Shajapur, Vyawara, Rajgarh, Guna

Shivpuri Mohana) total 109.79 KM. One railway track start from Bina Junction to Guna also comes under the control of Bhopal DRM which covers a distance of 98.31 Km.

The study area selected for rail side Plantation starts from Bhopal Junction to Bina Junction with a distance of 139 Km., and occupies 22.57% of the total area which comes under the control of Bhopal DRM., *Central Railway Bhopal (1999-2000).*

As per information obtained from the various station master/ Managers On Bhopal to Bina track the total number of trains plying per day varies within the range value of 120-140 trains, comprising of goods/ passenger/Mail/express trains. This track is one of the important electric track.

Table 1 shows the railway station and number of plantation sites selected for the study.

Table 1
Name of Station and Number of Plantation Sites

	Number of plantation sites				
Name of Station	*Old*	*Recent*	*Nursery*	*In running km (old plantation sites in Number)*	*Total Sites*
Sukhi Sewania	2	1	1	-	04
Salamatpur	3	1	2	-	06
Sanchi	4	2	1	4	11
Vidisha	3	1	1	1	06
Sorai	2	-	-	3	05
Between soraiand Sumer	1	-	-	4	05
Sumer	2	-	-	4	06
Gulabganj	2	1	1	-	04
Ganjbasoda	5	-	-	1	06
Bareth	2	-	-	3	05
Kalhar	3	-	-	1	04
Bina	6	3	4	-	13
Total	35	9	10	21	75

Source: Survey.

The maximum number of plantation sites under the category of old plantation exists at Bina 17.14% of the total selected sites, followed by Ganj Basoda with 14.28%, Sanchi , 11.42%. The recent Plantation of Railways occurred highest 33.3% at Bina and 22.2% at Sanchi. While 19.04% of the Plantation sites were observed at Sanchi, between

Sorai and Sumer. It is also evident from the above table that maximum number of Railway Plantation sites were surveyed at Bina with 17.33% of total surveyed sites.

Figure 1 shows the composition of different types of Railway Plantation selected for the purpose of study.

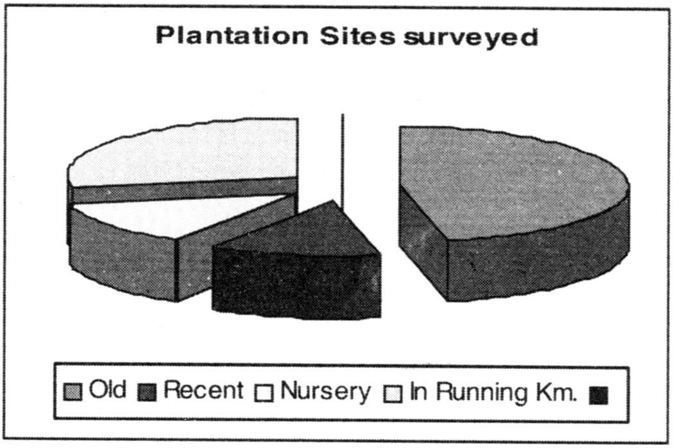

Figure 1

Table 2. Furnishes the details about the area of plantation existing in square metres under different category .The maximum area of plantation in sq mts comes under the category of old plantation followed by current plantation and nursery respectively.

As per ranking, kalhar Railway station covers an area of 20000 sq mts of plantation, followed by sanchi 16250, and Sorai 15000 sq mts. While sanchi covers an area of 25000 sq mts under the category of recent plantation. Sanchi Nursery, Bina nursery and the sukhi Nursery ranks as per the area cover in sq mts.

Table 3 provides the information about the category wise Species planted and existing at different railway station/ sites selected for the study, and number of Ecological quadrates laid to assess the vegetation status of plantation sites.

Above table reveals that 10 quadrates were laid at different plantation sites of Sanchi, followed by 8 quadrate at Bina and 5 quadrate each at Salamatpur, Sorai and Ganjbasoda. The size of ecological quadrate was 10 X 10 Mts.

Table 2
Station wise Area of Plantation Sites

Number of plantation sites and the area in Sq Mts.									
Name of Station	*Old*	*Area in Sq Mts*	*Recent Sq Mts*	*Area in*	*Nursery*	*Area in Sq Mts*	*In running km (old plantation sites in Number)*	*Area in Sq Mts*	*Total Area in Sq Mts*
Sukhi Sewania	2	10000	1	1000	1	1000	-	-	12000
Salamatpur	3	2200	1	200	2	100	-	-	2500
Sanchi	4	16250	2	25000	1	1500	4	2 rows of 6 mts x 3 Km (approx 36000)	78750
Vidisha	3	2300	1	900	1	900	1	Btewa River Bank 100 x150 Mts (aprrox 15000)	19100
Sorai	2	15000	-	-	-	-	3	Average strip of 6mts x 5 Km (approx 30000)	45000
Between sorai and Sumer	1	5000	-	-	-	-	4	Average strip 5mts x 6 Km (approx 30,000)	35000
Sumer	2	1500	-	-	-	-	4	Average strip 5mts x 6 Km (approx 30,000)	31500
Gulabganj	2	2000	1	150	1	150	-		2300
Ganjbasoda	5	4800	-	-	-	-	1	5mts x 1 Km. (approx 5000)	9800
Bareth	2	2400	-	-	-	-	3	6 Mts x 2 Km. (approx. 12000	14400
Kalhar	3	20000	-	-	-	-	1	5mts x 1 Km (approx. (5000)	25000
Bina	6	8500	3	4000	4	500	-	-	13000
Total	35		9		10		21		

Source: Survey.

Table 3

Name of Station	*Number of Ecological quadrate laid in the plantation sites*				
	Old plantation	*Recent plantation*	*Nurseries*	*In running (km old plantation sites in Number)*	*Total Quadrate laid each of 10 x 10mts size*
Sukhi Sewania	2	1	1	-	4
Salamatpur	3	1	1	-	5
Sanchi	4	2	1	3	10
Vidisha	3	1	1	1	6
Sorai	2	-	-	3	5
Between soraiand Sumer	1	-	-	2	3
Sumer	2	-	-	2	4
Gulabganj	1	1	1	-	3
Ganjbasoda	4	-	-	1	5
Bareth	2	-	-	1	3
Kalhar	3	-	-	1	4
Bina	4	1	3	-	8
Total	31	7	8	i4	60

Source: Survey

Figure 2 shows the plantation wise quadrate laid at different railway stations.

Table 4 shows the species planted and existing at the different plantation sites, under the category of old plantation 15 different

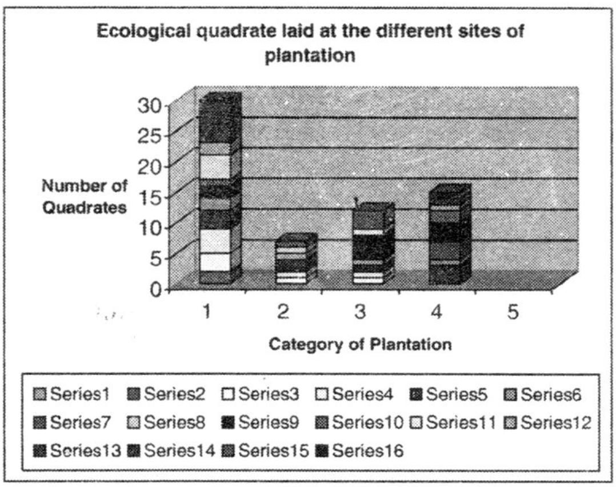

Figure 2

Table 4

Name of Station	Species planted/ existing at the different sites			
	Old plantation	*Recent Plantation*	*Nurseries*	*In running km (old plantation sites in Number)*
Sukhi Sewania	Soobabool	Gulmohar, sisam, Aam, Jamun, Neem babool	Gulmohar, sisam, Aam, Jamun, Neem babool	–
Salamatpur	Sisam, Soo babool, Eucalyptus, Ashoka Neem, Gulmohar	Jayson, Rose, Sada Shuhag, Kaner, Chandni	Bogan Biliya, banana, Papaya, Chandni, Rose	–
Sanchi	Soo babool, Sisam, Gulmohar Babool, Eucalyptus	Aam, Guava, Sisam, Sababool, papaya, Teak, Jamun, Kachnar	Aam, Guava, Sisam, Sababool, Papaya, Teak, Jamun, Kachnar, Ashoka, Bogan biliya, Eucalyptus, jaysaun, chandni, Kaner,	Babool
Vidisha	Jungle Zalebi, Babool, Sisam, Eucalyptus, Guava, Soo babool, Labhera, Gulmohar,	Kaner, Chandni,	Kaner	Babool, soobabool, Rinjha
Sorai	Sababool, Babool, sisam	–	–	Babool, Soobabool
Between soraiand Sumer	Babool,	–	–	Babool, Soobabool, Khejar
Sumer	Soo babool, Babool	–	–	Babool, Neem,
Gulabganj	Eucalyptus, Neem	Aam, Jamun, Papaya, Ashok, Sisam, Show, Plant, Bogan biliya,	Aam, Jamun, Papaya, Ashok, Sisam, Show, Plant, Bogan biliya, marry gold, Rose, Bogan biliya. Kaner.	–

Contd...

	Species planted/ existing at the different sites			
Name of Station	*Old plantation*	*Recent Plantation*	*Nurseries*	*In running km (old plantation sites in Number)*
Ganjbasoda	Soo babool, Eucalyptus, Acacia, Jungle zalebi, Sisam	–	–	Neem, babool Eucalyptus.
Bareth	Eucalyptus, Burar, Samiya, Kejhar, Babool, Soo babool	–	–	Babool, Soobabool
Kalhar	Soobabool, Babool, Eucalyptus, sisam,	–	–	Soobabool, Babool
Bina	Sisam, Babool, Soobabool, Eucalyptus, China tree, casurina, sewan, Gulmohar, Teak	Sewan, Sisam, bamboo, Jamun, sewan, Eucalyptus	Sewan, soobabool, Gulmohar, eucalyptus, sisam, Teak, bamboo, Jamun	–
Total Number of species	15	9	14	5

Source: Survey in the different plantation sites.

species are existing and most dominant species are Soobabool, babool, Sisam, Eucalyptus, neem, Samia, Sewan and Gulmohar. While under recent plantation category 9 different species are existing , Sisam, Aam, Soobabool, kaner, Chandi, Jamun, teak, papaya Bogan biliya. Besides under the category of nursery 14 different species are existing Aam, Jamun, Papaya, Ashok, Sisam, Show Plant, Bogan biliya,, marry gold, Rose, Kaner Sewan, soobabool, Gulmohar, eucalyptus, Teak,bamboo, are existing.

Table 5 shows the results of the ecological quadrate laid under the different category of railway plantation at selected railway stations/sites.

Table 5

Results of Ecological Quadrate Under the Category of Old Plantation Sites

Plantation Sites

1. Sukhi Sewania

Species	*Average Height (In Meters)*	*Average GBH (In CM)*	*Total Trees*
	Quadrate I		
Soobabool	11	42	12
	Quadrate II		
Soobabool	11.5	35.56	10
Khankhara	2	9	1
		Total Trees	11

2. Salamatpur

Species	*Average Height (In Meters)*	*Average GBH (In CM)*	*Total Trees*
	Quadrate I		
Sisam	4.3	33.8	8
	Quadrate II		
Soobabool	10.25	47	4
Kat Jamun	11	40	1
Babool	8.5	65	1
Ashoka	4	18	1
Eucalyptus	7	20	1
		Total Trees	8
	Quadrate III		
Soobabool	10.2	54.4	11
Neem	7	49	1
Sisam	4	36	2
Gulmohar	12.5	61	1
		Total Trees	15

3. Sanchi

Species	Average Height (In Meters)	Average GBH (In CM)	Total Trees
	Quadrate I		
Soobabool	4.5	14.5	47
	Quadrate II		
Sisam	4	23	8
	Quadrate III		
Soobabool	10.5	46.8	30
	Quadrate IV		
Soobabool	9.5	38	28

4. Vidisha

Species	Average Height (In Meters)	Average GBH (In CM)	Total Trees
	Quadrate I		
Sisam	4.	52	5
Babool	5	63	3
Jungle Zalebi	5.5	57	7
		Total Trees	15
	Quadrate II		
Guava	5.6	72	3
Soobabool	9	98	4
Eucalyptus	12	100	5
		Total Trees	12
	Quadrate III		
Eucalyptus	11	120	1
Sisam	5.5	57	1
Soobabool	8.5	84	6
		Total Trees	8

5. Sorai

Species	Average Height (In Meters)	Average GBH (In CM)	Total Trees
	Quadrate I		
Babool	6.5	58	2
Soobabool	8.5	52	9
		Total Trees	11
	Quadrate II		
Babool	5.2	32.9	9

6. Between Sorai and Sumer

Quadrate I			
Species	*Average Height (In Meters)*	*Average GBH (In CM)*	*Total Trees*
Babool	6	107	7

7. Sumer

Quadrate I			
Species	*Average Height (In Meters)*	*Average GBH (In CM)*	*Total Trees*
Soobabool	9.5	59	9
Quadrate II			
Babool	5.5	47	6

8. Gulabganj

Quadrate I			
Species	*Average Height (In Meters)*	*Average GBH (In CM)*	*Total Trees*
Eucalyptus	10.25	52.5	8

9. Ganjbasoda

Quadrate I			
Species	*Average Height (In Meters)*	*Average GBH (In CM)*	*Total Trees*
Acacia	5.5	45	3
Eucalyptus	12	72	2
Semal	10	110	1
Sisam	4	15	1
Ber	5	37.3	3
		Total Trees	10
Quadrate II			
Eucalyptus	10	57	6
Quadrate III			
Eucalyptus	14	63	15
Soobabool	13	60	2
		Total Trees	17
Quadrate IV			
Acacia	6.5	52	7
Eucalyptus	11.3	54	3
Jungle Zalebi	12	575	1
Sisam	6.5	41	1
		Total Trees	12

10. Bareth

	Quadrate I		
Species	*Average Height (In Meters)*	*Average GBH (In CM)*	*Total Trees*
Burar	12	67	1
Soobabool	8.5	38.4	8
		Total Trees	9
	Quadrate II		
Eucalyptus	7.5	32	9
Burar	10	80	1
Samiya	4.5	23.5	2
Khejhar	2.5	22	1
Babool	4	24	2
Soobabool	3	20	1
		Total Trees	16

11. Kalhar

	Quadrate I		
Species	*Average Height (In Meters)*	*Average GBH (In CM)*	*Total Trees*
Babool	5.5	57	13
Sababool	9	45	6
		Total Trees	19
	Quadrate II		
Babool	5	48	11
	Quadrate III		
Soobabool	9.5	52.3	16
Babool	6	59.5	5
		Total Trees	21

12. Bina

	Quadrate I		
Species	*Average Height (In Meters)*	*Average GBH (In CM)*	*Total Trees*
Sisam	4	24	7
Soobabool	8	33	6
Eucalyptus	7	26	2
Sewan	10	56	1
China Tree	3.5	18.4	1
		Total Trees	17

	Quadrate II		
Sisam	3.5	8	11
Babool	4.5	36	5
		Total Trees	16
	Quadrate III		
Sewan	4	27	3
Soobabool	5	26	4
Gulmohar	4.	22	1
Sisam	4.2	18	7
		Total Trees	15
	Quadrate IV		
Sisam	3.5	17	9
Teak Wood	3	13	8
Sewan	5.5	23	6
Sababool	5	18	3
		Total Trees	26

Source: Survey.

From the above ecological quadrate it could be concluded that

- 47 trees of soobabool were found in quadrate 1, at Sanchi with an average height of 4.5 Mts. While average GBH was 14.5 cm.
- 30 trees of soobabool were found in Q3 with average height of 10.5 Mts. And GBH 46.8 cm, at Sanchi.
- 28 trees of soobabool were found in Q4 with average height of 9.5 Mts. And GBH 38 cm, at Sanchi.
- The maximum GBH 120 cm of eucalyptus with 11Mts. height was recorded at Vidisha, followed by Semal tree with 110cm GBH and 10 Mts. height at Ganjbasoda.

ANALYSIS OF ECOLOGICAL QUADRATE LAID UNDER THE CATEGORY OF RECENT PLANTATION

Table 6

1. Sukhi Sewania

	Quadrate I		
Species	*Average Height (In Meters)*	*Average GBH (In CM)*	*Total Trees*
Gulmohar	1.5	5	5
Sisam	1.0	4	3
Jamun	2.	6	2
		Total Trees	10

2. Salamatpur

Species	*Average Height (In Meters)*	*Average GBH (In CM)*	*Total Trees*
	Quadrate I		
Kaner	1	5	4
Bogan biliya	.5	2	2
Chandni	.5	2.5	3
		Total Trees	9

3. Sanchi

Species	*Average Height (In Meters)*	*Average GBH (In CM)*	*Total Trees*
	Quadrate I		
Mango	1	3	3
Sisam	1.5	2	5
Jamun	1	2.2	4
		Total Trees	12
	Quadrate II		
Soobabool	1.5	4	5
Gwawa	1.0	3.5	3
		Total trees	8

4. Vidisha

Species	*Average Height (In Meters)*	*Average GBH (In CM)*	*Total Trees*
	Quadrate I		
Kaner	1.	3	8
		Total Trees	10

5. Gulabganj

Species	*Average Height (In Meters)*	*Average GBH (In CM)*	*Total Trees*
	Quadrate I		
Jamun	.5	2.5	4
Decorative plant	.3	1.0	5
Sisam	1.	2.	4
		Total Trees	13

6. Bina

Quadrate I			
Species	*Average Height (In Meters)*	*Average GBH (In CM)*	*Total Trees*
Sewan	3.5	18	9
Sisam	3	12	7
Teak	2.5	13	8
		Total Trees	24

From the above ecological quadrate it could be concluded that.

- 24 trees were found under the category of recent plantation consisting of Sewan, sisam and teak species, at Bina.
- The maximum GBH of 18 cm was seen of sewan plant with 3.5 Mts., of height was found, at Bina.
- Recently bamboo plantation is of economic value, The efforts have been made at Bina.

ANALYSIS OF RAILWAY NURSERIES

Eight railway nurseries were surveyed at six different railway stations. These nurseries are established with an object to provide saplings for plantation and to save time and cost factor for the transportation of saplings and plants from Govt Nurseries Betawa. Some of nurseries developed at Sanchi has received DRM and Gm award as per the information obtained from IOW Engineers and Station Master of Sanchi.

From the point of view of railways nursery established at Bina, some of the engineers have received training to grow saplings and how to prepare a bed for plants and how to transfer it in poly bags. The average size of bed is 1.2 x 10 Mts. each.

Bed I with more than 5000 sewan plants

Bed II with more than 5000 Ashok plants

Bed III with more than 10000 Eucalyptus saplings

Bed IV with more than 2500 Jamun plants.

The cost of nursery established at Bina is worth of RS 8000 while 4 Gardeners are obtaining the salary equivalent to grade IV class employee. These nurseries are protected by wall fence and wire fencing with attached gardener in each nursery.

ANALYSIS OF PLANTATION IN RUNNING KM BOTH SIDE OF RAILWAY TRACK

This is a very old plantation carried out by the railway authority a 15 or 16 years back. This plantation starts from Sanchi to Vidisha 3km and an average size of strip varies from 6 –10 Mts. At different places. The dominant specie is Babool. Fourteen quadrate were laid to assess the number of trees coming in a size of 10 x 10 Mts. of quadrate. The tree density varies from 4to 5 trees with an average GBH of 148 cm and 4.5 Mts. height. River side plantation near Betwa is a very good example .The objective of this plantation is to prevent soil erosion and reduce the sound intensity of plying train.

This plantation continued from Vidisha to Sorai 5.5 Km. Sorai to Sumer 8 Km and Sumer to Gulabganj 7.6 km. The Total number of trees varies from 6-7 per quadrate.

This plantation is protected by social fencing method and very beneficial from socio-economic and cultural point of view. The economic estimates of this plantation works out approximately 2-3 crores Rs.

COST ASPECTS OF PLANTATIONS

As per the discussions held with In-charge IOW Railways at different railway stations the budget of Rs 30000 is allotted to carry out the plantation activities under their section. The average expenses of plantation varies from the distance of Nurseries. Therefore to reduce the and to save the sapling costs the railway department has established good nurseries at junction station and managing stations. The fencing is important cost which depends and estimated on the basis of running Mts. However, Laxmi (1990), studied the cost effectiveness of fencing system and suggests the low cost model of protection and management of plantation.

The cost as incurred by the railway department on saplings differs from species to species. During survey it was informed by the engineers, Bina that they had purchased seeds from Nagpur. The following Table 7 furnishes a brief information about the purchase of seeds.

BENEFIT ASPECTS OF RAILWAY PLANTATION

The benefit aspects of railway plantation and the perception attitude & responses related to railway plantation were documented under the four different point of views.

Table 7
Seeds Purchased

Name of seeds	*Quantity purchased*	*Rate per Kg*	*Amount*
Teak	2	60.0	120.0
Sewan	2	60.0	120.0
Bamboo	2	120	240.0
Total	6		480.0

1. Ecological point of View
2. Economic point of view
3. Social point of view
4. Technical point of view

The views as expressed by the railway officials/ staff from all different five point of were gathered and analysed in table given below.

Table 8

Types of views Documented	*Percentage of response obtained*
Plantation maintains ecological balance and keeps moderate temperature near by the surroundings	40.0
Helps in soils conservation and moisture retainment.	16.0
Maintains the level of humus in soil	4.0
Changes has been occurred in ground water and surface water Level.	14.0
Establishment of nurseries for the plantation of different species.	6.0
To combat the threat of environmental degradation	20.0
Total	100.0

Ecological Point of View

Above Table 8 shows the responses related to ecological point of view and the same has been attempted on graphic version. 40 % of the response were related with ecological balance and moderate temperature nearby the surroundings. 20% of the response were related to combat environmental degradation, followed by 16% of response related with conservation of soil and moisture retainment. While 14 % of response related with changes in ground water and surface water level. Besides 10% of responses were related with maintaining humus level in soil and establishment of nurseries.

Figure 3 shows the graphic presentation of ecological views as obtained from the different sources during study.

Table 9 furnishes the perception attitude and responses of railway official/staff for plantations, from the economic point of view.

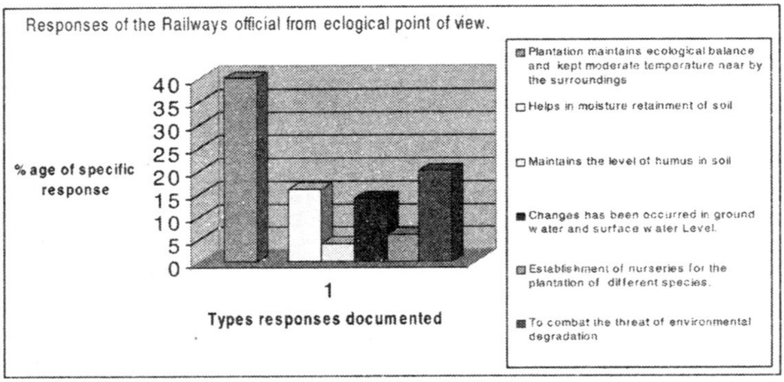

Figure 3

Table 9

Types of views Documented	*Percentage of response obtained*
Operation of the hat market in some of the plantation, where shop keepers sells different goods services and commodities.	5
30-40 peoples obtains fodder/grasses for their cattle for month from big plantations	15
15-20 peoples of nearby villages up to a distance of 2-4 km collects 5 –6 kgs of fuel wood from different plantation sites near by the track once in a week.	10
Railway department will get timber from various species of matured trees, worth of more than crore Rs.	40
Some passengers get fruits from the fruit bearing species like, Jamun, Aam, Ber etc.	5
Use of concrete sleepers in place of wooden sleeper to avoid felling of trees preserving present stock of plantation	25
Total	100

Economic Point of View

Figure 4 shows the perception, attitude and responses of the railway officials for the plantation from economic point of view. 40% of the

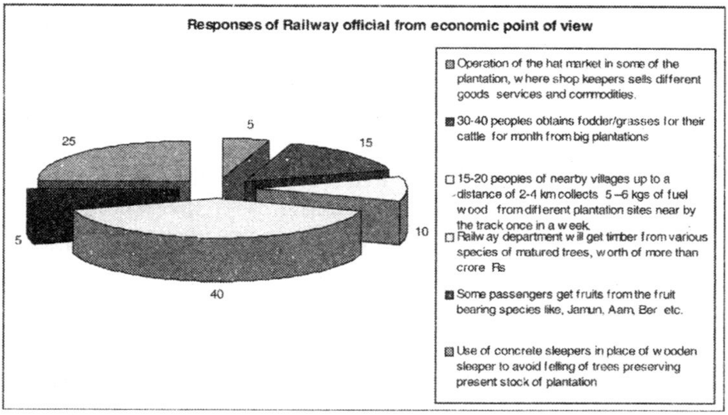

Figure 4

response were related to obtaining timber from various matured species, and the economic value of the existing plantation is worth of more than crore Rs. 25% of the response was related with use of concrete sleepers in place of wooden sleepers and preserving the existing stock of plantation While 15% of the response related with obtaining fodder/ grasses for cattle and 10% with the collection fuel wood.

Table 10 highlights the views of railway official for their plantation from social point of view. The following view related with railway plantation from social point has been documented and analysed as follows.

Table 10

Types of views Documented	*Percentage of response obtained*
Religious functions take place near "BABA KI MAZAR" on Thursday.	10.0
Helps and supports the survivability of poor.	18.0
Plantation is not only important from the point of view of human beings but also from the point of animals and birds etc.	22.0
Gang men enjoys their lunch under the shade of tree	20.0
Some of the local poor and passengers use to take rest and sound sleep under the cool shade of plantation.	28.0
Organising AKAND RAMAYNA under PIPAL tree.	2.0
Total	100.0

Social Point of View

Figure 5 shows the responses of the railway/passenger/ villagers for railway plantation from social point of view. 28% of the response related with passenger and common poor who enjoys sound sleep under the shade of plantation at different plantation sites. While 22% of the response related with the importance of plantation not only from the point of view of human beings but also from the animals, and birds point of view. 20% of the response related with the enjoying lunch under the shade.

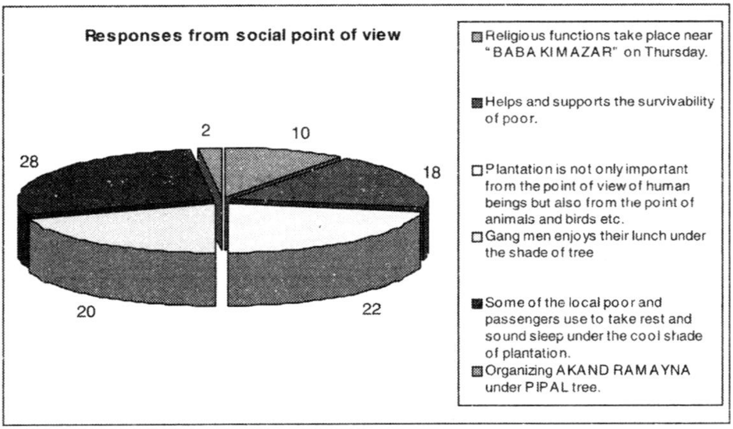

Figure 5

Table 11 points the importance of railway plantation from Technical point of view.

Table 11

Types of views Documented	*Percentage of response obtained*
Plantation checks the soil erosion and protects railway track from damage.	45.0
River bank plantation near by the railway bridge and at different elevation of track, checks the current of water flow help in soil and water conservation.	25.0
Fast growing species with an average height of 10Mts. And above, planted at a distance of 20-30 Mts. Away from the track so that traction should not be affected, or in nearby area the thinning is essential.	13.0

Contd...

Types of views Documented	*Percentage of response obtained*
Patrolling by the gang men, track engineers and vigil on plantation, shortening of trees below traction level.	7.0
Minimising the frequency of sound produced by trains plying per day, plantation absorbs the sound intensity.	10.0
Total	100.0

Technical Point of View

Above table shows that the maximum response 45% obtained for checking soil erosion and protect track from damage. While 25% of the response related with soil and water conservation. Where as 10% of the response related with frequency of sound produced by the plying trains.

Figure 6 represents the Technical aspects of railway plantation.

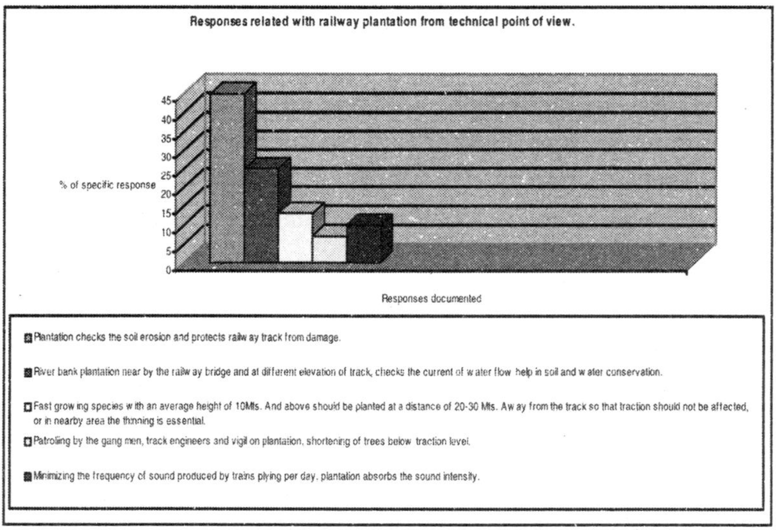

Figure 6

CONCLUSION

On the basis of facts and findings it could be concluded as follows:

- The study area selected for rail side plantation starts from Bhopal Junction to Bina Junction with a distance of 139 Km and covers 22.57% of the total area under the control of Bhopal DRM, Central railway Bhopal.

- The selection of Track was made on the basis of information obtained from various Station Masters/Managers on Bhopal to Bina Track and total number of Trains plying per day varies within the range value of 120-140 Trains, Comprising of Goods, Passengers, Mail/Express trains.
- Twelve Railway stations were selected with 75 Plantation sites consisting of 46.7% under the category of old plantation, 12% under Recent Plantation, 13.3% Under Nursery and 28.) % in Running Km between Bhopal to Bina Junction.
- As per ranking of plantation area *Kalhar* railway station covers an area of 20,000 Sq. Mts., followed by *Sanchi* with 16,250 Sq. Mts., and *Sorai* 15,000 Sq Mts. respectively under the category of old plantation. While Sanchi Covers an area of 25,000SqMts under the category of recent plantation.
- 60 Quadrate, each of 10x10mts size were laid in the 75 Plantation sites of selected railway land, to assess the tree dènsity and types of species planted.
- 51.6% of quadrates were laid under the category of old plantation, followed by 23.3% in old plantation in running Km.
- Under the category of old plantation sites on the basis of quadrates 15 species are existing and most dominant species are mentioned in Table 4.
- The results of quadrate laid under the category of old plantation sites were mentioned in Table 5 which indicates average height, GBH and total number of trees in each plantation sites. The relevant findings are mentioned on Page 19.
- Table 6 shows the result of quadrates laid under the category of recent plantation at six railway stations.
- Eight railway nurseries were surveyed at six different railway stations. Important nurseries are at *Bina, Sanchi and Gulabganj.*

- The dominant species of plantation , in running km is babool and the density varies from 4 -5 trees with an average GBH of 148 Cm and 4.5 Mts. height. This average strip 6-10 Mts. begins from *Sanchi to Gulabganj.*

BENEFIT ASPECTS OF RAILWAY PLANTATION.

- The benefit aspects of railway plantation is assessed on:
  1. Ecological Point of view.
  2. Economic point of view
  3. Social point of view.
  4. Technical point of view.
- The views as expressed by railway officials/staff from ecological point of view were gathered and analysed accordingly and results are mentioned in Table 8 and Figure 3.
- The results based on economic point of view are mentioned in Table 9 and Figure 4.
- The results based on social point of view are mentioned in Table 10 and Figure 5.
- The results based on technical point of view are mentioned in Table11 and Figure 6.

Issues Pertaining to Railway Plantation

- Function and management of railways plantation depends upon the limit of budget sanctioned by the authority and looking after the plantation.
- Encroachment on railways land by the farmers, affluent resident and existing socio- religious political pressure on authority.
- Increases possibility of animal accidents.
- Cultivation of railways land and obtaining surplus production by more than 100 farmers near by the track.
- Problem of harvesting of the matured trees, as per the order of supreme court.

Utilisation of Railway's Vacant Land in Some Other Ways

- Possibility of Pisi-culture development, where water availability lasts up to 10 months or entire year, leasing it out after fixing,

Time period, percentage to be obtained by railway, per annum and developing it in Eco-tourism site.

- Identification/listing of such farmers those who have encroached the railway land and obtaining the production of different crops. (measurement of area/per acre production and fixing out the percentage to be given to railways for the use of encroached land. This generated funds may be utilized for railways to develop the public/employee's utility.
- Identification of vacant land in colonies or other places where there will be no plan for laying out of railway track or where plantation can not be carried out, or barren land or degraded / denuded quality of soil exists, Railway department should come up with ambitious plan like construction of ware house specifically for commercial purpose, construction of houses/flats for the welfare of employees, which may be hand over to them after the assessment/valuation of land at market price, construction cost etc.

Overall Function and Management of Railway Plantation

Singh & Bhattacharya, (1999) studied the role & contribution of Indian Army and importance of forest from defence point of view. Further it highlights, various methods of protection, conservation and development of Indian forest while Jose (1990) mentioned the management of plantation in the study area.

Thus, the overall function and management of rail side plantation may be summarized as follows.

- The recent plantation and the nurseries are managed with wall fence and wire fence.
- Under the category of old plantation and Very old plantation the railways authority manages it through social fence method.
- In some of the plantation the management and functions govern by the specific staff of IOW and attached gardener and Malis in the specific sites.
- At the time of study some of the local resident at selected station entered in the plantation sites was returned back by the gardener " How they entered in the plantation".

- The row plantation either side of the railway track managed by the local staff of railway/ gang men with the local resident.
- Incoming future the level of people's participation and railway staff will check the illicit felling of plantation as observed during survey.
- The railways ambitious plan regarding function and management will come in future in the collaboration with soil and forest department respectively.

ACKNOWLEDGEMENT

Authors sincerely acknowledge Dr. Ram Prasad, Director, Prof. S. M. Hasan, Shri. S. K. Vidhan, Ex-Finance Officer, Shakti Saran, Finance Officer Shri R.S. Bhadoria, Asst. Manager (M), Shri D. K. Verma, Asstt. Manager (H), Dr. D. Dugayya of Indian Institute of Forest Management, Bhopal for their support in bringing out this useful document. We are also highly indebted to Prof. Snehalatha Shrivastav, Chairman, Board of Studies (Economics), Prof. R. D. Singh, Director, Centre for the Study of Environment and Sustainable Development, Barkatullah University, Bhopal. Authors also acknowledge Brig. P.C. Roy and Brig. K. K. Nathni from Survey of India, Dehradun for initial discussions and their views on the topic. Authors also express their sincere respect to Shri Ravindra Sharma, Shri Pradeep Kumar, Shri M. P. Dubey, IRS, Shri A. K. Singhal, Div. Engineer, Shri R. N. Sonkar, Div. Engineer, Sr. DN North Shri M. K. Agarwal, Shri D.C. Dubey (AEN), Sr. SE P-Way Shri D. K. Saxena, Shri K. N. Saxena, Section Engineer, Vidisha and Shri S.C. Sukla, Sr. P-Way, and other staff of Indian Railways for their valuable suggestions & guidance during the study period. Our sincere thanks are due to Shri Kohli Saheb and Ex. S/Maj. Munshi Lal, Defence Research and Development Establishment, Gwalior for their moral support. Authors are highly indebted to Shri KVC Sekhar, IIFM for his technical expertise in composing and designing of this valuable document to give it ornamental shape to the win words as well as graphics. Authors have received continuous co-operation and support from all, without which it would not be possible to develop this important document.

References

Arya, A. K. (1990) , "A Rational Approach Towards Greening Wastelands". OT No. 11, *Indian Institute of Forest Management, Bhopal.*

Central Railway Bhopal Division (1999-2000), " Saghan Vrakcharopan Karyakram".

Jose, P. D. (1990), "Management of Plantation" OT No. 19, *Indian Institute of Forest Management, Bhopal*

Laxmi. M.G. (1990) " Cost effective fencing system : A study " . OT No. 40, *Indian Institute of Forest Management, Bhopal.*

Natasha landell-Mills & Jenson Ford (1999), "Privatising Sustainable Forest Trees", IIED, London.

Pon. T. Rajesh (1990), "Optimization of Land Use for the Production/Revenue of TAFCORN" OT No. 28, *Indian Institute of Forest Management, Bhopal.*

S.P. Singh & P. Bhattacharya (1999), " The Green Warriors, Protection Conservation and Development of Indian Forest- Study of 3. EME Centre Bairagarh, Bhopal", Wasteland News August Sept., pp. 76-79.

Wasteland News (1993), "Huge Potential along Railways Goes Untapped", *SPWD*< Vol. VIII, No. 2. p. 39.

11

TRAINING APPROACH-A STUDY WITH REFERENCE TO NEW GENERATION BANK: ICICI BANK LTD.

Anjali Ganesh & A. Raghurama

INTRDUCTION

It is unbelievable to everyone if newspapers or the late night editions of the TV news do not carry anything about ICICI, one of the India's biggest development financial institution and a tremendously growing New Generation Private Sector Bank. ICICI Bank Ltd. is a new breed of Indian banks: ambitious, globally competitive, and finely tuned to customer needs and internet savvy.

Industrial Credit and Investment Corporation of India (ICICI) Bank Ltd. was originally promoted in 1994, *(http://www.icicibank.com)* by ICICI Limited, an Indian Development Finance Institution. The growth of the bank over the years has repeatedly proved the ability of the institution in adapting to new technologies and products within a short span of time. The major cause for the exponential growth of ICICI Bank Ltd. is its willingness to adapt to both internal and external changes. It has developed such a dynamic workforce, which is most willing to adopt new things.

ICICI Bank Ltd. is one of the best employers to work for in India, due to the excellent HR practices with its employee-centric approach. Participation of the employees in the activities of the institution is a key to the success of any organisation. The co-operation from the employees to the management of the bank has been outstanding. The new generation bank approaches the training priorities of its employees in a unique way. Historically, everybody talked about three types of capital-finance, technology and human. (Jayakar Roshni and Arara Sunit 2001). The bank makes the human capital, the centrepiece of its strategy. 'Speed' is another capital, which the bank has made the focal point along with human capital around which technology and finance revolve. ICICI Bank Ltd. encourages managers to try new techniques and technologies by empowering them.

Training Needs of ICICI Bank Ltd. is very high as it rides on technology. Training is imparted with the perspective of encouraging learning and helping the employees to handle the products of the bank efficiently by imbibing the skills of the prudent banker. The employees are always brainstormed on, 'not knowing something is not something to hide, but something that the person could correct'. In the context of this, the study is carried on with the following objectives.

OBJECTIVES

1. To understand the training approaches (practices) of ICICI Bank Ltd. for its employees.
2. To know the differences in the training practices between ICICI Bank Ltd. and Corporation Bank and Karnataka Bank Ltd.
3. To analyse the opinions of the employees of ICICI Bank Ltd. regarding its training practices.
4. To suggest measures based on the findings of the study.

METHODOLOGY

With a view to fulfilling the objectives of this study, the whole population of fifty employees of ICICI Bank Ltd. in Dakshina Kannada (D.K.) district were contacted and interviewed personally. This bank's network in D.K. District as of now is limited only to Mangalore taluk.

BACKGROUND INFORMATION

ICICI Bank Ltd. has its regional office in Bangalore situated in Koramangala and its corporate office situated in Mumbai. There is a 'Training Centre', which is located in the regional office of its own. There is no separate Staff Training College (STC) of its own meant for employees of ICICI Bank Ltd. unlike in the case of Corporation

Bank and Karnataka Bank Ltd. So, staff structure of Training Centre is different from other commercial banks that will have a regular full time principal of the cadre of Assistant General Manager (AGM). Simplified staff structure does not conclude that the employee's training in ICICI Bank Ltd. is taking a back seat.

There is "Training Co-ordinator", who is an officer of the supervisory cadre of the same bank, who takes care of the training programmes as and when hosted. Training details and requirements of the top-level executives of ICICI Bank Ltd. are taken care of by the HRD division of Head Office, Mumbai. The Training Co-ordinator, in consultation with the regional offices, prepares training plan jointly. Regional Offices in turn will consult the bank branches of their jurisdiction, for preparing the training plan, only after identifying the training needs of the employees. HRD division by referring to the list of employees who are freshly recruited decides about sending them for training programmes to the Training Centre. In case of special training programmes such as 'FOREX', 'advances' or 'recovery', an employee concerned receives information about it couple of weeks in advance so that he/she could cope mentally to accept and concentrate on such training.

Eligibility of the Employees

All the employees are eligible to undergo the required training depending upon the skill and creativity required to carry on the job. New inductees have to undergo compulsory induction programme, in the form of 'new employee orientation'. Programme regarding the information of products and services of the bank are also provided. This programme is for duration of five days, held in Training Centre. This programme takes place after fifteen days of induction of the employees. For this programme, usually, the trainer will be an expert from the same bank. This is a sort of mentoring exercise followed by the ICICI Bank Ltd. to imbibe the necessary skills into their employees.

There are other categories of functional training programmes depending upon each employee's need for it, his access to the particular line of activity or on the introduction of the new product by the bank, the functional training programmes are mostly outsourced by ICICI Bank Ltd. to resource persons from IIMs, RBI, BTC and NIBM. This is because ICICI Bank Ltd. believes that it is better its employees to be experts on the product or service it is selling and someone else be an expert on other tasks. One such other task is training also. The outsourced training programmes are conducted in prestigious hotels and eye-catching resorts that have a very sound ambience for learning. It is a pleasant learning exercise for ICICI bankers.

Important Training Programmes

A major challenge of ICICI Bank Ltd. is its online training, which is compulsory for all the employees. When ICICI's e-technology initiative was implemented, employees had to learn to live with different structures. Bank gives employees an opportunity to move freely within the organisation. Should there be any requirement in an existing department or a new area, that the bank is entering, the information is available on the 'ICICI Universe', part of ICICI's intranet. ICICI Bank Ltd. is a pioneer among Indian banks to launch its own website on 26th February 1996. (Rao, Madanmohan 1997). Employees are trained in such a way as to use web-enabled applications on the bank's intranet. This conveys that ICICI Bank Ltd. rides on technology.

ICICI Bank's online training (learning) with the help of e-learning solution is taken care of by Brain-visa, *(http://www.brainvisa.com)*-a software company that plans for a distributed installation of the solution to meet the increasing requirements. Online training aims to train employees of ICICI Bank Ltd. spread over wide locations on changes in products, technology and regulations. The employees also need to be trained on their roles in the new environment. One of Brainvisa's largest installations, the 'Learning Matrix' is positioned internally at ICICI Bank Ltd. Hundred hours of online learning courses are developed and delivered through the system which performs functions such as learning resource co-ordination, training co-ordination, tracking and monitoring, content management, enabling instructor activities, learner portal and competency management.

All the employees have to undergo compulsory 'Certification Test' through 'Learning-Matrix, depending upon their area of work within a stipulated time schedule. The several products of ICICI Bank Ltd. which the employees can get themselves trained online are e-Bank, Credit Card, Debit Card, D-Mat, House Loan, Car Loan, NRI Account, ATM functioning and the like.

A few important training programmes that are imparted to the employees of ICICI Bank Ltd. which are the essential banking functional related training programmes that are also given by Corporation Bank and Karnataka Bank Ltd. with slight changes in the nomenclature of the programmes.

(a) *Leadership Training:* This training is imparted to develop the leadership and vision of current and potential strengths and weaknesses by taking up initiatives in the areas of strategic planning, policymaking and goal setting.

(b) *Marketing, Customer Service and Selling Skills:* This training programme is on how to improve customer relations and provide customer service. This course helps to build the attitude, skills and habits needed to demonstrate the effectiveness of their products and services and to influence the purchasing decisions of prospective and existing customers.

(c) *HR Skills for Management Effectiveness:* This training is provided to enhance one's effectiveness in maintaining better human relations, by creating awareness on the importance of managing the people and development of varieties of skill in a working environment.

(d) *Interpersonal Communication:* It is training in Communication and Co-operation among individuals and groups including conflict resolution, stress management, team work and group dynamics.

(e) *General Banking:* This sort of training is meant to equip the officers with analytical skills in matters in the areas of credit, advances, lending, and recovery, interpretation of financial statements and details of other development schemes.

(f) *Branch Management:* It is a training imparted to the branch managers to give an exposure in the field of planning, organising, problem solving and decision making processes that are applicable to the branches of the bank.

It is learnt from database that on an average, an employee undergoes about 62 men hours of training at ICICI Bank Ltd. every year, including specialized functional training. ICICI Bank Ltd. also offers sabbaticals, up to four years. A fee reimbursement plan is available to employees, where the tuition fees for courses related to the business are reimbursed. This is how the employees get encouragement for pursuing their education and training. As per Zachariahs(2002), corporates like ICICI Bank Ltd. are opting for soft skills to make hard sell. It matters little whether an employee is a new entrant or a CEO, they are all grabbing, not market share, but social graces. ICICI Bank Ltd. brings 'Business Etiquette' or 'soft skills' into HR focus. Employees of ICICI Bank Ltd. have to undergo such training from front line staff to middle management. ICICI Bank Ltd. feels that knowing soft skills are more important than the knowledge of banking regulations. This sort of training is gaining currency around the world as it attempts to win a lot of goodwill–both at a personal and professional level.

ICICI Bank Ltd. also sends its top executives for 'Intrapreneurship Development', an executive development programme to unleash the entrepreneur within. The training is imparted by Entrepreneurship Development Institute of India (EDI), set up in 1983, as an autonomous institution registered under the Societies Registration Act sponsored by All India Financial Institutions like IDBI, ICICI, IFCI and SBI with an active support of Government of Gujarat. (*ediindiaadl@sancharnet.in*). The duration of this eight to ten hours/day residential programme ranges from five to six days on full time basis. Training methods comprise of case-discussions, role-plays, simulation exercises, lectures, discussions, counselling and audio-visual aids. The participants would be exposed to a variety of innovative situations.

ICICI Bank Ltd. also conducts executive training and knowledge enhancement workshops and courses for finance practioners and intermediaries, delivered by global subject experts through Invest India Economic Foundation (IIEF), India's leading private sector agency in financial policy analysis, investor education and executive training. (*http://www.iief.com*).

FINDINGS OF THE STUDY

Difference in Training Approach of ICICI Bank Ltd.

Employees of ICICI Bank Ltd. in D. K. District feel very much excited about their training system, since they enjoy being trained and they feel that the training is a change from the routine banking work, resulting in learning and development. Most laudable aspect of training in ICICI Bank Ltd., in comparision to other banks (CB and KBL) is that there is a correlation between the type of training imparted for the employee and the job handled by him/her. Thus the training inputs are properly utilised by the employees at work. Since employees are trained through online as well as by the training institutes, depending upon the functions handled by them, it could be inferred that the training needs of employees are properly identified.

But as far as training evaluation practices are concerned, ICICI Bank Ltd. is considered on par with other commercial banks, (CB and KBL), wherein the behaviour and results evaluation is totally neglected. Truly speaking, the banks are not practicing the full-fledged training evaluation.

Relevance of Training

Employees of ICICI Bank Ltd. in D.K. District opined that the present model of training is well focused on vital areas of banking and are very much relevant to their work.

Training Infrastructure

As far as infrastructure and other facilities for training are concerned all the employees are fully contented, since they are usually trained in resorts and in star hotels where the ambience is very much conducive and motivating to learn and develop.

Development of Skills through Training

The respondents were asked to appraise their skills after undergoing the training programmes such as Resource Mobilization, Credit Management, Recovery Management, Bank Marketing and Customer Service, HR Skills and Branch Management.

Graph 1 shows the percentage of attendance of employees of ICICI Bank Ltd. in various training programmes.

At least twenty two employees are of the opinion that the training may not help in developing certain important banking skills like analytical, risk management, problem solving, inter-branch reconciliation and communication skills. But they feel that the training will definitely enhance their HR, marketing, accounting, cash management and IT related skills. However, ICICI Bank Ltd. believes in enhancing the soft skills as well as technical skills of its employees through specific training programmes at all levels.

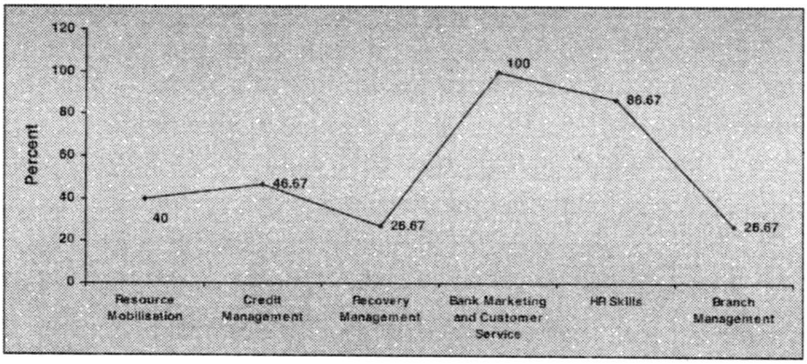

Graph 1: Category-wise Analysis of Attendance of Employees in Various Training Programmes

SUGGESTIONS

Based on the findings, few suggestions are provided.

1. The banks should develop training Evaluation Practices seriously, taking into consideration its drawbacks. For the purpose of proper evaluation of training, the banks should set up an 'Evaluation Unit', which exclusively deals with an analysis of pre and post training performance of the employees.
2. More and more seminars on Agriculture and Rural Development should be arranged in the common interest of the economy of the country as well as for the knowledge of the employees.
3. Instead of spending the valuable time on formal functions like inauguration and valediction, the training sessions and programmes should be well planned with intensive brainstorming sessions in the beginning to understand the pre-training status of the trainees personally and can be wound up by taking a feedback by the trainees about the benefits derived by them after undergoing training.
4. The training practices must always have an in-built flexibility and the trainer must have the freedom to include extra topics relevant to the programme if found necessary.

5. Compulsory introduction of workshops and seminars on Yoga, Meditation and Relaxation Techniques on a regular basis should be introduced, as they are greatly beneficial to the employees to overcome stress in their life.
6. Sufficient training programmes must be arranged in the field of risk management so as to handle and minimise the risks like operational risks, credit risks, liquidity risks, foreign exchange risks, market risks, strategic risks and the like.

CONCLUSION

Any form of classroom training is rather theoretical than practical in nature. The utility of it can be maximised only by applying it into practice. Empowerment of the trainees to apply the training inputs into practice works wonders to transform the organisation from stereotypic culture to non-stereotypic one. For this, the change in the mentality should begin with the top management itself, which percolates to all the divisions in the bank. However, training can provide the employees more with the theoretical inputs, it is up to the employees to perform well on their job by applying training knowledge, learning from peers, gaining exposure and gaining experience of banking functions.

References

ediindiaadl@sancharnet.in–EDI (Entrepreneurship Development Institute of India).

http://www.icicibank.com

http://www.iief.com–Invest India Economic Foundation–Profile.

http://www.brainvisa.com–Brainvisa Technologies, Clearing Solutions.

Jayakar Roshni and Arara Sunit (Jan. 21st 2001), ICICI, The Metting Pot, *Business Today*, 10(1), pp. 169-180.

Rao, Madanmohan (May 15th 1997), ICICI Bank: A Pioneer Among Indian Banks on the Net, *India Line*, *http://www.brainvisa.com*–Brainvisa Technologies, Clearing Solutions.

Zachariahs Candice (June 17th 2002), Corporates opt for Soft Skills for Hard Sell, *India Times*, and *http://learning indications.com*

12

INDIAN WOMEN WORKFORCE: STRIKING A BALANCE BETWEEN WORK-LIFE!

Smita Singh

"Whatever women do, they must do twice as well as men to be thought half as good. Luckily, this is not difficult."
– Charlotte Whiton

Work-life balance has gradually become a major concern spreading across gender, generations and organizations. This brief paper aims at examining literature related to work-life balance, exploring its significance with special focus on working women and addressing implications of ignoring the issue as well as forward strategies for achieving improved work-life balance. There is substantial literature which suggests that women experience greater work-life conflict as compared to men. While some suggest that this is the result of their hormonal response to different stressors (Jick & Mitz, 1985) there are others who argue that these responses are the result of differences in role expectations and socialisation of men and women (Duxbury & Higgins, 2001). 'Women, irrespective of their involvement in paid work, are significantly more likely than men to bear the primary responsibility for home chores and childcare (Statistics Canada, 2000*a*). At both their workplace and homes, women, world over, are exposed to diverse and a greater number of stressors than men and this calls for examining the issue in depth.

There is a significance difference in the working roles of women and men and substantial light has been thrown on the same by studies conducted by Super (1977), Schein (1978), Arnold and Feldman (1986) and Bradwick (1980). The life phases of women have been divided into four parts by Bradwick:

(i) Early adult transition years (17-28 years)–there is a preoccupation with getting settled in life and getting married. Even for working/professional women, there is a preoccupation with traditional roles.

(ii) Second adult life phase (30-40 years)–is the settling down period where women concentrate harder on juggling work with home responsibilities. Those who are married but have postponed having children now look to starting and completing their families. This leads further to stress, feeling of personal inadequacy and anxiety.

(iii) Middle adulthood phase (40-50 years)– women tend to experience greater assertiveness and professional accomplishment at work. With greater freedom due to grown up children and thus free time in hand, women experience a 'professional resurgence'.

(iv) Older life phase (50years and above)–since this is the period when most have retired and are left single due to widowhood/ divorce etc., the main focus is on managing separation and loneliness.

These phases become more relevant given the impetus women have gained working in the organised sector in India. The Indian economy is in a phase of transition, rapidly evolving from a traditional, conservative economy to a modern, liberated one and the increasing participation of women is evident in all spheres. "Growing employment opportunities for women mark a significant improvement in the social status and gender justice besides imparting economic power", said ASSOCHAM President, Mr. Venugopal N Dhoot. The 2007 Assocham Eco Pulse Study on 'Women Employment Growth Rate and Gender Budgeting' has revealed a 3.35 per cent growth in the employment rate of women against an approximate 8 per cent fall in case of men between 1998 and 2004. Further, the total number of women employed in public and private sector rose up to 49.34 lakh in

2004 from 47.74 lakh in 1998. During the same period the employment of men fell from 233.92 lakh (1998) to 215.09 lakh (2004).

This rapid increase of women in the Indian workforce calls for attention to the issue of work-life balance. Assocham, in its study released on the eve of International Women's Day, 2008, reveals that Indian women are putting in on an average 60 hours at their workplaces compared to 48 hours three years ago, all in a bid to get an equal footing with their male counterparts. Inspite of assuming greater professional responsibilities, they experience difficulty in shedding their role as housewife and mother. Their conscious engagement in the corporate sector coupled with emerging pattern of nuclear families has subjected them to tremendous work pressures.

WORK-LIFE BALANCE DEFINED

During ones' life-time an individual plays different roles and each of these impose some demand on his/her time and energy. When the participation in one role makes participation in another role increasingly difficult, it leads to work-life conflict. Thus, work-family or work-life conflict occurs when the cumulative demand of these many work and non-work life roles are incompatible in some respect so that participation in one role is made more difficult by participation in the other role" (Duxbury & Higgins, 2001, p. 3) or "Work-family conflict is a form of inter-role conflict that arises when role pressures from the work and family domains become mutually incompatible in some respect." (Greenhaus & Beutell, 1985, p. 7).

While the role conflict had always existed, it has suddenly become very relevant due to the changes taking place in the composition of the work force. The new workforce is older, more ethnically diverse, and has a larger proportion of working women, working mothers, dual-income families, employees with responsibilities for the care of aging parents, fathers with dependent care responsibilities, and sandwich employees (i.e., those with both childcare and eldercare responsibilities). (Duxbury & Higgins, 2001). The new millennium has seen a rise in the number of dual income families with both partners juggling work responsibilities with household chores, which once came under the purview of the stay-at-home spouse.

Work-life conflict can be better understood as having two aspects to it: work-to-family conflict and the family-to-work conflict. While work-to-family conflict is 'inter-role conflict in which the general demands of, time devoted to and strain created by the job interfere with performing family related responsibilities'(Netemeyer et al., 1996, p.401). Family to work conflict refers to the reverse. Time demands and psychological strain created by employees' efforts devoted to family activities interfere with performing work responsibilities. (Ilies, R, 2007, p. 1368).

As seen above, the common perception about the impact of an overlap or a commitment concurrence between the two domains of family and work, is interference leading to conflict. The premise rests on the scarcity hypothesis (Goode, 1960) and the identity theory (Burke & Reitzes, 1991). The Identity theory states that individuals have multiple role identities and with each of these they attach certain expectations. For each of these identities, the individual strives to strike a balance between his expectations and experiences. Roles recognised by an individual as having greater expectations and hence, higher commitment, would have greater time and energy devoted to them, to help translate the expectations into reality. (Burke & Reitzes, 1991).

The Scarcity hypothesis states that the physical and psychological resources available with an individual are fixed in nature. The greater the amount allocated to one domain, the lesser would be available for the other domain or roles. (Goode, 1960) It is this depletion that leads to *interference* and consequently to compromises in the performance and results.(Graves, Ohlott & Rudermann, 2007).

While the detrimental effects of work-life conflict, a result of negative spill over or *interference*, has been well researched and documented, the outcome of a positive spill over has not been explored as well. The view promoting positive spill over or *enhancement*, holds that 'experiences in one domain generate resources that can be transferred to the other domain.' It is this transfer of resources that is termed as *enhancement* and which is presumed to contribute positively to satisfaction, attitudes and performance. (Graves, Ohlott & Rudermann, 2007). Work-family enhancement, which basically implies strengthening or enhancing the quality of one role by the other, has also been termed as work-life enrichment, work-family facilitation and positive spill over.

The above suggests that the spill over from one domain to the other can be either positive or negative. Commitment to family concerns need not necessarily be detrimental to performance in the work domain. *Family-to-work* spill over in the negative sense is regarded as *family-to-work interference*. This negative spill over leads to resource depletion, conflict and lowered performance and reduced satisfaction in either/or both of the family and work domains.

Family-to-work Interference has been defined as the occurrence of an interrole conflict where an individual's attention to his/her family leads to counterproductive behaviours at work. (Greenhaus & Beutell, 1985). This could also imply decreased efforts put in work situations due to 'reduce(d) time, energy and attention in the work role.' (Graves, Ohlott & Rudermann, 2007). A negative spill over is associated with *psychological strain*, a state where the individual is unhappy and anxious. Increased interference abets psychological strain, promoting a less favourable view of the individual's life and career situations.

When the spill over from either of the domains is positive in nature, it leads to enhancement and enrichment of the experience in the other domain. *Family-to-work enhancement* or positive spill over thus, can be termed as 'inter-role facilitation' (Graves, Ohlott & Rudermann, 2007). This results when the experiences in the family domain contribute positively, improving the individual's energy levels, work relevant skills and over all well being. Outcomes of positive spill over or family-to-work enhancement are three pronged–*life satisfaction*, *career satisfaction* and *work performance*.

Early literature on work-family issues states that women experience significantly greater work and family related stressors than men. (Anderson & Leslie, 1991; Duxbury, Higgins, & Lee, 1994). Researchers have brought to light the stress experienced by individuals in parental roles, (Barnett & Baruch, 1985), however, there are also indications of parenting having a positive influence on those seeking work-life balance. Often this influence is associated with successful parenting which increases the feeling of competence and helps reduce the 'sense of overload in multiple role demands' (Erdwin, Buffardi, Casper, & O'Brien, 2001).

ANTECEDENTS OF WORK-LIFE CONFLICT FOR WORKING WOMEN

When exploring the antecedents of Work-life conflict, the oft cited article by Greenhaus and Beutell (1985) is of special relevance. Herein are identified the three main factors leading to work-life conflict– time based conflict, behaviour based conflict and strain based conflict. (Greenhaus & Beutell,1985). All the three also figure in our model as contributing to work-life conflict. Undeniably all working women are faced with the delicate task of balancing their family and work lives.

Time based conflict can be understood as any 'additional time spent in one domain that precludes individuals from investing that time in another domain.' (Messersmith, 2007). One of the main contributors to time based conflict is work or role overload, when competing roles' demands exceeds the available time. Women are saddled with the primary responsibility for household work; structural changes in family patterns (joint to nuclear) and the demands of modern working make reconciliation of time required for work and family as a key issue. Women assuming multiple roles results in work–family conflict because time and energy is shared, clubbed and extended across the two spheres of activity.

Increased level of conflicts from the two domains of family and work results in higher absenteeism, burn-out and reduced work performance for women as stated by Frone *et. al,* 1992. Sinclair 1998, Bakker 2000 have described work-life balance as double life perspective between career and children. Role overload is the result of domestic contingencies and unpredictable extensions in work schedules.

Behaviour based conflict refers to situations where behaviour patterns expected in one domain are in conflict with those expected in another. Literature on work-life conflict discusses states that 'when individuals are expected to behave in an impersonal or emotionally reserved manner at work but are then asked to be emotionally open ... at home', it results in behaviour based conflict. Behaviour based conflict can be an issue for working women who are expected to behave as hard core, tough professionals and decision makers at their work places and are then expected to be sensitive, submissive and decision takers as they transit into their family roles. The same woman who is expected to deftly handle problems in her professional life and be twice a good as her male counterparts to be appreciated, is expected to transform into the ideal home-maker and adjust to the patriarchal diktats once back home. This accounts for severe behaviour based conflict. According to Duxbury and Higgins (1991) women who are highly involved in their work role have more work-life conflict due to the increased anxiety and guilt felt by them linked with their views regarding their ability to perform traditional family roles.

On the other hand, *strain based conflict*, refers to the stress created in one role affecting another domain. (Greenhaus & Beutell,1985). This is more related with psychological factors and is 'actualised when employees have difficulty leaving the pressures of work behind when transitioning to their personal roles.' (Messersmith, 2007). The strain experienced by the individual causes adverse psychological and physical impact and this often spills over to the other areas of an individual's life (Edwards & Rothbard, 2000). Technology has contributed in a big way to strain based conflict. Even though technology has brought about greater flexibility for people, it has also lead to employees spending more working when at home, rather than engaging in non-work responsibilities. Indian women have traditionally been accorded a status lower than that of men in the family. She is supposed to be 'self-sacrificing, self-effacing' and her 'enabler role gets precedence over the performer role' (Rajadhyaksha & Bhatnagar, 2000). Working mothers bear the burden of guilt of not being able to do justice with their roles of wife, mother and nurturer. Since the Indian society is 'a complex combination of custom, functionality and religious belief' (Chitnis, 1988) where individuals live by their 'ascribed' rather than 'achieved' status (Rajadhyaksha & Bhatnagar, 2000) which magnifies strain based conflict for women.

SIGNIFICANCE OF WORK-LIFE BALANCE

The importance of work-life balance issues cannot be ignored today, when there are sweeping changes taking place in the way business is conducted and when expectations from the staff are scaling new heights every day. Significant changes in the composition of the work-force are foreseen.

1. There are an increasing number of women in the work-force. It is also expected that women would be assuming greater responsibilities, seeking to return to work sooner after

childbirth and an increase in dual-earner households. (Holmes *et al.*, 2007)

2. With the generation of Baby Boomers gradually ageing, there will be greater caring responsibilities. By 2010, nearly ... million people will have to shoulder caring responsibilities. (DPW, 2001) The 'baby bust' generation would have to assume responsibility for both dependent children and ageing parents. This 'sandwich generation' would be facing extraordinary demands trying to balance family and work. (Vanier Institute, 1994).
3. With increased exposure and better avenues, more and more young people are going to opt for working while pursuing studies, leading to more instances of role overload.
4. The role of men as the breadwinner is gradually changing. Men are increasingly playing an active role in bringing up children, staying at home to look after the baby or nurse a sick child. (Thompson *et al.*, 2006).
5. The government schemes of extending the service tenures, thus raising the retirement age, is likely to call for introduction of flexibility in work environment. (Holmes *et al.*, 2007).
6. The rapid pace of technological changes have blurred the boundaries between work and non-work areas. Technological advancements have had a hand in decreasing job security, swallowing up positions at an alarming rate and accelerating work-life issues. While connectivity in the form of mobiles and internet eases life, it also hastens the pace of work, depriving workforce of much needed rest.
7. Use of technology has also made skills up-gradation a continuous and relentless process.

STRATEGIES FOR MANAGING WORK-LIFE IMBALANCE

A burnt out employee is useless for the employer and this is a fact that most employers are recognising today. Therefore, strategies to manage work-life imbalance need to be chalked out and implemented. This paper makes an attempt at summarising some such strategies for mitigating work-life imbalance.

Introducing Family-Friendly Policies

Literature related to implementation of family friendly policies suggests that employees form a favourable perception of work-life balance if such policies are implemented. White et al. have found that employees with greater discretionary power over their working hours, place and time of work are likely to experience much less negative spill over from work to home. Outcomes of research on the different policies implemented to mitigate work-life imbalance indicate that on-site child care reduces work-life conflict of working parents (Goff, Mount, & Jamison, 1990).

Similarly virtual work, may allow for greater autonomy and flexibility in deciding what to do and when and where to do it (Greenhaus, Parasuram, Granrose, Rabinowitz & Beutell, 1989). Virtual work means 'employees are electronically linked to the organization, yet physically located in the home' (Messersmith, 2007). However, virtual work has its own connotations. Studies also reveal that it may not be the panacea for all ill. It has actually been associated with an increase in work-life conflict due to the blurring of boundaries between work and personal life. (Duxbury, Higgins & Thomas, 1996; Raghuram & Wiesenfeld, 2004). Therefore, implementation of virtual work policies calls for clear drawing of lines demarcating work lives and personal lives.

Orientation Strategies

Since role ambiguity and role conflict equally contribute to increased work-life conflict, proper orientation of the employees could work to reduce these. Nielson, Carlson and Lankau, 2001 have in their empirical research drawn conclusions that employees in mentoring relationships are likely to experience much less work-family conflict than otherwise. Their adaptation to their work roles is faster and have demonstrated higher organizational attachment (King, *et al,* 2005).

Another dimension to this is educating the managers and the employees regarding the pitfalls of burn-out and work-life imbalance. Explicit communication that 'balanced employees tend to be more effective and better organizational members' (Messersmith, 2007) would positively contribute towards its achievement. This is likely to reflect in the employee and employer commitment to maintaining work-life balance.

High Involvement Work Practices

High Involvement Work Practices (HIWP) include measures like reward and incentive plans, information sharing, merit based promotions, information sharing (Messersmith, 2007). There is evidence that higher levels of compensation and rewards are likely to reduce turnover intentions (Bartol, 1983). Further, the negative consequences associated with work-life conflict are largely offset by additional benefits accruing to the employees.

Opportunities for career enhancement and promotions reduce dissatisfaction (Jiang & Klein, 1999; Cougar, 1988). Therefore if the employees can be offered development and career growth opportunities, there is an increased likelihood of their experiencing reduced work-life conflict. Results in literature reviewed suggest that high involvement work practices could well serve as 'important buffering mechanisms that reduce the negative consequences of work-life conflict' (Messersmith, 2007).

CONCLUSION

It is a fact that the present work scenario makes greater demand on the personal resources, both time and energy, of women in professional roles. Research by Rajadhyaksha & Bhatnagar, 2000, concludes that for women professionals significant inter-correlations were observed among the reward value of commitment scores of the family roles while such inter-correlations were found to be absent for occupational and other life roles. This leads to the conclusion for working women homemaker and marital roles are equally important and therefore the strategies for managing work-life conflict need to take this aspect into account.

References

Anderson, E. A. & Leslie, L. A. (1991), Coping with Employment and Family Stress: Employment Arrangement and Gender Differences. *Sex Roles*, 24, 223-237.

Arnold, H. J. & Feldman, D.C. (1986), Organizational Behaviour. New York: McGraw-Hill.

Bartol, K. M. (1983), Turnover among DP Personnel: A Causal Analysis. Communications of the ACM, 26, 807-811.

Blood R. O. & Wolfe, D. M. (1960), *Husbands and Wives*. New York: Macmillan.

Bradwick, J. (1980), The Seasons of a Women's Life. In D.G. McGuigan (Ed.), Women's Lives: New Theory, Research and Policy. Ann Arbor, MI: The University of Michigan Press.

Chitnis, S. Feminism (1988), Indian ethos and Indian Conditions. In Rehana Ghadially (Ed.), Women in Indian Society: A Reader. New Delhi, Sage.

Cougar, D. J. (1988), Motivators and Demotivators in the IS Environment. *Journal of Systems Management,* 39 (6), 36-41.

Duxbury, L. & Higgins, C. (2001), Work-Life Balance in the New Millennium: Where Are We? Where Do We Need to Go? *Work Network, Canadian Policy Research Networks, Inc.*

Duxbury, L., Higgins, C. & Lee, C. (1994), Work-family Conflict: A Comparison by Gender, Family Type, and Perceived Control. *Journal of Family Issues*, 15, 449-466.

Duxbury, L. E., Higgins, C. A. & Thomas, D. R. (1996), Work and Family Environments and the Adoption of Computer Supported Supplemental Work-at-home. *Journal of Vocational Behaviour,* 49, 1-23

Erdwin, C. J., Buffardi, L. C., Casper,W. J. & O'Brien, A. S. (2001). The Relationship of Women's Role Strain to Social Support, Role Satisfaction, and Self-efficacy. *Family Relations*, 50, 230-238.

Graves, L. M., Ohlott, P. J., & Rudermann, M. N. (2007), Commitment to Family Roles: Effects on Managers' Attitudes and Performance. *Journal of Applied Psychology*, Vol. 92, No. 1, 44-56.

Goff, S. J., Mount, M. K. & Jamison, R. L. (1990), Employer Supported Child-care, Work-family and Absenteeism: A Field Study. *Personnel Psychology,* 43, 793-809.

Greenhaus, J. H. and Beutell, N. J. (1985), Sources of Conflict Between Work and Family Roles. *Academy of Management Review*, 10, 76-88.

Greenhaus, J. H. & Powell, G. N. (2006), When Work and Family are Allies: A Theory of Work-family Enrichment. *Academy of Management Review*, 31, 72-92

Greenhaus, J. H., Parasuram, S., Granrose, C., Rabinowitz, S., & Beutell, N. (1989), Sources of Work-Family Conflict Among Two Career Couples. *Journal of Vocational Behaviour,* 34,133-153.

http://www.pcr.uu.se/conferenses/myrdal/pdf/singh.pdf

http://www.ilo.org/dyn/gender/docs/RES/292/F267981337/Breaking%20Glass%20PDF%20English.pdf

http://suryamurthy.wordpress.com/2007/03/07/women-beat-their-men-counterparts-in-employment-growth-rate/

Jick, T. and L. Mitz (1985), "Sex Differences in Work Stress," *Academy of Management Review,* 10: 408-420.

King, R. C., Weidong, X., Campbell Quick, J. & Sethi, V. (2005), Socialisation and Organizational Outcomes of Information Technology Professionals. *Career Development International,* 10, 26-51.

ILO (2004), 'Breaking Through the Glass Ceiling', update.

Levinson, D. J. (1986), A Conception of Adult Development. *American Psychologist,* 1986, 41 (1), 3-13

Messersmith, J. (2007), Managing Work-life Conflict Among Information Technology Workers. *Human Resource Management,* Vol. 46, No. 3, 429-451.

Neilson, T. R., Carlson, D. S. & Lankau, M. J. (2001), The Supportive Mentor as a Means of Reducing Work-family Conflict. *Journal of Vocational Behaviour,* 59, 364-381.

When can Employees have a Family Life? The Effects of Daily Workload and Affect on Work-family Conflict and Social Behaviours at Home (Remus Ilies, *et. al.*, 2007, *Journal of Applied Psychology,* Vol. 92, No. 5, 1368-1379)

Only 3.3 pc working women reach top positions http://indiapost.com/article/india/1804/

http://www.indianmba.com/Faculty_Column/FC660/fc660.html 'Incongruence in the Roles played by Employed Women in Work-Family Interface-An Approach to Role conflict'.

http://www.dancewithshadows.com/society/work-stress.asp, 'Job-related Stress Spreads to More Sectors in India, Shows Study'

http://economictimes.indiatimes.com/articleshow/2845334.cms, 'Large Number of Women Work with Low Salaries: Report'.

Lambert, S. J. (1990), Processes Linking Work and Family: A critical Review and Research Agenda. *Human Relations*, 43, 239-257

Raghuram, S. & Wiesenfeld, B. (2004), Work Nonwork Conflict and Job Stress Among Virtual Workers. *Human Resource Management,* 43, 259-277.

Rajadhyaksha, U. & Bhatnagar, D. Life Role Salience: A Study of Dual-career Couples in the Indian Context. *Human Relations,* 2000, 53(4), 489-511.

Schein, E. H. (1978), Career Dynamics: Matching Individual and Organizational Needs. Reading, MA: Addison-Wesley, 1978.

Statistics Canada (2000*a*), *Women in Canada 2000: A Gender Based Statistical Report*, Statistics Canada, Ottawa, Catalogue No. 89-503-XPE.

Simon, R. W. (1995), Gender, Multiple Roles, Role Meaning, and Mental Health. *Journal of Health and Social Behaviour,* 36, 182-194.

Super, D. E. (1977), The Psychology of Careers. New York: Harper & Row.

Wadley, S. (1988), Women and the Hindu Tradition. In Rehana Ghadially (Ed.), Women in Indian Society: A Reader. New Delhi, Sage.

Zedeck, S. (Ed.). (1992), *Work, Families, and Organizations*. San Francisco: Jossey-Bass.

13

MICRO CREDIT: A WAY FOR THE UPLIFTMENT OF THE RURAL WOMEN

P. Sundara Pandian

INTRODUCTION

Approximately 400 million people in India living below or close to the poverty line could be roughly translated into 75 million households out of which around 60 million are rural household. So poverty in India has predominantly a rural character. While there are several structural dimensions to the rural poverty it is generally accepted that it arises due to the lack of capital or lack of surplus. The rural poor is perpetuating poverty and is the victims of the "vicious cycle of poverty".

In India 75 million households depend on moneylenders to meet financial needs; almost 90 per cent of people in rural India have no access to insurance; 50 million households are landless and need small credit to start some economic activity. And even families earning Rs. 4000-5000 a month in urban areas spend huge portions of their earnings to service debt.

INABILITY OF BANKS

India has one of the largest networks of bank branches in the world, but the hundreds of millions of poor in the country are largely out of it. Banks were nationalised three decades ago with the hope-and promise-that their services would reach the poor. But that goal is not even close to being met today. With 65,000 commercial bank branches, 14,522 branches of regional rural banks and 100,000 cooperative bank branches, the country is teeming with institutions that should be able to meet the credit needs of the people.

MICRO CREDIT

"Micro-credit" can be defined as small loans made to individuals to undertake self-employment or to start very small businesses. This type of financing may be provided through a number of different sources: independent non-profit organizations, community economic development programs, commercial financial institutions, etc.

Microfinance emerged in the 1970s as social innovators began to offer financial services to the working poor—those who were previously considered "un-bankable" because of their lack of collateral. Micro credit can aid employment and sustain households giving them opportunities they never had before. It is called micro credit with good reason. The size of the loan is typically small. The borrower is usually battling against poverty. The repayment schedule is simple and short. And, the activity for which the loan is taken is often of a small nature.

In India, micro credit has worked largely through self-help groups (SHGs). Predominated by women, these are formed with simple rules-save, accumulate and give loans to each other. Globally, it is slowly proving one of the most effective strategies to neutralise poverty. Micro credit lending institutions are currently estimated to reach some two million households in India.

HOW MICROFINANCE WORKS

The most common microfinance product is a micro credit loan—usually less than Rs.5000. These tiny loans are enough for hardworking micro-entrepreneurs to start or expand small businesses such as weaving baskets, raising chickens, or buying wholesale products to sell in a market. Income from these businesses provides better food, housing, health care and education for entire families, and most important, additional income provides hope for a better future.

The global repayment rate for micro credit loans is higher than 95 per cent, which allows MFIs to re-lend these funds to even more clients. By giving the world's poor a hand up, not a handout, microfinance can help break the cycle of poverty in as little as a single generation. Micro credit loan cycles are usually shorter than traditional commercial loans—typically six months to a year with payments plus interest, due weekly. Shorter loan cycles and weekly payments help the borrowers stay current and not become overwhelmed by large payments.

Number of MFIs and Total Client Numbers Reporting to Micro Credit Summit

Year	*Number of MFIs*	*Number of Total Clients*	*Number of "Poorest" Clients**
1997	618	13.5 million	7.6 million
1998	925	21 million	12.2 million
1999	1,065	23.6 million	13.8 million
2000	1,567	30.7 million	19.3 million
2001	2,186	55 million	26.9 million
2002	2,572	67.6 million	41.6 million
2003	2,931	80.9 million	54.8 million
2004	3,164	92.3 million	66.6 million

*(< $1 per day or bottom half of those living below national poverty line when first loan is received).

UPLIFTMENT OF WOMEN

There are many reasons why women have become the primary target of microfinance services. At a macro level, it is because 70 per cent of the world's poor are women. Women have a higher unemployment rate than men in virtually every country and make up the majority of the informal sector of most economies. They constitute the bulk of those who need microfinance services.

Targeting women has also proved to be a successful, efficient economic development tool. Rural poor women, who are in the forefront of the micro credit movement, use the small loans to jumpstart a long chain of economic activity from this small beginning. As they have enormous pride in their integrity, they repay quickly and reliably, not wanting to be seen as defaulters. Then, they begin again, this time with a bigger loan - and keep expanding their profit base until they do not need the loans any longer. Micro credit has given women in India an opportunity to become agents of change. The movement has made them more confident than ever helping them to explore new horizons, new dreams.

SHGs AND MICRO CREDIT

The major spin-off of the micro-credit movement at the grassroots level has been the fact that women have used this system to come out and join a mainstream activity in the village. In many areas, particularly where there has been support from strong SHGs, women have gained a voice and been able to use this space to come out of their traditional roles into a more 'proactive' male space. Women have been able to mobilise capital, and in the process have acquired skills that have enhanced their economic, social and political power. This positive growth has usually been where SHGs are linked with NGOs that have facilitated training and capacity-building with additional inputs.

Millions of poor women are today using small loans to rewrite their present and future. Many of them have not even seen the corridors of a high school, but are using common sense to propel their entrepreneurship and group business activities. In India, a number of self-help groups (SHGs) were created in the 1980s to provide credit facilities to the poor, especially women, in both urban and rural areas. These SHGs stumbled upon a surprising finding: by targeting women, repayment rates came in well over 95 per cent, higher than most traditional banks. Impressed by the repayment rates, institutions like National Bank for Rural Development (NABARD) and the Small Industries Development Bank of India (SIDBI) began increasing their lending to SHGs in India.

Growth in the number of self-help groups and the amount of loan disbursed to them is the two important indicators to judge the success of the programme. In India the SHG-bank linkage programme has emerged as the largest micro credit programme in the world (National Bank for Agriculture and Rural development, 2004). The pilot project started in 1992 has turned into a national movement, linking more than one million SHGs with bank credit and leading to the socio-economic empowerment of women. It is also important that the bank loans enable the group members to undertake income generating activities which leads to sustainable development. The number of Self-help group linked with banks increased from 255 in 1992–1993 to 10, 79,091 in 2003–2004 registering a growth of nearly 4,231 times higher than the base year. The amount of bank loan disbursed reveals a staggering growth. It increased from 0.10 million US$ in 1992–1993 to 867 million US$ in 2003–2004, 8,670 times higher than the base year. The increasing number in linking self-help groups with banks and the loan provided by the banks reveal the success and acceptance of micro credit programme among the poor people and the sustainability of the programme.

Number of SHGs Linked with Banks and the Amount of Loan Disbursed (Amount in Million Us$)

Year	*Number of SHGs linked with Banks*	*% of change over previous year*	*Bank loan*	*% of change over previous year*
1992-1993	255	-	0.10	-
1993-1994	620	143.14	0.20	100.00
1994-1995	2122	242026	0.78	290.00
1995-1996	4757	124.17	1.81	132.05
1996-1997	8598	80.74	3.33	83.98
1997-1998	14317	66.52	6.40	92.19
1998-1999	32995	130.46	13.57	112.03
1999-2000	114775	247.85	44.53	228.15
2000-2001	263825	129.86	105.26	136.38
2001-2002	461478	74.92	215.20	104.45
2002-2003	717360	55.45	455.00	111.43
2003-2004	1079091	50.43	867.00	90.55

It was not easy getting small groups of women to overcome typical resistance and struggle against stereotypes in rural India. But, gradually, the movement has created a sense of belonging among the women members, a sense of purpose and a new determination. They see the benefits of good communication, cohesion and cooperation. There is a sense of pride through decision-making and problem solving.

CONCLUSION

A recent World Bank report confirms that societies that discriminate on the basis of gender pay the cost of greater poverty, slower economic growth, weaker governance, and a lower living standard for all people. Micro-credit is often portrayed as a "win-win" option, wherein investors profit handsomely while the poor gain access to resources that allow them to help themselves.

Women are usually the primary or sole family caretakers in many developing countries. Helping them gain additional daily income improves the condition of their entire household. Putting extra income in women's hands is often the most efficient way to affect an entire family, as women typically put their children's needs before their own. Children are more likely to complete their education and escape the poverty trap than their parents are. Giving women access to micro credit loans therefore generates a multiplier effect that increases the impact of a microfinance institution's activities, benefiting multiple generations.

References

Annual Report, National Bank for Agriculture and Rural Development, Mumbai.

Bansal, H. (2003), 'SHG-bank Linkage Programme in India: An Overview', *Journal of Micro Finance*, Vol. 5, No. 1, pp. 21–49.

Chakrabarti, R. (2004), The Indian Microfinance Experience–Accomplishments and Challenges, *www.microfinacegateway.org*.

Krog, J. (2000), Attacking Poverty with Decentralization and Micro Credit: Indian Experiences, *www.ulandslaere.au.dk.*

Mohanan, S. (2000), Micro Credit and Empowerment of Women-Role of NGOs, *Yojana,* Vol. 44, No. 2, pp. 22–28.

Wilson, K. (2002), 'The New Microfinance-An Essay on the Self-Help Group Movement in India', *Journal of Microfinance,* Vol. 4, No. 2, pp. 21–245.

14

PEOPLE'S PARTICIPATION IN RURAL DEVELOPMENT PLANNING IN TRIPURA

Jayanta Choudhury

INTRODUCTION

Development is that strategy by which person, family, community or society can take their own responsibility to change their own situation. And to achieve this goal in a systematic way is called planning. Planning should be designed to maximize welfare of the people. In our country there are two types of planning. One is centralized planning and other is decentralized planning. Since independence in our country the strategy of planning was centralized planning which was based on top-down approach. Centralized planning means complete control over major part of economy where economic decision are take up central planning authority. During the planning period it shows that in this planning system the top down approach could not prove effective because consulting with the people, understanding there need, involving then for mobilization or corrective efforts to deal with the problem have been mostly neglected. India is a developing country and 70% area of this country is rural area. There are certain specific characteristics of the developing countries such as poor economic road regional imbalances and uneven distribution of resource, rural urban disparity high degree of income inequalities etc. And this planning is mostly inappropriate to reduce this problem.

To develop the country equitable distribution of the benefit between different regions and also between section of population is very important it is for this region the Government of India is keen to modify the planning process in the country by introducing decent relished planning.

Decentralized planning is a system through which planning process is brought close to the people who are the ultimate target after development. It is a multi level planning system in which planning is attempted at different political administrative and executive levels. So that, there is greater integration between developmental needs and socio economic classes with the regional sub national and national level development policies and goals. Decentralized planning is neither a substitute to centralized planning nor a bottom of process of planning. It is in fact a two way process which begins at both top level (national or state level) as well as grass roots level (Local level) simultaneous and merge with each other at the point below which centralized planning become irreverent and above which micro planning is meaningless.

PANCHYAT RAJ INSTITUTION : FOUNDATION FOR DCENTRLISATION

Development experiences is that development can not be imposed from outside. It is the people themselves who have to come forward for development and to improve their socio-economic condition.

Decentralization, interpreted in simple terms, would mean moving away from the center or *deconcentration*. In the context of development, which is our concern here, decentralization means transfer of certain authority and power in the matter of formulation and implementation of development plans from the highest organization or institution at the national level or state level to organisations or institutions at the sub-state level.

The lower level, which includes district, block and panchayat will have a particular role in the planning exercise and will be vested with the powers and the responsibilities associated with the role. In a truly decentralized situation such power will include the power to determine goals and targets and to raise resources locally.

Decentralized Planning can, thus, be defined as a type of planning where local organisations and institutions formulate, adopt, execute actions and supervise the plan without interference by the central body.

In Tripura, about 85 per cent of people live in the rural areas, and most of them are economically and socially backward. To improve the condition of these people is the major objective of the village development plan.

Panchayati Raj was first introduced in Tripura during 1959, by enacting Tripura Panchayat Raj Act, 1959 (adopted from U.P. Panchayat Raj Act with some modifications). In this Act, single tier (Gram Panchayat) was proposed. Tripura Panchayate Raj Rules was framed in 1961. Under the Tripura Panchayat Raj Rules, 1961 (which continued till 1978), the Gram Panchayats were constituted through open election by raising hands. The Rules were amended in 1978 to ensure the constitution of the Gram Panchayats under adult franchise by secret ballot with participation of political parties. At the block level, Block Development Committee (BDC), an advisory body, was constituted with the elected Pradhans of the Gram Panchayats and the MLAs from the block area. The BDCs were encouraged to act as de *facto* Panchayats samitis.

Following the 73rd amendment of the Constitution in 1992, Tripura was one of the first states to enact Tripura Panchayats Act, 1993 with a provision for setting up of three tier Panchayat system- Gram Panchayat at Village level, Panchayat Samiti at Block level and Zilla Parishad at District level. During 1994, various functions of 12 departments were assigned to the Panchayat bodies. Again curing 2000, some more functions were transferred to the Panchayats. The state Finance Commission was set up in 1994 which has submitted its report in 1996 and is accepted by the Govt. The second SFC has already started functioning. Two elections of the PRIs have been held (1994 & 1999) so far. Similar reforms were done in the Nagar Panchayats following the 74th amendment.

The Tripura Tribal Areas Autonomous District Council was set up on 18th January, 1982 as an autonomous Body in the state under the 7th schedule of the Constitution. Later, with the objective of entrusting more responsibility and to give more power to the TTAADC, Provisions of the 6th Schedule to the Constitution of India were extended to Tripura from 1st April, 1985 by the 49th Amendment of the Constitution. The TTAADC covers an area of 7133 sq. km., which are about 68 per cent of the state's total area. As per the 1991 Census, the total population in the District Council area is 8.87 lakh which is about one-third of State's population. Of this, 6.62 lakh are tribal, which is about 66 per cent of tribal population.

Before the 73rd amendment, or more specifically, before the enactment of the Tripura Panchayats Act, 1993, the one tier Gram Panchayat used to just act as an implementing agency of the various labour intensive schemes, recommending the names of the beneficiaries. But the 73rd amendment enabled the Panchayats to function as "Institutions of self-governance" by empowering the panchayats to have some original functions and some agency functions.

The original function of the Panchayats is the preparation of plans for economic development and social justice, while the agency function relates to the implementation of schemes for economic development and social justice as may be entrusted to them including those in relation to the matters listed in the Eleventh Schedule. It may be mentioned here that there can not be two sets of schemes, one for economic development and another for social justice because any plan for economic development must automatically enhance and/or promote social justice. Active participation of the deprived masses in every stage of planning is the essential precondition in order to enhance/ promote social justice by developmental planning.

PAST SYSTEM OF PLANNING

Notwithstanding wide differences of opinion among scholars regarding details, they agree that the centralized system of planning has been a failure in addressing fundamental problems of development faced by the country, such as mass poverty and unemployment. Even though it would be too simplistic to attribute the above failure exclusively to what may be referred to as 'centralization', there is growing consensus around the view that over-centralization had been a major debilitation feature of he Indian System.

Commonly identified evils, that are attributable more to centralization than to any other important feature of the system, are;

- Widespread apathy among people.
- Lack of involvement of people in nation building activities.
- Indifference to the development needs of the people.
- Channeling of resources for wrongly perceived goals.

- Disregard of local specificities even where it matters most.
- Insensitive to local knowledge.
- Lack of efforts at integration of isolated development interventions which often tend to work at cross purposes.
- Spiraling of corruption.

All the same, it would be unrealistic to assume that planning of everything is best done at the local level. While optimal solutions for many problems are to be found at the local level, there are also issues, which require to be addressed at higher levels. It is also important that development interventions are integrated both horizontally and vertically among various tiers of decision-making so that complementarities are maximized and conflicts are reduced to the minimum.

OBSTACLES TO DECENTRALIZATION

Desirability of a decentralized system of planning was never in doubt. The slogan 'gram raj' is as old as the freedom movement. During the post-independence period, the demand for making the country's governance more democratic through a meaningful process of decentralization of power continued to enjoy pride of place on the national agenda.

In spite of such conviction and support, the process of decentralization could not make much headway in the country. The failure of earlier efforts is usually attributed to a variety of reasons, viz.,

- Resistance offered by the vested interests nurtured by the centralized structure.
- Lack of pressure from below due to the absence of representative governments at levels below the states.
- Paucity of expertise and preparedness at the local level, etc.

There were many efforts in the past to identify factors constraining the process of decentralization and to suggest concrete measures to overcome the hurdles. Not to be lost sight of are also some important experiments at the field level, including the efforts of states like Rajasthan, Karnataka and West Bengal and many micro-level interventions under the auspices of various agencies, which provided valuable insights for future attempts in the same direction. But the country had to wait till 1993, when the 73rd and 74th constitutional amendments were enacted, to see a comprehensive and determined effort to tackle the various factors that hinder the process of decentralization.

Nevertheless, the constitutional amendments, at their best, serve only as a favourable framework. As the inter-state variations in the responsibilities, powers, and resources devolved to the newly constituted Panchayat Raj Institutions would amply testify, the constitutional amendments leave many important parameters of the process of decentralization to be determined by the State legislatures even now. The State Governments can either make use of the constitutional provisions to establish true local self governments or misuse the loopholes to maintain the status quo.

It has been the experience in Tripura that success of government initiatives and legislations depend a lot on the environment in which such moves are made and the pressure exerted from below. This is more so because what is envisaged in the context of decentralized planning is a total restructuring of the planning and execution system.

The state government has already set a good example for the rest of the country with respect to division of responsibilities, devolution of power and resources, provision of facilitating services, and complementary changes in administrative procedures and practices.

Tripura was one of the first few states to frame its Panchayati Raj Act on the pattern envisaged in the 73rd amendment of the Constitution. It was again one of the first to set up the State Finance Commission and accept many of its recommendation. As per the recommendations of the State Finance Commission, funds and responsibilities are being devolved to the Panchayati Raj Institutions. Even though the 73rd amendment to the Constitution and the recommendations of the State Finance Commission are not applicable to the ADC areas, the Government was conscious of the fact that these areas can not be left behind as far as the devolutions are concerned. A separate arrangement was accordingly worked out to devolve funds and responsibilities to the ADC areas.

Devolution of powers, responsibilities, and resources and the complementary measures taken at the government level are necessary conditions, but not sufficient in themselves to ensure genuine democratization of the planning process. Hardly any tier of the Panchayati Raj Institution can claim to have prior experience in the art of development planning. Nor are they equipped with expertise, infrastructure or the required information base to take up the task of making development plans, all by themselves, for their respective regions. Further, many of them may not even be prepared to come out of the shell of inactivity with which they have been accustomed for long.

DEVELOPMENT CHALLENGES BEFORE THE STATE

The development dialogue that follows is phenomenal in terms of widespread participation, range of issues raise, amount of details and insights generated, etc. For our purpose, it suffices to note the consensus in favour of a decentralized process of decision making and revival of the old legacy of collective intervention by the people in development activities.

The decline in the quality of services, especially of those supplied by the public sector, needs urgent remedial measures, for it has already started affecting the quality of life of people, especially, vulnerable sections of the society. The over centralized system of development planning and implementation is totally unsuitable to take on these challenges. This is especially so with respect to land and water management, development of agriculture and allied sectors, rural and cottage industries, drinking water, sanitation and many of the social service sectors. In view of the consensus in favour of a decentralized system, the state also witnessed some important moves to evolve a viable mode of decentralized system of administration and planning.

GRAMODAYA–A NEW INITIATIVES

Under the above background, 'Gramoday' is an effort to consolidate and articulate public opinion in favour of decentralized planning and thereby help the government to translate its commitment to concrete actions. 'Gramoday' is a system of multi-level planning, where the lowest unit is allowed to plan and implement everything that can be performed most effectively at that level and only the residual is left to the higher levels.

The primary objective of the 'Gramoday', is to motivate and empower the Panchayati Raj Institutions to take up the new challenge of development planning. It is sought to be achieved by mobilizing people regardless of their political affiliations, religion, caste, etc, to help the Panchayati Raj Institutions in all the stages of development planning from plan formulation and implementation to maintenance.

Enthusiasm of the masses and their wholehearted participation is the key to success of any effort at decentralization. Government orders and directions alone are no guarantee for informed and enthusiastic participation of the people. This is especially so in the context of the contemporary reality of near total alienation of people form development activities. Therefore, a mass awareness Programme is found to be necessary to mobilise people and motivate them to take up different tasks related to planning from below.

The centralized system of planning is insensitive not only to local conditions but also to local knowledge on development problems with which people of each locality are richly endowed. In this respect, what 'Gramoday', has sought to do is to establish a system at the village level in which the villagers themselves harness such scattered information and knowledge to be used in evolving future development activities. But local experience and knowledge constitutes only one of the many pieces of information required for making development plan at the local level. The local knowledge needs to be blended with information on modem technological alternatives, alternative sources of funding, ongoing development programmes of line departments and other agencies, etc, In short, the Plan Campaign has to ensure that minimum necessary skills of development planning are imparted to the local people and the representative, governments at that level. In other works, what is being sought through the Campaign is not just nominal participation but informed participation of the people.

EVOLUTION, STRUCTURE AND PROCESS OF GRAMODAY

The Tripura State Planning Board was reconstituted in early 1998. It held its first meeting on the 6th July 1998. During this meeting, 4 (four) sub-committees for the primary sector, secondary sector, tertiary sector and tribal welfare were formed for formulating sectoral plans. On the basis of recommendations of these sub-committees, "Approach to People's Plan in Tripura" was prepared which clearly identifies the areas of strengths and weaknesses, sets lout the objectives of the State

Government, chalks out the strategies for the development of each of the above four areas and lists the steps to be taken for this purpose. "Approach to People's Plan in Tripura was approved by the Council of Ministers on 27th January 1999 and placed before the State Planning Board on the 25th February 1999.

Among many other initiatives mentioned in the "Approach to People's Plan in Tripura", preparation of area-based plans taking into account local resources and with active participation of the people was adopted as a strategy of decentralized planning in the state. Three consecutive workshops (May 3-4, June 12-13, September 11, 1999) were organized at the state level to give a concrete shape to the idea of participatory planning and resource mapping. Experts from Kerala State Planning Board, Geological Survey of India (GSI), North-Eastern Regional Institute of Water and Land Management (NERIWALM), National Remote Sensing Agency (NRSA), Action Aid India, etc. were invited to share their experiences. After several rounds of discussions, the concept of 'Gramoday' got crystallized.

It was then decided to launch 'Gramoday' first in the West Tripura district and after learning from the experiences of West Tripura, to extend it subsequently to all the districts of the state. The district level training of Sector officers in West Tripura district was organized on January 18, 2000. 'Gramoday' was formally launched at Harishnagar J.B. School in Bishalgarh Block on 7th February 2000 by His Excellency the Governor of Tripura. The work was reviewed and experiences of West Tripura district were shared in a workshop held on the 16th October, 2000. It was decided to expand 'Gramoday' to the entire state during 2000-01 for formulation of plan for 2001-02.

At the very begging a format was prepared and supplied to all the panchayats. The format devised for the 'Gramoday' has *4 (four)* parts as indicated below:

1. *Part–I–Village Profile*–It includes the basic data of the village.
2. *Part–II–Identification of Gaps*–On the basis of data collected and norms/requirements, the gaps in resources/infrastructure existing in the village are to be identified in this part.
3. *Part–III–Perception of the People*–Views and observation of the local people on their developmental needs are to be recorded in this part.

4. *Part–IV–Village Development Plan*–This is the last part and is the plan for development of the village, prepared on the basis of perception of the people recorded in Part-III and with reference to information available in Part–I and II.

Series of workshops were held at the district level in all the four districts. At the end of workshop in each district, district level resource persons were identified and dates for the training of sector officers were fixed.

Within a block, for the purpose of 'Gramoday', all the villages are grouped into sectors. Each sector comprises of about 5-6 villages. Generally, an officer (Sector Officer), not below the rank of an extension officer of a line department be in-charge of the sector for imparting training, supervision and coordination of works, and called Sector officer.

In each village, a Village Planning Team had been constituted by the Sector Officer, in consultation with the Village Pradhan. The Village Planning team consists of 2-3 government officials and 2-3 volunteers form the concerned village, and essentially consist of Gram Pradhan, Panchayat Secretary and VLW of concerned village. Panchayat Secretary is the convenor of the Team. The volunteers preferably have an educational background of Madhyamik and above. The number of members may vary either way (by 2-3 members), depending on the availability of good volunteers and the need of the area. To accommodate additional volunteers/ experts, sector/subject wise task forces or sub-committees may be constituted.

The sector officer is mainly responsible for the training of the Planning Teams, supervision and co-ordination of the 'Gramoday', at the sector level. He also acts as moderator for the village level meetings.

The Village Planning Team is the most crucial and important component in the organizational hierarchy of the 'Gramoday'. This Team is primarily responsible for undertaking the works of:

- Awareness campaign.
- Collection of information.
- Understanding and recording the perception of people, and
- Preparation of the development plan at the village level.

At the block level, a Block Level Planning & Coordination Committee, consisting of officials from the major development departments and some non-officials is formed for Sector Officers/ VPTs, examining the plan proposals (panchayat/ block) for their technical viability, compilation of plan proposals form the panchayats, and supervision and co-ordination of the 'Gramoday' at the block level. The BDO acts as convenor of the Block Level Planning & Coordination.

THE OBJECTIVES

In order to ensure maximum active participation of the people in the planning process, they must be assured that their suggestions/ advices, derived from their knowledge and wisdom, are not going to be wasted. Active participation of people and formulation of plan proposal are the two essential components of any micro-level plan exercise. The unique feature of 'Gramoday' is that both these components are given maximum priority for the preparation of the village/ panchayat development plan. Active participation of he people does not mean just giving importance to their advices in the formulation and implementation of schemes. It means the enhancement of the level of their consciousness and increase in their level of self-confidence in the process.

The primary objective of 'Gramoday' is to empower the local bodies so that they formulate their plan proposals with maximum people's participation. However, its real agenda has been much more challenging than the immediate objective of drawing the plan proposals.

Defined in the broad sense, 'Gramoday' is an attempt to conceptualize, operationalise and institutionalize a system of multi-level, people centered planning process suitable to the regional specifications of Tripura. As a corollary of the above objective, it also aims at bringing about a major transformation in the attitude of various participants in the development process, viz, officials, elected representatives, intelligentsia and the people at large. It is also an effort to make the local people aware of the locally available resources. What is needed is a new development culture itself. It is also of equal importance that the system of multi-level planning thus put in place helps the State to overcome its contemporary development crisis:

Needless to assert that the broad goals of 'Gramoday' identified above could be broken into a series of detailed objectives, viz.,

- An assessment of locally available resources.
- Reconstructing the received ideas on decentralization and people's planning.
- Enabling the State Government to translate its commitment to concrete actions by mobilizing people in support.
- Harnessing popular opinion and will to overcome resistance offered by vested interests.
- Correcting popular and well entrenched but wrong notions of development by initiating development dialogues and introducing plausible alternatives.
- Involving mass organizations of the people in development activities.
- Imparting knowledge and skills needed for local level planning and
- Evolving and institutionalizing a systematic procedure by which development needs of the people are articulated, suitable solutions arrived at, prioritized, integrated into comprehensive development plans, implemented, and Monitored with maximum people's participation at all levels.

Last but not the least is the objective of horizontal and vertical integration of planning between various tiers.

Importance and timeliness of 'Gramoday' is best understood in the light of the following:

- Prevailing criticism of centralized planning and administration in the country.
- Failure of past efforts at decentralization and the intimidating long list of obstacles that new attempt at genuine decentralization face.
- Contemporary development challenges of the State which by consensus demand a decentralized approach to planning as also a revival of the participatory spirit to protect the widely acclaimed gains of the past.

GRASSROOT REALITY

For better understanding, about the actual process of Gramodaya, a micro level rapid appraisal was conducted with few necessary components of decentralized planning in two villages – one non-ADC village and another ADC village in West Tripura district. Rangutia village is a non-ADC village having seven wards while Sepaipara is an ADC village having four wards under Mohanpur R.D. Block.

Planning Process

In each ward, meeting (Gram Sansad) is organized. In this meeting all adult members of that ward and Panchayat member are need to be present. In this meeting all people can express their needs, problems which are noted in the ward register copy.

Then after completion of all ward level meetings, one meeting is take place in the Panchayat office or other place where the elected Panchayat members, Panchayat Secretary, other Panchayat worker, Pradhan (Chairman of GP), Upa-Pradhan (Vice-Chiarman of GP), BDO, other relevant officials of the block are present. In the present of above mention persons and with the help of register book of each ward the action plan of next year made.

After the preparation of the action plan, every person of each household of that village is invited formally to be present in the Gram Shabha. In this Gram Shabha, the BDO, Panchayat body and others officers of the block are present.

Gram Shaba starts when the one-third of the population is present. The action plan is read by someone in front of the whole population and after the reading of the action plan, if there is any objection and suggestion of the people, it also get importance and included in the action plan. Approved action plan is sent to the block for approval and funding.

People's Participation

The planning system is good, villagers can participate. But in this system, the Panchayat Secretary and Pradhan and Upa-Pradhan control the process. In Ward Sansad, people express their need and view but it is totally depends on the members what will be registered in the list or not. But ultimately, only the Panchayat member and other officers determine the plan. Again, when plan is ready it is red by someone for the village people and all the calculation of fund is also shown and asked to people if they have anything to say but in such big gathering hardly anyone get chance to express their view. Sometime, it may be due to hesitation. So ultimately people's view is not taken properly.

In ADC village the situation is more pathetic. In the Panchayat (VDC), all the members are tribal who are not so much educated and therefore totally dependent and guided by Panchayat Secretary who have very little knowledge about local needs and local language. For example, villagers wanted a health centre various times but it never get important in the village planning. The whole planning system is centered only. Some elite classes, people express their views and suggestions in favor of the tribal villagers.

Utilization of Local Resources

There is no village resource which can be used in implementation of plan without human resource. Human resources are used in the plan. Sometime it is seen that the human resource is not trained enough to utilised village resources and therefore trained manpower has to brings from outside. Again the work is not enough according to the human resources. So the problem arises regarding the distribution of work.

Implementation of Plan

The overall responsibility of implementation of the plan in each word is given to the elected ward member and the people of that word along with concerned officer. The labour is taken from the village and the secretary and Prodhan and the up Prodhan ascertains the work. In implementation of plan one management committee is made. To implement the plan in a specific ward the responsibility is given to the elected ward member and other people of that ward. But it is given when the work is generally small, when a big size of work the responsibility is given to the contractor.

In A.D.C. Village the Pradhan, Upa-Pradhan and Panchayat Secretary are related with the implementation of plan.

MAJOR PROBLEMS

1. The process of Gramoday is not followed properly during preparation of village. Only information format are filled up and send to upper levels.

2. There is lack of active participation of the people in the grass root level planning. This is due to lack of awareness and lack of importance given by the authorities.
3. Elected Panchayat members are not trained properly for Panchayat activities and don't have the required skilled for planning.
4. In the village level, hardly any VPT exists. Therefore Panchayat Secretary is responsible for the village planning and as a result the quality of the planning widely varies panchayat to panchayat.
5. Gram sabha is full of different agendas. Planning hardly gets any important both by the villagers as well as by the panchayat functionaries. Villagers are mostly interested on development schemes, from which they are 'personally' benefited.
6. There is some bias in the Panchayat activities. Therefore some people think Gram Sabha is a political meeting rather than public meeting and become reluctant to attend and give their opinion.
7. The fund is neither available in time, nor up to the requirement. The fund is given quarterly so sometime it make problems of implementation. Beside this to get the approval of various estimation, is a long term process which spoil the time and this is the reason of delay in project implementation in the village.
8. The line departments participate half-heartedly. They have their own departmental target and planning. They are not interested to be integrated in the Gramoday. This is the biggest obstacle towards success of this innovative planning system in Tripura. It became an isolated activity of Planning & Coordination department.

STEP FORWARD

For minimize the above problems and prepare meaningful and effective planning, following measures may be taken.

1. Gramodaya process needs to follow for the preparation of not only village development plan but also preparation of block, district s well as state plan. Then only the objectives of decentralization of planning can he achieved.
2. Active people's participation is the heart of decentralized planning. Adequate attention should be given for ensuring people's participation.

3. Gram Sabha meeting are vital for the identification of the felt need for preparing the plan. Quality meeting in Gram sabha must be ensured. In such meeting people can't expresses their view and can't understand all distribution of fund and work. Therefore to make understand the people about the fund and work another meeting would take place in the ward level after the preparation of plan.
4. Education level of the villagers particularly among the tribals should be improved by giving all the facility of education. It will widen the meaningful participation in the development process.
5. Panchayat members should not ignore the local people during preparation of plan.
6. Political bias should be avoided because it has been disturbing of social harmony and for these people also think about Panchayat system as a part of political party which is controlled by political members. Therefore people are interested to participate in Gram Sabhas.
7. Some specific and mandatory training program need to organized for the elected members and panchayat functionaries.
8. For improving decentralize planning the Gram Panchayat must be equipped with necessary manpower and infrastructure.
9. Utilization of local resources in a proper way among the local people is very much necessary and for that creation of proper socio-economic information for each village is quite essentials.
10. In Panchayat there should be co-ordination between Panchayat members and government functionaries, locally active NGOs, CBOs, clubs and other developmental agencies.
11. Panchayat should try to augment its income. For these, they should identify the under utilized and unutilized resources and make commercial uses of the available resources.
12. The Gram Sabha should he organized in holidays so that all people of the village can participate and can express their view.

13. Fund which is allotted to the Gram Panchayat is not enough. More funds are needed to meet the need of the people of the village.
14. Panchayat should give importance to the socially excluded classes of the village.

References

Abdul Aziz (1995), Decentralisation-Mandal Panchayat System in Karnataka, National Institute of Rural Development, Hyderabad.

Arun Ghosh (1988), "Decentralized Planning, West Bengal Experience", *Economic and Political Weekly,* March 26.

B. M. Sanyal (2001), India: Decentralised Planning Themes and Issues, Concept Publishing Company, New Delhi.

Cheema, G. S. and Rondineli, D. A. (Eds.) (1983), Decentralization and Development: Policy Implementation in Developing Countries, Beverley Hill, Sage.

Das Gupta, Ashim (1994), 'Panchayati Raj and Decentralized Planning in West Bengal in Decentralized Planning and Panchayati Raj. (Proceedings of the D.T. Lakdawala Memorial Symposium), Institute of Social Sciences, New Delhi, Concept Publishing Company, New Delhi.

G. Thimmaiah (1998), Democratic Decentralisation; Lessons from India, Man & Development, CRRID, Vol. XX, No. 3, Chandigarh.

G. Palanithuran (1999), New Panchayati Raj System at Work : An Evaluation, Concept Publishing Company.

Govt. of India (1993), Planning Commission, Report of NDC Committee on 'Microlevel Planning and Involvement of People at Grassroot Level, New Delhi, April.

Hazra, A. & Choudhury, J. (2005), 'Participatory Micro Planning for Village Eco-Development' in *Decentralized Planning and Participatory Rural Development (Ed),* Concept Publishing Company, New Delhi, pp. 92-105.

Institute of Social Sciences, Decentralized Planning and Panchayati Raj (Proceedings of the D.T. Lakdawala Memorial Symposium), Concept Publishing company, New Delhi, 1994.

Iqbal Narain, 'The idea of Democratic Decentralization', *Indian Journal of Political Science*, Vol. XXI, No. 2.

Meenakshi Sundaram, S. S. (1994), Decentralization in Developing Countries, Concept Publishing Company, New Delhi, p. 11.

Mishra, S. N. (1984), Rural Development Planning-Design and Method, Satvahan, New Delhi.

Misra, R. P., and Sundaram K.V. (1980), Multi-level Planning and Integrated Rural Development in india, Heritage Publishers, New Delhi.

Mukherjee, Amitava (1991), Methodology and Database for Decentralized Planning, Vol. 3 (Parts A,B and C), Heritage Publishers, New Delhi.

Reddy, Y. Venugopal (1979), Multilevel Planning in India, Vikas Publishing House, New Delhi.

Shaikh, Maqsood Ali, *et al.* (1983), Decentralization and People's Participation, National Institute of Public Administration, Dhaka.

Shalini Rajneesh (2002), Rural Development Through Democratic Decentralisation Deep & Deep Publications, New Delhi.

United Nation Development Programme: Decentralisation in India Challenges & Opportunities, Discussion Paper Series I, New Delhi, 2001.

United Nations, Decentralization for National and Local Development, New York, 1962.

United Nations, Local Participation in Development Planning, New Delhi, 1987.

United Nations, Popular Participation and Decision-making for Development, New York, 1975.

Vyas, V.S. *et al.* (1985), Decentralized Planning in India, Oxford and IBH Publishing Co., New Delhi.

Yadav, R. P. and Kafle, M. P. (1980), 'Development Planning in Nepal', Paper to the Expert Group Meeting on Development Planning at District Level, Kathmandu, Nepal, Oct. 24, Nov. 1. (mimeographed)

Yugandhar, B. N. and Mukherjee Amitava (1991), Readings in Decentralized Planning (with Special Reference to District Planning, Vols. I & II, Concept Publishing Company Ltd., New Delhi.

15

PARTICIPATION OF WOMEN IN DECENTRALIZED RURAL GOVERNANCE: A STUDY OF PRIs IN UTTAR PRADESH, INDIA

Kamal Kumar

The essential feature of development is that, it represents a transformation of society. It embraces a movement to modernize and adopt a liberal method from traditional relations, traditional cultures and social norms, traditional ways of dealing with health and education and traditional methods of production. All societies are a blend of the old and the new. However, change is not an end in itself, but a means to other objectives. The changes that are associated with development provide individuals and societies with more control and influences over their own destiny. Development enriches the lives of individuals by widening their horizons of choice and freedom and reducing their sense of isolation. Thus, a development strategy must be aimed at facilitating the transformation of society in identifying the barriers to, as well as potential catalysts of change.

PARADIGM SHIFTS IN RURAL DEVELOPMENT

Rural development had received priority since the 1920s and several programmes and experiments were in existence in different parts of the country, 'carried out by charismatic leaders with or without outside resource support (and those) executed through individual initiatives generally but with the resource support of the state' (Ray n.d.: 2). Some such programmes that may be mentioned are: 'Tagore's 'Srineketan' experiment, Hatch's 'Martandam' experiment in Kerala,

Gandhi's 'Wardha' and 'Sabarmati' experiments, Bryne's 'Gurgaon experiment, Krishnamachari's 'Baroda' experiment and Firka Development Scheme in then Madras. While there experiments influenced the form and programme of rural development that was started in 1952, Albert Mayer's Etawah project and S. K. Dey's Nilokheri experiment were coterminous with independence. In fact, the Etawah project proved to be a 'trial run' for the Community Development Programme [Jha 1999:20).

The ultimate objective of rural development was the eradication of poverty and thus improving the quality of masses. In formulating rural development policy the whole approach has been fundamental and it has to be targeted towards alienating rural poor from this culture of poverty, much has been perpetuated over the ages. In a democratic society, the basic objectives of rural development are (i) raising community solidarity, (ii) raising agricultural needs and (iii) institutionalization of equality and part and parcel of rural development efforts. The concept of rural development has undergone many changes depending upon the requirements and social transformation of Indian democratic system. The Government of India was committed to formulate plan policies on rural development during the successive Five Year Plans, which are shown in Chart 1. After the independence, the Community Development Programme was launched in year 1952 with 55 pilot projects on experimental basis. By early 1960's, the programme was extended to almost all the 5011 CD blocks of the country. It was emerged that the developmental process would allow benefits to percolate to the lowest short of the society on its own. It failed to achieve the desired results mainly because of the lack of functional responsibility and coordination of the part of administration. The food shortage in 1960's led to the policy shift and more emphasis on rural development was laid on production-oriented programmes like IADP and IAAP. This was followed by the adoption of a new strategy of agricultural development based on high yielding varieties of crops in the late 1960's. During 1970 Area Based Programmes were introduced like SFDA, DPAP, MFAL etc. 1980's emphasized on strengthening socio-economic infrastructure in rural areas, alienating disparities under Integrated Rural Development Programmes, creating new employment opportunities etc. 1990's era witnessed the policy shift and decentralized, people's centred and

Chart 1
Policy Shifts in Rural Development

Five Year Plan	*Period*	*Rural Development Policy*
Ist	1951-56	Community development as method and national extension service as the agency.
IInd	1956-61	Cooperative farming with local participation.
IIIrd	1961-66	Panchayati Raj–three tier model of democratic decentralization.
IVth	1969-74	Area based programme.
Vth	1974-78	Introducing concept of minimum needs programme.
VIth	1980-85	Emphasis on strengthening socio-economic infrastructure in rural areas, alleviating disparities under Integrated Rural Development Programmes.
VIIth	1985-90	Emphasis on creating new employment opportunities, special programmes for income generation through asset endowments, Land reforms, participation of people of the grass roots level.
VIIIth	1992-97	Emphasis on building up rural infrastructure, priority on rural roads, especially in tribal, hill and desert areas, minor irrigation, soil conservation, social foresting and participation of people in rural development programmes.
IXth	1997-02	Jawahar Gram Samridhi Yojana, Swarn Jayanti Gram Swarojgar Yojana, Pradhan Mantri Sarak Yojana, Sarva Shiksha Abhiyan etc. implementation.
Xth	2002-2007	Construction of roads, capacity building, human resource development, communication technology transfer, education women empowerment, self help groups and micro credit etc.

Source: *Indian Journal of Social Development,* Vol. 1(1), June, 2001 & 10th Five Year Plan, Government of India.

human face development approach and strategy was adopted. Chart regarding policy shifts in rural development is shown below:

DECENTRALIZATION OF GOVERNANCE

Advocacy for decentralization has been a part of the liberal political tradition (Smith 1985: 19-30). It is argued that decentralization is beneficial for the functioning of a democratic system at the national level, as also at the level of locality, 'Each can be further sub-divided into three sets of inter-related vales. At the national level, these vales relate to political education, training in leadership and political stability. At the local level, the relevant values are equality, liberty and responsiveness' (*ibid*: 20). These six vales in support of decentralization have been well argued in the literature, some of them in the context of local government. The benefits of democratic decentralization are elaborated thus: 'Decentralization combined with democratization (usually in its electoral, representative form) might provide greater transparency, accountability, responsiveness, probity, frugality, efficiency, equity and opportunities for mass participation. (Crook and Manor 1998:2).

Decentralization became important after independence from the point of view of the twin objectives of the Indian polity, namely, democracy and development. The early 1950s saw the introduction of the constitution, the electoral process and planned development. The need for decentralization was realized on all these counts and different forms and institutional schemes have been introduced since 1950.

EVOLUTION OF PANCHAYATS IN INDIA

Self governing village communities characterized by agrarian economies existed in India during the Rig-Vedic period. The historical and mythological evidences also indicate that republics existed in India for a long period which ensured people's participation and involvement in decision making process and development. However, Panchayats could not get their due status and importance in the development planning in India until 1992. The post independence phase of Panchayati Raj is marked with significant developments. Gandhiji was very much concerned about functional democracy at the grass root level and he advocated the concept of village republics however, no constitutional status was given to panchayats. Article 40 in the Directive Principles of State Policy made a provision that state governments to establish village republics (Panchayats) and ensure democratic decentralization. However, this could not make much head way in fulfilling the dreams of rural masses. The Balvantrai Mehta Committee (1957) suggested a set of institutional arguments resulting in creation of a three tier system of panchayat to organize and manage rural development activities. The village panchayat, panchayat samiti and zila parishad constituted the three tiers of PR, located at the village, the block and the district levels respectively. While the village panchayats and district boards were already functioning units of local government, the block development committees that existed as advisory bodies at the block level, were converted into panchayat samitis. Since the scheme of decentralization was conceived as a means to facilitate programmes of development, the middle tier of panchayat samiti at the block level was to be 'the basic institution in the entire scheme of Panchayati Raj' (Mehta 1962: 472).

The PR scheme, both in terms of its conception and evolution combined the development imperative with an attempt to provide democratic institution at local levels. Balvantrai Mehta scheme combined the past experience of local bodies and the new functions of development [Lele 1965: 18-19].

The Rationale and the effect of different types of elections on the working of PR bodies were subjects of elaborate discussions (Santhanam Committee Report, 1963). But the prevailing conception was that 'politics' is divisive and that PR institutions should be 'non-political'. The PR institutions were not regarded either as a 'political means' to bring abut change in rural India, or as part of the overall political process in the country, or as institutions reflecting social division in society. But the logic of a democratic process at different levels affected changes on all the three counts and the 'Second Generation' of PR institutions in West Bengal, Andhra Pradesh and Karnataka brought in the new role of PR as 'political' institutions. By 1959, all the states had passed the Panchayati Raj Act and by mid 1960, panchayat had reached all the parts of the country. In the 1960's despite the focus of government attention, Panchayati Raj System failed. The support for decentralized Panchayati Raj declined because most of the state politicians were reluctant to devolve powers to local institutions of governance. Thus by 1970's, most of the Panchayati Raj Institutions had become defunct and were dissolved. The Balvantrai Mehta Committee appointed in 1956 to examine this problem, felt that: Development cannot progress without responsibility and power. Community development can be real only when the community understands its problems, realizes its responsibilities, exercises its necessary powers through its chosen representatives and maintains a constant and intelligent vigilance on local administration. With this objective, we recommend an early establishment of statutory elective bodies and devolution to them of the necessary resources, power and authority (Asoka Mehta Committee Report 1978: 2-3). The Asoka Mehta Committee Report represented a landmark in so far as (a) it treated the PR clearly as 'an extension of democracy' and recommended 'establishment of democratic bodies below the state level'; (b) it declared 'the need of providing constitutional sanction to panchayati raj' and (c) suggested 'to transfer substantial quantum of powers from the State Government to the local bodies'.

The bifurcation of the two arenas of politics at the centre and in the states became fully operative in the 1980s, with the emergence of regional parties which came to power in many states. The non-Congress chief ministers introduced a 'new level of intensity in the debate on federal restructuring' (Arora 1992:6). They became assertive especially after the formation of a joint forum which met at regular intervals raising substantive issues of centre-state relations. The report of the Sarkaria Commission on centre-state relations appointed in 1983 gave a place of importance to democratic decentralization. The Economic Advisory Council appointed by the prime minister in 1983 (under the chairmanship of Professor Sukhamoy Chakravarty) pleased for 'functional reasons for decentralization'.

Rajiv Gandhi took up the issues of decentralization as a different note of providing 'responsive administration' and effective planning. The 'spent practically the whole of 1989 in having his reform package discussed at a series of meetings' (Arora 1992: 18) with district officials, district council presidents and chief ministers. The effort again was to reach out to the districts directly, but with due realization of the importance of PR institutions. A comprehensive 64th Constitution Amendment Bill passed by the Lok Sabha by a two-thirds majority fell through in the Rajya Sabha in October 1989 by a margin of two votes. The Congress government revived the proposal and democratic decentralization finally received constitutional status in 1992 with the 73rd and 74th Amendments, extended to the Scheduled Areas by an Act of 1996.

The Constitution Amendments of 1992 along with the extension to Scheduled and Tribal areas have been hailed as important landmarks in the system of decentralized governance. To accord constitutional guarantee to PR institutions by itself is a major step which has long been demanded from various quarters. A fixed tenure for the panchayats and holding of elections at the proper time under the supervision of an independent Election Commission appointed in the states is a major step. Besides reservation of seats for the SCs and STs in proportion to their population, the Amendments provide for the reservation of one-third of the seats of members as well as of chairman of PR institutions for women.

Held after the 73rd Amendment and the state legislations following it, the elections had guaranteed representation of women at all the three tiers of PRIs through the provision of one-third reservation. Equally guaranteed was the reservation of women from SC & ST, as the Amendment required that at least one of the women had to be from SC or ST. Unlike in the case of SC & ST reservation where the number of reserved constituencies was in accordance with the proportion of population, in case of women, it was simply and uniformly 33.3 per cent. Consequently, whereas elections to PRIs were held after April 1993, wards or constituencies were reserved for women. (Kaushik 1999: 239).

These provisions are rightly regarded as important steps towards 'empowerment' of women– an issue debated forcefully in the last two decades (Seminar 1997). The number of Panchayati Raj Institutions in India is reported to be 227698 at village level, 5906 at block level and 474 at district level. The total representatives were reported to be more than three million who were elected through democratic process and out of them one million are women representatives.

BACKGROUND OF WOMEN REPRESENTATIVES

The socio-economic characteristics of women representatives are not different from any other women in Indian society. Most of the women who stood for the elections were in the age group of 35-55 years. Less than one fourth of the women, compared to three fourth of man, had past political experience. Most of the Women were from the dominating caste, however, reservation for down trodden castes added a margin of representation for these groups. Less than five per cent of women as against twenty per cent of men were found professionally educated. The majority of women representatives were engaged in domestic work, household activities including agriculture operation and other unorganized economic activities. They lack resources and need capacity building. Most of the elected women representatives are not aware about their duties as panchayat functionaries. Thus, the effective functioning of panchayats could not be ensured. Caste polarization is prevalent and panchayats and women representatives work with their own caste group. They depend heavily on their husbands and in laws to resolve the problems presented to them. Women representatives at the higher tiers are often more educated and experienced and therefore they are more vocal and participative in meetings as compared to women members in gram panchayat meetings. Women's participation in constituted committees is negligible and male members dominate such committees. Male members attempt to dominate the meeting without giving any space to women members to participate. Women members also lack confidence and are less vocal in the meetings. Social customs and values also prevent women to speak before men. Physical violence in panchayat elections and meetings often impedes women's participation in Panchayati Raj. Government officers are also indifferent towards women representatives but they respond immediately to male representatives. It is rightly observed that women representatives are for name sake, the real power lies with husband, or male members of the household.

WOMEN'S REPRESENTATION IN PANCHAYATS IN U.P.

Women representation in the first PRI's election in 1995, after the enactment of new Panchayati Raj System in Uttar Pradesh (including Uttaranchal) was reported to be 33 per cent and 33.32 per cent respectively against total number of Pradhans and Members at Gram Panchayats. Similarly at Block level panchayats 33.29 per cent and 33.32 per cent women were elected as Pramukh and Member while at the district level panchayat women constituted 34.96 per cent and 32.37 per cent respectively as Adhyaksha and member (Table 1).

The second elections held in 2000 for PRIs (excluding Uttaranchal) demonstrated much higher share of women's representation as against the one third reserved seats. While comparing the statistics of the two elections, it is found that there has been an increase of 4.69 per cent in representation of women at district level

Table 1
Women Representation In Panchayats in U.P. (1995)
(Including Uttaranchal State)

	Gram Panchayats		*Kshetra Panchayats*		*Zila Panchayats*	
Particular	*Pradhan*	*Member*	*Pramukh*	*Member*	*Adhyaksh*	*Members*
Total	58620	673601	904	57288	83	2528
	(100.00)	(100.00)	(100.00)	(100.00)	(100.00)	(100.00)
ST	117	1347	2	114	-	5
	(0.20)	(0.20)	(0.22)	(0.20)	-	(0.19)
Male	78	898	1	76	-	4
	(0.13)	(0.13)	(0.11)	(0.13)	-	(0.16)
Female	39	449	1	38	-	I
	(0.07)	(0.00)	(0.11)	(0.07)	-	(1.04)
SC	12341	141456	189	12030	18	531
	(21.05)	(20.94)	(20.91)	(20.99)	(21.68)	(21.00)
Male	8269	94304	126	8020	11	354
	(14.11)	(13.99)	(13.94)	(13.99)	(13.25)	(14.00)
Female	4072	47152	63	4010	7	177
	(6.95)	(6.99)	(6.97)	(6.99)	(8.43)	(7.00)
OBC	15827	181872	243	15469	25	683
	(26.99)	(26.99)	(26.88)	(27.00)	(30.12)	(27.02)
Male	10604	121248	162	10313	17	456
	(18.09)	(17.99)	(17.92)	(18.00)	(20.48)	(18.04)
Female	5223	60624	81	5156	8	227
	(8.90)	(8.99)	(8.96)	(9.00)	(9.64)	(8.08)
Unreserved	30335	3248926	470	29675	40	1309
	(51.75)	(51.80)	(51.99)	(51.80)	(48.19)	(51. 78)
Male	20324	232618	314	19784	26	873
	(34.67)	(34.53)	(34.73)	(34.53)	(31.32)	(34.53)
Female	10011	116308	156	9891	14	436
	(17.08)	(17.27)	(17.25)	(17.26)	(16.89)	(17.25)

Source: U.P. State Election Office, Lucknow.

panchayat members and 4.63 per cent in gram panchayat members. Again, at Kshetra Panchayat level there has been an increase of 3.42 per cent of women representatives as Pramukh and 2.5 per cent increase in case of Kshetra Panchayat members. Interestingly, women represented 37.95 per cent, 35.82 per cent and 37.06 per cent respectively as members of Gram Panchayats, Kshetra Panchayats and Zilla Panchayats. Similarly, women constituted 35.32 %, 36.71% and 53.62% as heads of Gram Panchayats, Kshetra Panchayats and Zilla Panchayats in the state (Table 2).

Table 2
Women's Representation in Panchayats (2000) in U.P.

Particular	*Class*	*Women*	*Male*	*Total*
Member Gram Panchayats	ST	0.02	0.03	0.05
	SC	10.34	13.72	24.06
	OBC	10.92	17.79	28.71
	General	16.67	30.52	47.19
	Total	37.95	62.05	100.00
Member Kshetra Panchayats	ST	0.03	0.03	0.06
	SC	8.65	14.93	23.58
	OBC	10.51	19.01	29.52
	General	16.64	30.21	46.85
	Total	35.82	64.18	100.00
Member Zila Panchayats	ST	0.09	0.00	0.09
	SC	9.74	14.72	24.46
	OBC	11.43	19.29	30.72
	General	15.80	28.03	44.73
	Total	37.06	62.94	100.00
Pradhan Gram Panchayats	ST	0.02	0.04	0.06
	SC	8.05	13.71	21.76
	OBC	11.88	21.68	33.56
	General	15.37	29.25	44.62
	Total	35.32	64.68	100.00
Kshetra Panchayats Pramukh	ST	-	-	-
	SC	9.89	10.01	19.90
	OBC	12.73	15.58	28.31
	General	14.09	37.70	51.79
	Total	36.71	63.29	100.00
Adhyaksh Zila Panchayats	ST	-	-	-
	SC	13.04	7.25	20.29
	OBC	15.94	15.94	31.88
	General	24.64	23.19	47.83
	Total	53.62	46.38	100.00

Source: U.P. State Election Commission Lucknow.

The next panchayat elections were held in 2005-06 and women in Panchayati Raj Institutions reached upto 39.19 per cent. Their share has expanded much higher as against the statutory provision of 33 per cent. This has been reflected more pronouncing in case of Adhyaksh Zila Panchayat (75.71 per cent) followed by Member Zila Panchayat (51.83 per cent) and Pradhan Village Panchayat (50.22 per cent) (Table 3). A comparative analysis of women representation in Panchayati Raj Institutions shows higher increase in Adhyaksha Zila Panchayat (40.75 percentage points) while at block level their representation as Block Pramukh increased by 18.54 percentage points. Even their share in the representation of Village Pradhan has also increased by 17.22 percentage points (Table 4).

Table 3
Women's Representation in Panchayats (2006) in U.P.

	The Categories of Elected Candidates				
Name of the Post	*ST*	*SC*	*OBC*	*Gen.*	*Total*
Member, Village Panchayat	345	69971	85314	94613	250243 [38.40]
Pradhan, Village Panchayat	61	4961	12536	8545	26103 [50.22]
Member, Kshetra Panchayat	53	6340	9219	9268	24880 [38.23]
Member, Zila Panchayat	1	271	409	376	1057 [40.22]
Pramukh, Kshetra Panchayat	1	108	190	125	424 [51.83]
Jyeshtha Up-Pramukh	0	20	92	136	248 [30.28]
Kanishtha Up-Pramukh	0	37	89	115	241 [29.46]
Adhyaksh, Zila Panchayat	0	10	28	15	53 [75.71]
Total	461	81718	107877	113193	303249 [39.19]

Source: U.P. State Election Commission Lucknow.

Table 4
Increasing Representation of Women in PRIs

	1995	*2000*	*2005*	*Change*
Village Punchayat				
Pradhan	33.00	35.32	50.22	17.22
Member	33.32	37.95	38.40	5.08
Block				
Pramukh	33.29	36.71	51.83	18.54
Member	33.32	35.82	38.23	4.91
District				
Adhyaksh	34.96	53.62	75.71	40.75
Member	32.36	37.06	40.22	7.86

Source: U.P. State Election Commission Lucknow.

PROBLEMS OF WOMEN REPRESENTATION

In many countries including India cultural traditions holds women back from playing prominent role in economic life. Political participation of women, no doubt has increased at the grass root level, however, their participation in parliament and state assemblies continues to remain very low. Their representation is reported to be just 8.5 per cent in parliament, is 10.8 per cent in Central Council of Ministers. Their participation in state assemblies has shown a declining trend. In 1984-85 their number was reported to be 141 which declined to be 135 in 1987-88 and further to 113 in 1989-90 and 62 in 1993-94. Thus, women's participation in the political institutions and decision making bodies has been reported to be less effective.

Women have been enthusiastically participating in politics but not without difficulties, challenges and problems. Their low level of passive participation in decentralized rural governance and its programmes and schemes is the key problem for the administrators and policy makers. The proxy in election process, meetings, participation in development programmes and decision making has caused a serious damage to the dream of women's empowerment and hence concern for all. Husbands, in-laws and close relatives have become the main decision makers relegating the actual women representatives to the background. The role conflict on the part of these representatives has also increased while managing house hold responsibilities and political activities simultaneously. Since, male dominating society is reluctant in accepting the women as decision makers, they are being abused and harassed by officials, caste leaders, other elected representatives and also power brokers. Thus, desire for political power, status and sustainable source of black money has also caused social concern affecting women representative.

SUGGESTIONS

- Women PRI members need to be more aware of their rights and responsibilities so as to discharge their functions effectively without the male interference or help.
- Electoral reforms need to be effected so as to encourage Women PRI members to take total charge of their functions, without male dominance.

- Socio-cultural value system does not allow women to come out and participate actively in the development and decision making process. Thus, the traditional set up needs to be reformed, so that women contribute significantly to family, society, and nation as a whole.
- NGOs also need to closely coordinate with PRIs through it's women representatives. NGOs may be strengthened by providing opportunities and resources for orienting PRI members and extending support in execution of development programmes.
- There is urgent need to improve rural governance, greater accountability and transparency through convergence and better coordination with various rural development programmes and their concerned departments.
- More functional and financial devolution of powers to the Panchayati Raj institutions is needed so that the unfinished agenda of democratic decentralization may be completed.
- Women representatives in the Panchayati Raj institutions need orientation training for their capacity building in order to cope up with the emerging problems pertaining to functioning of PRIs, procedures and process of development planning and execution of development programmes.
- The role of civil societies may be further increased so that they may impart orientation training to women members in Panchayati Raj institutions for their active role in development and decision making process.

References

Arora, Balveer (1992), 'India's Federal System and the Demands of Pluralism: Crisis and Reform in the 80s', in Choudhury, Jyotipaul (Ed.), India's Beleaguered Federalism: The Pluralist Challenge. Tempe, Arizona: Centre for Asian Studies, Arijona State University.

Asoka Mehta Committee Report (1978), Report of the Committee on Panchayati Raj Institutions, Government of India, Ministry of Agriculture and Irrigation, Department of Rural Development.

Crook, Richard, C and Manor, James (1998), Democracy and Decentralization in South Asia and West Africa, Cambridge University Press.

Jha, S. N. & Mathur, P. C. (Ed.) (1999), Decentralization and Local Politics, SAGE Publication, New Delhi, Thowand Oaks, London.

Kaushik, Susheela (1999), 'Women in Panchayat Elections' in Jha, S.N. and Mathur, P.C. (Ed.), Decentralization and Local Politics. Sage Publications, New Delhi, Thousand Oaks, London.

Lele, Jayant, K. (1965), Role of Local Government in Rural Development. Ph.D. Thesis, Cornell University.

Mehta, B. (1962), 'The Panchayat Samiti at the Block Level as the Basic Unit of Panchayati Raj', *The Indian Journal of Public Administration,* Vol. VIII, No. 4, October-December.

Ray, C.N. (n.d.), Rural Development Programmes in India: Overview of Their Organizational Form (Mimeo.), Lucknow: Giri Institute of Development Studies.

Santhanam Committee Report, (1963), Report of the Committee on Panchayati Raj Elections. Ministry of Community Development and Cooperation, Government of India.

Seminar (1997), Empowering Women: A Symposium on Political Reservation for Women, September.

Smith, B. C. (1985), Decentralization: The Territorial Dimension of the State, London: Allen and Unwin.

16

PERFORMACNE OF JOINT FOREST MANAGEMENT IN TAMILNADU

V. Selvam & I. Sundar

INTRODUCTION

Joint forest management as a concept demands attitudinal changes among the foresters and among the forest abuttant community members. Foresters have to develop a positive minds set for participatory culture with the inclusion and formal induction of village community in forest Management and have to develop a positive attitude towards beneficial effects and impacts of peoples participation based partnership in forest protection and conservation. People have to change their attitude of treating forester as their enemy or as a person saying "no" to everything they need and preventing them from enjoying their access to forest resources. Mutual attitudinal changes can result in mutual rapport building and mutual trust building resulting in strong bondage of partnership.

Tamil Nadu Afforestration Project (TAP)

The major Joint Forest Management project being implemented in Tamilnadu is the Tamilnadu Afforestation Project (TAP). The TAP has been launched during 1997-98 in Tamilnadu with a massive tree planting programme to bring about balanced ecological upgradation and for meeting the requirements of the local people with respect to wood and non-wood forest produce. The scheme envisages ecological restoration of Forests with fullest participation of people through JFM.

The project is implemented with the assistance of Overseas Economic Co-operation Fund, Japan. The objectives of the project are given below.

OBJECTIVES

General Objectives

To launch a massive tree plantation programme in the State of Tamilnadu to bring about balanced ecological upgradation and to meet, to the extent possible, the requirements of the local people with respect to wood and non-wood forest products.

Specific Objectives

- Improving the productivity of the forest by creating heterogeneity of tree species and through intensive soil conservation and water harvesting measures.
- Preserve areas which are rich in biodiversity.
- In consonance with these concepts, optimise use of land resources on scientific basis and provide employment opportunities in rural areas.
- Enhancing the capabilities of the Tamilnadu Forest Department by establishing Geographic Information system, various training programmes, and re-orientation in the management of natural resources through Joint Forest Planning and Management.

This project is scheduled for five years with an annual target of 200 Villages and each village covering approximately 300 Ha of degraded forests. The target for five years is given below.

Joint Forest Management	3,02,000 ha (Planting)
Buffer Zone activities	1000 Villages
Incentive for local Tree	250 lakhs (Seedlings) cultivation
Conservation Programme	1,00,500 ha and 500 kms
Production Programme	650 ha. 1000 km (Planting)
Conservation of Species	2226 ha. (Planting)
Total financial outlay	Rs. 475.51 Crores.

TAP FIELD ZONATION

Local Bio-diversity Conservation

Under this component 200 programme villages are identified and work will be taken up on watershed basis following the Joint Forest Management (JFM) concept. The watershed improvement work will consist both planting and soil and moisture conservation work. The improvement treatment of each watershed will be done zone-wise (eg. Lower, Middle and Upper and buffer) based on the character of terrain and existing vegetation cover. The watershed on a holistic basis irrespective of ownership of land will be treated for effective action.

LOWER ZONE

The lower zone will be planted with the species to meet the immediate needs of the village community and also for long term benefits. 500 seedlings/ ha. are to be planted in this zone in addition to soil and moisture conservation measures like gully plugging. 450 seedlings of miscellaneous species will be planted which can meet the need of the local villagers for fruit, fodder, Naval, Cashew, Sitha, Nelli, Mango, Neem, Achan, Poovarasu, Sissu, Mungil, Vagai, Usil Perumaram, Odai, Kapock etc., will be planted here. For the balance 50. 25 good quality tamarind seedlings and 25 vegetative propagated cuttings are to be planted in this zone.

MIDDLE ZONE

In middle zone (asset creation zone) species to meet the long term needs of the village community will be planted. Usually fruit bearing and small timber etc. will be planted here. 300 seedlings /ha. are to be planted in this zone in addition to soil and moisture conservation measures like gully plugging, check dams, contour trenches, vegetative barriers 250 Nos. of seedlings of Misc. species like Bamboo, Illupai, Naval, Nelli, Sissu, Vagai, Achan, Poovarasu etc., will be planted here for the remaining 25 good quality tamarind seedlings and 25 vegetative propagated cuttings are to be planted in this asset creation zone. The rate of financial allocation per Ha. for planting work and soil and moisture conservation measures in middle zone should be 55: 45 respectively.

Stages of Implementation of Joint Forest Management

In order to counter the forest degradation, Joint Forest Management (JFM) was introduced in planning, conservation, afforestation and benefit sharing. In order to restore the degraded forests in Tamilnadu, a massive JFM based afforestation project called Tamilnadu Afforestation Project Phase-I (TAP-I) was implemented at a cost of Rs.688 crores over 8 years from 1997-98 to 2004-05 with a soft loan from Japan Bank for International Co-operation (JBIC), which included Rs 205 crores as State Government share. The project was implemented on watershed basis with active participation of people. It aimed at restoring degraded forests and also alleviating poverty in the project village.

An extent of 4.80 lakh ha. of degraded forests and community lands has been covered. 1367 Village Forest Councils formed with 4.66 lakh villagers as members. 23454 check dams and 2201 percolation ponds constructed for rainwater harvesting. A combined storage of more than 800 million cubic feet of water created. Forest fringe villages had a rise in water table ranging from 5% to 10% despite severe drought. This also helped augmenting agricultural production. Introduction of Geographical Information System (GIS) in implementation and monitoring of the project.Computerization down to the level of the Forest Range Office. Community assets like overhead tanks, borewells, hand pumps, VFC buildings, etc. provided to improve the quality of life in all project villages. 4722 rural development works implemented by 22 line departments by cross sectoral linkage. Rs. 41.30 crores worth of works benefited 946 project villages spread over 27 districts. The 3 districts not covered were Chennai, Nagapattinam and Thiruvarur. 1,75,000 forest dependents and villagers benefited through alternate employment. 60 million person days of employment generated. Rs.53 crores of Micro-credit distributed to villagers. Fund will revolve and rejuvenate village economy. Active participation of women 3891 Self Help Groups (SHG) benefitting around 60,000 women formed.

The Afforestation programme has two sub components viz.

- Integrated Watershed Development Programme (IWDP)
- Integrated Tribal Development Programme (ITDP)

Due to anthropogenic impact and exclusive biotic pressures a sizeable chunk of the forests have undergone retrogenic changes in their structure and composition. Poverty leading to destruction of forests and destruction of forests leading to poverty constitute a vicious cycle. Realising the immediate need to treat about 1,77,500 hectares of degraded forests in another 800 villages including 150 tribal villages, the Tamil Nadu Afforestation Project Phase-II assisted by Japan Bank for International Cooperation with an outlay of Rs. 567.42 crores, is being implemented over a 8 years span upto 2012-2013.

Minimum basic infrastructure facilities are being provided to improve the quality life of rural people who live in the fringe areas of reserve forests. Besides afforestation for ecological restoration of the natural capital, alternate employment opportunities are being created to improve the income level of the rural population.

Micro-finance facilities are also being extended to poor women, dependent on forests for their livelihood. During the year 2006-2007, 45,250 ha. of degraded forests in 205 fringe villages including 40 tribal villages have been covered at a cost of Rs.101.42 crores. During 2007-2008, it is proposed to implement the project at a cost of Rs.115.22 crores, over an extent of 51,500 ha. of degraded forests in 230 forest fringe villages including 40 tribal villages.

Effects of Project Implementation

Under this project, some 160 million trees were planted in a total area of 457,454 ha which outperformed the initial target of 470,500 ha. This afforested area accounts for 19.8% of the total forest area of the state standing at 2,304,400 ha in 2005, making some contribution to increasing the state's forest coverage.

Through this project, Joint Forest Management (JFM), a participatory forest management, was implemented. JFM initiatives included the afforestation planning that accommodates community needs through the village forest committees (VFCs) set up by local residents for the consultation with the state forestry department, the executing agency, and other operation and maintenance of the forest area managed by village forest committees. It is observed that this project had the effect of improving the environment by reducing pressures on the forests from illegal logging or grazing. In addition, it is estimated that the project also made some contribution to poverty reduction, as some 170,000 people or about 40% of the total village forest committees membership (some 460,000) started businesses under the livelihood improvement activities, including microfinance via the village forest committees.

Therefore, this project has largely achieved its objectives and its effectiveness is high.

Relevance

This project has been highly relevant with India's national policies and development needs at the times of both appraisal and ex-post evaluation. In Tamil Nadu State, the regeneration of degraded forests was given the highest priority in the planning stage. This recognition remains relevant at the time of the expost evaluation, and special emphasis is placed on sustainable forest management through JFM and the diversification of income sources for forest-dependent people.

Efficiency

The project period was much longer than planned (161% of the planned period), and the project cost slightly exceeded the plan (110% of the planned cost). However, a major reason for those was the additional undertakings associated with changes in the project scope. Therefore the efficiency of the project is high.

Sustainability

The sustainability of the livelihood improvement activities is unclear. However, the training for forest department officials, village forest committees members and NGOs has remained in place in Phase II of this project, and no major problems have been observed in the capacity of the executing agency nor its operation and maintenance system; therefore sustainability of this project is high.

In light of the above, this project is evaluated to be highly satisfactory. A major in its success was the temporary financial support at the early stages of the project, when the yields of forest products were small and funds for livelihood improvement activities were in short supply.

Tamil Nadu JFM, like many other JFM initiatives in the country, provides forest products as the major incentive to the participating villagers. All the forest produce such as fuel, fodder, green manure, and NTFP that can be harvested from the restored forests on a sustainable yield basis goes to the village forest committees members free of charge (with priority given to the poor and landless). Any surplus produce can be sold by the village forest committees, and any proceeds are then to be distributed equally among the village forest committees members after remitting 25% to a specially constituted Village Development Fund.

The Village Development Fund is meant to meet various costs incurred by the village forest committees in managing joint forest management and to undertake general development activities to benefit the village. Village-level development activities include laying roads, providing drinking water facilities, and constructing community halls etc. About 70% of the Village Development Fund is used to compensate individuals or small groups who were dependent on forests but lost access to them due to restrictions (e.g., grazing) that came about after the onset of joint forest management. Similar individual incentives are also provided to some community members who are interested in working for JFM to compensate for their time and effort, even if they were not previously forest-dependent. The individual benefit component generally includes activities such as the establishment of self-help groups, provision of micro-credit and vocational training etc.

While the Forest Department's project funds fully pay for afforestation and water harvesting, the Village Development Fund provides the funds for the village development and individual assistance components. In addition to the proceeds from the sale of forest produce, other sources of money for the Village Development Fund include village forest committee membership fees, fines and penalties, taxes, and general contributions from village forest committee members (monetary or labor). Discussions with forest officials indicate an assumption on the part of program planners that forest protection would generate enough on-site benefits for joint forest management to pay for itself after three years.

Joint Forest Management Outcomes

As discussed in the second section, successful conservation investments can yield benefits at three levels: local, regional, and global. To date, little effort has been made to measure these impacts and so it is difficult to assess the overall outcomes of joint forest management. Some specific studies of local impacts have been undertaken, but there has not been any attempt to disentangle the effects of different investment components. Regional and global effects have not been assessed.

Local Impacts

At the local level, soil and water conservation activities undertaken have not only checked erosion and impounded water, but also revived many natural springs, despite harsh agro-climatic conditions prevailing in the project areas (Sivanappan 2002; Swaminathan and Vidhyavathi 2002; Business Line 2000). In 20 of the sample watersheds where hydrological observations were made, an increase of 3.8% to 14.2% in the ground water table was recorded (Sreedharan 2002). This is consistent with the performance of water harvesting structures elsewhere in India (Hanumantha Rao 2000).

With the increased moisture, barren areas were put into production, and positive changes were observed in agricultural yields and cropping patterns in several project areas (Neelakantan 2000). Heavy investment in water harvesting and revegetation, along with the active cooperation of villagers through joint forest management in protecting plantations, are considered the major reasons for success. Significant reductions in goat populations, cattle grazing, wildfire occurrence, and forest encroachments were also recorded in almost all the joint forest management villages (TNFD 2002). As many FD officials and VFC presidents recall, villagers came in their hundreds to put out forest fires in joint forest management areas. Support from local leaders for forest protection, sometimes at the expense of political and economic hardship in their villages, was extensive.

Despite the resurgence of vegetation, the degraded forests failed to produce enough forest produce to be harvested by the village forest committees. The areas under joint forest management are characterized by very little topsoil, low nutrient availability, and severe soil compaction caused by decades of cattle movement. As a result, no joint forest management forests in the state yielded significant quantities of forest products.

Regional Impacts

At the regional level, the joint forest management areas in Tamil Nadu are critical catchments for major rivers, reservoirs, and irrigation tanks in the state. For example, the industrial city of Coimbatore is fully dependent on the Siruvani river for its municipal water supplies, and the forests of Coimbatore division form its main catchment area. Similarly, the Krishnagiri Reservoir, which is the life support system for farmers in Dharmapuri district, largely draws its water from innumerable streams that flow through the forests of Hosur division. Although it is suggested that JFM efforts will help increase water supplies by reducing siltation of lakes and reservoirs, the regional hydrological effects of these forests are poorly understood, and there is no data available on how much water these forests utilize through evapotranspiration or the relative magnitude of the effects of evapotranspiration and reduction in siltation. It is important to keep in mind, then, that in the early stages of joint forest management, revegetation takes the form of grasses and shrubs as well as small trees. Accordingly, the water consumption of this vegetation does not resemble that of a dense forest of large trees. This article has already mentioned recreation, tourism and scenic beauty as potential regional forest benefits. No data are available on these potential impacts either.

At a national and international level, forest conservation and regeneration sequesters carbon, thereby helping to stabilize global climate change (Verweij 2001). In addition, the forests of the Western Ghats that span the Tamil Nadu-Kerala border are home to significant biodiversity (Menon and Bawa 1997), including medicinal plants and important megafauna such as elephants and tigers with high international appeal. To date, the authors are not aware of studies that have attempted to measure the effects of joint forest management on such global public goods.

Benefits to Local Resource Management Institutions

Providing such environmental services imposes certain costs on joint forest management villages. These occur at two levels. One is the cost involved in ensuring compliance with the community's forest protection obligation. The other cost is the hardship incurred by the existing forest users such as cattle grazers and fuel wood collectors who were required to restrict their access to joint forest management forests in order to help restore them. The poor and landless, particularly those women for whom such activities constitute their primary source of livelihood, have been significantly affected.

The main incentive available to the VFCs, for either meeting operating costs or for compensating individuals affected by JFM, is primarily the proceeds from the sale of forest products, maintained through the Village Development Fund. The very low productivity of degraded forests in these areas, however, makes this rather pointless. Thus, although the joint forest management program document (GoTN 1997) talks of estimating and distributing forest benefits to VFCs, no forest benefits come out of JFM forests in significant quantities anywhere in the state. For Tamil Nadu's 799 VFCs, with a membership of 285,643 villagers, the total estimated value of forest produce taken in kind during 2000-2001 was a meager Rs. 793,465 (approx. US$ 17,600), or about Rs. 3 (less than seven US cents) per capita (RUPFOR 2002).

On the other hand, in the absence of any direct forest benefits, seed money provided to the VFCs for village development (Rs. 600,000 over three years), proved to be a major incentive to the villagers. Compared to other areas in the state, the villages situated in and around forests historically lagged behind with regards basic necessities and development assistance, and the onset of joint forest management provided a major opportunity for local leaders to help remedy this situation. Among survey respondents who reported obtaining benefits from joint forest management, three quarters listed access to loans, employment, and other development benefits. In addition, about half of all respondents said that obtaining more of these same benefits would be the main way of improving joint forest management.

Several villages came forward to take up the onerous task of protecting the forests through joint forest management, anticipating some developmental assistance made available in the form of seed money. Furthermore, catering to local communities' long pending concerns helped attract influential people in the villages, rendering much visibility and popularity to the program among the local populace. There were cases of state level political functionaries seeking selection of certain villages for joint forest management, and local leaders taking the issue of election of VFC president to the highest court in the state. These instances indicate the kind of enthusiasm and interest joint forest management has generated among local communities.

Environmental Service and Sustainability

The availability of seed money to joint forest management-participating villages was restricted to the first three years, which is a very short period compared to the long gestation period required for joint forest management to yield substantial forest products. As the non-existence of promised forest benefits became apparent, the interest and involvement of local villagers in joint forest management began to decline drastically after the third year of the project. At the end of three years, the death of these local management institutions became imminent, greatly undermining the concept of joint forest management and local forest management. Some VFCs, realizing the potential of the water harvesting measures under joint forest management to improve the water situation in the villages, tested a series of innovative ideas to augment the VFC's resources and thus sustain people's interest in joint forest management. These included levying a tax on farmers cultivating land close to water harvesting structures constructed under JFM (and thereby making use of an enhanced water supply), and selling silt obtained from the water tanks in forest areas. According to the foresters and VFC functionaries interviewed in the study, all these measures to generate money from forest improvement met with little success. The challenges include problems associated with devising proper pricing mechanisms, the general reluctance of people to pay for anything from the forest, poor institutional enforcement, and almost no extension/outreach efforts undertaken to highlight the water service benefits realized. These issues are discussed further below.

Challenges

As mentioned, the initiation of water augmentation activities, while providing benefits to some villagers, imposes costs on certain other groups- such as cattle grazers using the forest catchment. In addition, half the respondents did not perceive any of the above-mentioned benefits. This led to the idea of taxing those who benefit in order to compensate those adversely affected. This taxation approach was thought of for two main purposes. One was for VFCs to have some money to meet their costs, and the second was to ensure that there was no ill feeling within the village that only certain people were receiving benefits whilst others were not. However, this approach did not work since water harvesting efforts led to enhanced ground water, which is both legally and practically very difficult to regulate.

Furthermore, the water harvesting structures are placed in and around forest areas according to the terrain and technical requirements of the local area and not according to the needs or interests of the individuals who might benefit from them. So, for the people farming nearby, this increased water could be construed as an accidental benefit rather than something that is born out of their active interest or involvement in joint forest management. Moreover, once the structure is constructed, the farmer will receive a benefit irrespective of his/her interest or involvement in or contributions to joint forest management.

Opening up joint forest management to all willing households in a village led to the recruitment of a large number of villages belonging to various groups and castes, anticipating various development benefits. Managing such heterogeneous groups led to high transaction costs related to negotiating and enforcing contractual agreements. Moreover, in several places, the watershed boundaries did not tally with village/hamlet administrative boundaries. Although social fencing is supposed to be the forest protection norm in joint forest management, with different hamlets being grouped together as a single joint forest management village, covering such distant and scattered habitations suddenly meant that the VFCs had to hire forest protection "watchers". With no resources to pay for these watchers, in many places forest protection came to a standstill after 3 years, according to VFC presidents and field level forest officials. Although there is a proviso to help affected forest dependents, insufficient resources to effectively implement this further complicated the compensation scenario. In such instances, erstwhile forest users showed their potential not to abide by joint forest management agreements. Many respondents surveyed cited a lack of equity in the distribution of these compensation benefits as an area for improvement in joint forest management.

The Forest Department (FD) and local community heads provided most of the leadership in forming VFCs and developing institutional mechanisms as part of joint forest management. While villagers were mostly engaged in village development and forest protection, the FD undertook watershed development. In many instances, these two activities ran separate from each other. There were also no explicit mechanisms to explain to the public the link between watershed management and increased water availability. Facilitating public participation in forest management is new to the FD (Matta *et al.* 2005) and very limited resources and a lack of expertise has hindered the undertaking of any extension/outreach activities. Furthermore, the FD kept to itself detailed records on the hydrological changes occurring in the project areas and largely assumed that the benefits would become automatically apparent to the local public. Most villagers viewed the seed money provided for the village development as yet another form of top-down 'rural development' or 'social welfare' support. Consequently, for many villagers, the link between watershed protection efforts and increased groundwater levels was not apparent, although the local media and general public in certain far-flung places praised such efforts. Even if some villagers perceived the link, they did not play a big role in the VFCs. Thus, a failure to strongly attribute the benefits produced by watershed protection significantly affected the sustainability of VFCs and in turn that of JFM. It seems that under current conditions the emergence of successful institutional arrangements to make local people pay for water appears very unlikely. Legally they are not obliged to do so, and culturally and politically they are not accustomed to it. Some radical changes will be needed for such a local payment mechanism to function and it is difficult to envision such a transformation in the short term.

Opportunities

The overall analysis of joint forest management in Tamil Nadu indicates that the assumption implied in government orders that the improvement of degraded forests can generate enough forest produce to make it a self sustaining scheme in joint forest management villages has failed to work in practice. The efforts of local resource management institutions, after the withdrawal of seed money in the third year, remain under-compensated when compared to the costs being incurred.

Another significant outcome of institutional development and local resource management through VFCs is that forests were no longer being treated as open access resources. The VFCs' control rendered the forests the status of a property. The regulations on the use of forest resources through peoples' institutions brought about a general feeling among the villages that forests are of some 'value' and not free for all, as was preceived previously by many. Furthermore, the political processes and the interactions among villagers that have developed since the onset of joint forest management has not only led to greater discussion and debate over forest uses or abuses but also to substantial collective action in the villages, resulting in improved forest protection. Elections to the VFCs became an important and prestigious issue. VFC presidents and other functionaries proudly display their newfound status on wedding invitations and at other local functions. The formation of self-help groups, strengthening micro-credit and income generation institutions, and ensuring women's participation and capacity building led to considerable community mobilization and organization. Every JFM village now has tie-ups with local commercial banks and other professional development institutions. Thus, the costs to society in the event of failure of these VFCs are very high when one takes into consideration the unseen benefits the VFCs are having in terms of general environmental health and quality of life.

Making these local resource management institutions function could be a financially viable proposition if the offsite benefits they render are taken into account. As mentioned above, VFCs' efforts in JFM can contribute to a number of off-site benefits and perhaps these positive externalities justify compensation. Unfortunately, many of these potential benefits do not receive much attention and they have not been studied, so it is not possible to assess their value at this time. It is also difficult to find precedent for such an approach in India; the few examples available concern the reduced siltation of downstream water bodies. For example, Chopra *et al.* (1990) cite annual savings of US$200,000 in saved dredging and related costs in the case of Sukhna Lake, Chandigarh, which involved similar afforestation and watershed improvement. Sehgal and Abrol (1994) cite alarming levels of siltation in a number of important reservoirs in India, suggesting potential high off-site benefits would come from improved soil conservation and revegetation in associated catchment areas.

It appears that several individuals and organizations interested in conservation have already taken notice of the benefits of forest protection and have come forward to help the VFCs in isolated cases. The cash and kind support of the TVS Group of Companies, a major industrial house in Tamil Nadu, for watershed rehabilitation in the state demonstrates the potential for industrial financing of environmental restoration (TERI 2002). The TVS Group, in collaboration with local NGOs and the Forest Department, is actively promoting the forest regeneration and protection efforts of VFCs in selected joint forest management villages in two districts. Several religious and philanthropic organizations have also shown a keen interest in post- joint forest management forest protection and rehabilitation in several places. What is needed is a concerted effort to galvanize these interests and develop appropriate institutional mechanisms to make VFCs sustainable.

Interestingly, the public interest in supporting joint forest management may stem from the kind of misconception of forests' hydrological effects as cited by Calder (2002), Kaimowitz (2002) and others, and as discussed earlier. In particular, the hydrological benefits of Tamil Nadu's joint forest management program are almost certainly due to water harvesting investments that have nothing to do with forests and trees per se, yet they are popularly associated with joint forest management's afforestation efforts. It seems reasonable that developing mechanisms to compensate local villages for providing environmental services will require greater effort to identify what those services are and estimating how much they are worth. Clearly, someone who pays for watershed services must know what he or she is purchasing.

Payments for Environmental Services (PES) schemes, while rare in India, are spreading elsewhere in the world and such experiences could help guide India in this respect. In Costa Rica, for example, upstream landowners receive payments for watershed protection and carbon sequestration, with a national agency working as an intermediary to reduce transaction costs (Subak 2000). In Southeast Asia, the Rewarding Upland Producers for Environmental Services (RUPES) program uses a variety of rewards systems, including cash but also secure land tenure, and, unlike in Costa Rica, it works with groups of land users rather than just individuals (ICRAF 2003). The latter aspect of the program could provide some useful guidance for JFM.

Measuring and valuing environmental services remains a major hurdle in PES schemes all over the world. On the other hand, if the objective is simply to give people in forest fringe areas a greater incentive to protect such resources, measuring the precise level of forest benefits is less critical. joint forest management program managers and VFC functionaries confidently estimate that VFCs can be made viable at a cost of as little as Rs.100,000 per year (about US$2,200 or a few dollars per ha), the payment being dependent on the quality of forest protection that they provide. At this point in time, given the extreme state of degradation of many of India's forests, additional regeneration will provide clear off-site benefits so their precise measurement is probably unnecessary. In the future, as the ability to measure and value off-site services develops, it might be possible to identify appropriate beneficiary organizations to fund VFCs as indicated above. On the other hand, if detailed measurements of the hydrological effects of forests were to reveal that forests are in fact net consumers of water, some downstream interests might turn against forest protection. More realistically, it may prove that the off-site benefits of forest management are sufficiently diffuse that individual sources of demand could be difficult to identify.

CONCLUSIONS

Joint forest management appears to have halted the degradation of forests for the time being. The problem, however, seems to be in ensuring the sustainability of the program in the absence of some immediate and perceived benefits to the local people involved. The current joint forest management approach that offers forest products as the only benefit to participating villagers may not be appropriate, at least in places where joint forest management is implemented in particularly degraded forests. Especially in water-starved states such as Tamil Nadu, the stated principle for long-term joint forest management planning should seemingly concentrate on supplying long-term environmental services rather than providing some immediate forest usufructs. The experiences of some eco-development projects in India (Pandey and Weils 1997; Chopra 1998; Mishra 1999) and further afield (Brown *et al.* 2002) suggest that a program to compensate local people for providing environmental services could be a viable venture. While such an approach will face challenges of its own both in ensuring conservation (Ferraro 2000) and providing benefits to the poor (Smith and Scherr 2003; Landell-Mills and Porras

2002), it is worth exploring the possibilities for joint forest management given the contradictions of the program's current approach. We hope this article will set a new trend in joint forest management thinking and pave the way for research to identify and estimate off-site benefits of joint forest management, and develop innovative mechanisms for sustaining local resource management institutions.

References

Anon (2000), State of Forest Report 1999, Forest Survey of India, Dehradun India.

Anon (2001), World Development Report 2000/2001 Attacking Poverty, The International Bank for Reconstruction and Development. Washington, D.C. USA.

Andersen, K. E. (1995), Institutional Flaws of Collective Forest Management. Ambio 24(6):349-353.

Aylward, B. and S. Tognetti (2001), Valuation of Hydrological Externalities of Land Use Change: Lake Arenal Case Study, Costa Rica. Land-Water Linkages in Rural Watersheds Case Study Series. FAO, Rome, Italy.

Bahuguna, V. K., V. Luthra, B. Mcman and S. Rathor (1994), Collective Forest Management in India. Ambio 23(4-5): 269-273.

Baland, J. M. and J. P. Platteau (1996), Halting Degradation of Natural Resources: Is There a Role for Rural Communities? FAO, New York and Oxford: Clarendon Press, Oxford, UK.

Brown, D., K. Schreckenberg, G. Sheperd and A. Wells (2002), Forestry as an Entry Point for Governance Reform. ODI Forestry Briefing No. 1, April.

Bruijnzeel, L. A. (2000), Hydrology of Tropical Montane Cloud Forests: A Reassessment. Land Use and Water Resources Research 1:1-18.

Business Line (2000), Effective Way to TAP Water in Dharmapuri Dist. News article published in the Business, *Daily Business Line* on June 2.

http://www.blonnet.com/businessline/2000/06/02/stories/1402601a.htm

Calder, I. (2002), Forests and Hydrological Services: Reconciling Public and Science Perceptions. Land Use and Water Resources Research, 2:2.1-2.12.

Chopra, K. (1998), Economic Aspects of Biodiversity Conservation: Micro and Macro Strategies for Intervention, *Economic and Political Weekly,* 33(52), 3336-3340.

Chopra, K., G. Kadekodi and M. N. Murthy (1990), Participatory Development: People and Common Property Resources. Sage Publications, New Delhi, India.

Corbridge, S. and S. Jewitt (1997), From Forest Struggles to Forest Citizens? Joint Forest Management in the Unquiet Woods of India's Jharkhand. *Environment and Planning*, 29(12), 2145-2164.

Datta, S. and V. Varalakshmi (1999), Decentralization: An Effective Method of Financial Management at the Grassroots (Evidence from India). *Sustainable Development,* 7(3), 113-120.

Dhar, S. K. (1994), Rehabilitation of Degraded Tropical Forest Watersheds with Peoples Participation. Ambio, 23(3), 216-221.

ECCM (2002), Estimation of Carbon Offset by Trees. ECCM Technical Document No. 7.

Edinburgh Centre for Carbon Management, Edinburgh, Scotland.

Ferraro, P. (2000), Global Habitat Protection: Limitations of Development Interventions and a Role for Conservation Performance Payments. *Conservation Biology*, 15(4), 9990-1000.

Ghate, R. (2000), Joint Forest Management: Constituting a New Commons: A Case Study from Maharastra, India. Paper submitted for the Eighth Biennial Conference of the IASCP, Indiana University, May 31-June 4, 2000.

GoI (1990), Involvement of Village Communities and Voluntary Agencies for the Regeneration of Degraded Forestlands. Government of India, Ministry of Environment and Forests, New Delhi. Letter, 6-21/89, pp. dated June 1, 1990.

GoTN (1997), Government of Tamil Nadu Environment and Forests (FR. VI). Department Orders MS. No. 342 and 343, dated August 8, 1997.

Hanumantha Rao, C. H. (2000), Watershed Development in India: Recent Experience and Emerging Issues, *Economic and Political Weekly,* 4, 3943–3947.

ICRAF (2003), RUPES Program Brochure. International Centre for Research on Agroforestry, Nairobi, Kenya. On the web at: *www.worldagroforestrycentre.org/sea/Networks/RUPES*

Jeffery, R and N. Sundar (eds). (1999), A New Moral Economy for India's Forests? Sage, New Delhi, India.

Kaimowitz, D. (2002), Useful Myths and Intractable Truths: The Politics of the Link Between Forests and Water in Central America. Center for International Forestry Research (CIFOR), Bogor, Indonesia.

Kant, S. and J. C. Nautiyal (1994), Sustainable Joint Forest Management Through Bargaining: A Bilateral Monopoly Gaming Approach. *Forest Ecology and Management,* 65(2-3), 251-264.

Kerr, J. in Collaboration with G. Pangare and V. Lokur Pangare (2002), An Evaluation of Watershed Development Projects in India. Research Report 127. International Food Policy Research Institute (IFPRI), Washington, D.C.

Khare, A., M. Sarin, N. C. Saxena, S. Pali, S. Bathla, F. Varnia and M. Satyanarayana (2000), Joint Forest Management: Policy Pactice and Prospects. Policy that Works for Forests and People Series, No. 3. IIED, London and WWF-India, New Delhi.

Kumar, S. (2002), Does Participation in Common Pool Resource Management Help the Poor: A Social Cost-benefit Analysis of Joint Forest Management in Jharkhand, India. *World Development,* 30(5), 763-782.

Landell-Mills, N. and I. Porras (2002), Silver Bullet or Fool's' Gold? A Global Review of Markets for Forest Environmental Services and their Impact on the Poor. IIED, London, United Kingdom.

Lele, S. (2000), Godsend, Sleight of Hand, or Just Muddling Through: Joint Water and Forest Management in India. Natural Resource Perspectives No. 53. ODI, United Kingdom.

Lise W. (2000), Factors Influencing People's Participation in Forest Management in India. *Ecological Economics,* (34), 379–392.

Matta, J. R., J. Kerr and K. Chung (2005), From Forest Regulation to Participatory Facilitation: Forest Employee Perspectives on Organizational Changes and Transformation in India. Forthcoming in *Journal of Environmental Planning and Management.*

Menon, S. and K. S. Bawa (1997), Applications of Geographic Information Systems, Remote-sensing, and a Landscape Ecology Approach to Biodiversity Conservation in the Western Ghats. *Current Science,* 73(2), 134-145.

Miles, M. B. and A. M. Hubernan (1994), Qualitative Data Analysis. Sage, California, USA.

Mishra, T. K. (1999), Forestry Research in India, *Economic and Political Weekly of India,* 34 (16-17), 942-944.

Neelakantan, K. S. (2000), From Barren Fields to Grapevine Yards. *Indian Forester,* 126(5), 505-08.

Ostrom, E. (1992), "The Rudiments of a Theory of the Origins, Survival, and Performance of Common Property Institutions" in D.W. Bromley (ed.),

Making the Commons Work: Theory, Practice and Policy. ICS Press, San Francisco, California.

Ostrom, E., R. Gardner and J. Walker (1994), Rules, Games and Common-pool Resources. University of Michigan Press, Ann Arbor, Michigan.

Pagiola, S., J. Bishop and N. Landell-Mills (eds). (2002), Selling Forest Environmental Services: Market-based Mechanisms for Conservation and Development. Earthscan Publications, London, United Kingdom.

Pandey, S. and M. P. Wells. (1997), Eco-development Planning at India's Great Himalayan National Park for Biodiversity Conservation and Participatory Rural Development. *Biodiversity and Conservation,* 6(9), 1277-1292.

Rangachari C. S. and S. D. Mukherji (2000), Old Roots, New Shoots. Winrock-Ford Series, New Delhi.

Ravindranath, N. H., D. N. Pandey, I. K. Murthy, R. B. Deepti Jain and M. Poffenberger (eds.). (2001), Communities and Climate Change: The Clean Development Mechanism and Village-based Forest Restoration in Central India. A Case Study from Harda Forest Division, Madhya Pradesh, India. Santa Barbara: Community Forestry International.

RUPFOR. (2002), *http://www.rupfor.org/jfm_india.htm* (JFM Fact Sheet: Tamil Nadu)

Sanders, D., P. Huszar, S. Sombatpanit and T. Enters (eds). (1999), Using Incentives in Soil Conservation. Science Publishers, Enfield, New Hampshire.

Saxena, N. C., M. Sarin, R. V. Singh and T. Shah. (1997), Independent Study on Implementation Experience in Kanara Circle, Bangalore: Karnataka Forest Department.

Sehgal, J. and I.P. Abrol (1994), Soil Degradation in India: Status and Impact. Oxford and IBH, New Delhi.

Singh, C. (1991), JFM: Analysis of Forestry Notifications. Wasteland News, August-October.

Sinha, V. K. (1999), Current Practices of Joint Forest Management in Western India: A Case Study from Rajpipla Forests. PhD Dissertation. State University of New York.

Sivanappan, R. K. (2002), Watershed Development and Management Strategies and Case Studies. Proceedings of the Workshop on Joint Forest Management and Watershed Development, January 21-22, 2002, Chennai, TNFD. 108-133 pp.

Smith, J. and S. J. Scherr (2003), Capturing the Value of Forest Carbon for Local Livelihoods. *World Development,* 31(12), 2143-2160.

Sreedharan, C. K. and M. K. Sarkar (1998), People's Participation and Joint Forest Management in Tamil Nadu. *Indian Forester,* 124(1), 7-13.

Sreedharan, C. K. (2002), Joint Forest Management for a Human-habitat Harmony-Successful Trends in Tamil Nadu. Proceedings of the Workshop on Joint Forest Management and Watershed Development, January 21-22 2002, Chennai. TNFD. 1-25, pp.

Subak, S. (2000), Forest Protection and Reforestation in Costa Rica: Evaluation of a Clean Development Mechanism Prototype. *Environmental Management,* 26(3), 283-297.

Sundar, N. (2001), Is Devolution Democratization?, *World Development,* 29(12), 2007-2023.

Swaminathan, L.P. and A. Vidhyavathi (2002), Impact of Soil and Water Measures of Joint Forest Management: A Case Study in Salem Division. Proceedings of the Workshop on Joint Forest Management and Watershed Development, January 21-22, 2002, Chennai, TNFD, pp. 298-303.

TERI (1998), Looking Back to Think Ahead. Tata Energy Research Institute, New Delhi.

TERI (2002), Corporate in Green Voyage: Partnership between the Forest Department and TVS-SST in Tamil Nadu. TERI, New Delhi.

TNFD (1997), Tamil Nadu Afforestation Project (TAP) Proposal to Overseas Economic Cooperation Fund of Japan (Now Known as the Japanese Bank for International Cooperation). TNFD, Chennai.

TNFD (2002a), Progress Report on the Performance of Tamil Nadu Afforestation Project (TAP) TNFD, Chennai.

TNFD (2002b), *http://www.forests.tn.nic.in/water_harvesting.htm*

van Noordwijk, M. (2005), Separating Watershed Myth from Watershed Science in Policymaking and Project Design. Paper presented at World Bank workshop entitled Landscapes, People, and Water: Reviewing the State of the Art in Managing Watersheds, February 24-25, 2005, Washington, D.C.

Varughese, G. (2000), "Population and Forest Dynamics in the Hills of Nepal: Institutional Remedy by Rural Communities" in Gibson, C. G., M. McKean and E. Ostrom (eds.) People and Forests. The MIT Press, Cambridge, Mass.

Verweij, P. (ed.) (2001), Understanding and Capturing the Multiple Values of Tropical Forests. Proceedings of the International Seminar on Valuation and Innovative Financing Mechanisms in Support of Conservation and Sustainable Management of Tropical Forest. March 20-21, The Hague, Netherlands.

Vira, B. (2000), "Implementing Joint Forest Management in the Field: Towards an Understanding of the Community–bureaucracy Interface" in Jeffery, R and N. Sundar (eds.), A New Moral Economy for India's Forests? Sage Publications, New Delhi.

Wade, R. (1988), Village Republics, Economic Conditions for Collective Action in South India. South Asian Studies. Cambridge University Press, Cambridge, United Kingdom.

17

FISCAL DECENTRALISATION IN INDIA: AN OVERVIEW

G. Senthilkumar

INTRODUCTION

There are a number of additional reasons for the analysis of fiscal decentralization in India. The adoption of market oriented reforms since 1991 has redefined the role of the State and this has necessitated a reexamination of fiscal arrangements between different levels of government. In fact, there have been opposing forces at work. While on the one hand, the transition from centralized planning and market based resource allocation has enhanced the role of subnational governments in delivering social and physical infrastructure, increasing trend in regional inequalities has necessitated greater central role. Inter-regional distribution of incomes has shown increasing inequality during the 1990s (Rao, Shand and Kalirajan, 1998). There is also considerable debate on the trends in poverty with official statistics showing increasing trend in recent years. Efficient antipoverty interventions warrant a solution within the co-operative federalism framework (Inman and Rubinfeld, 1992). It must be noted that despite a decade of fiscal adjustment, fiscal imbalances at both central and State levels continue to pose serious threat to macroeconomic stability in the country.

Another important reason for the examination of fiscal decentralization in Indian context is the statutory recognition of the third tier of fiscal structure and evolution of a formal three-tier federalism subsequent to the 73rd and 74th Constitutional amendment in 1992. The introduction of the third tier of fiscal authority has met with varying degree of successes in delivering public services in different States and it is important to examine extent of sub-State decentralization in different States. The analysis assumes importance also due to the fact that the institutional environment for the delivery of services has significantly changed with the advent of a coalition of parties in power at the Central level and emergence of regional parties in the States and as partners in Central coalition.

The functions related to money supply, external borrowing, international relations, defense, atomic energy, space, national highways, airways, international waterways, and those having significant scale economies are assigned exclusively to the center. The functions involving benefits spanning across States and matters with significant developmental potential are undertaken concurrently with the States. These include economic planning, energy, education, health and family welfare. The functions with statewide implications are assigned to the States. Most progressive tax handles have been assigned to the Center. The tax handles have been assigned to the States include land revenue, tax on agricultural incomes and wealth, stamp duties and registration fees, tax on sale and purchase of goods, excise duties on the sale of alcoholic products, tax on motor vehicles and tax on goods and passengers transported through roads and inland waterways. However, from the viewpoint of revenue productivity, the tax on the sale and purchase of goods is the most important. The residual functions and residuary tax powers also vest with the Center.

Intergovernmental Fiscal System

India, as a democratic polity, evolved as a two-tier classical federation with constitutional demarcation of functions and finances between the centre and the States with separate legislative, executive and judicial arms of government constituted at the two levels. The seventh schedule to the constitution specifies legislative domains of the two layers of government in terms of Union (central), State and concurrent lists. The constitution also requires the President of India to appoint a Finance Commission every five years to review the finances of the centre and the States and recommend devolution of taxes and grant in aid for the ensuing five years.

Pre-reform Fiscal Arrangements

Though constitutionally a federal country, owing to relatively high degree of centralization India is characterized as quasi-federal. In shaping decentralization in India, both historical factors and the public sector have dominated. In the latter, the heavy industry-based import substituting industrialization strategy has played an important role. Centralization inherent in the constitution was accentuated by an autarchic economic regime, public sector domination in industry and the financial sector and state engineered allocation of resources. Since 1991, market oriented reforms have been introduced to liberalize the economy from the dirigisme.

In the pre-reform system, the constitutional division of functions was only between the centre and States. In the two-tier federal structure, local bodies below the State level in both urban and rural areas were merely the State government agencies. Although many States did have a third tier, elections to the level were infrequent and supercession of the elected bodies in them was rather common. More important, the State governments were reluctant to devolve fiscal responsibilities to the third level. Not surprisingly, fiscal decentralization was limited to the State level.

Furthering Fiscal Decentralization Through Constitutional Amendment

An important development in fiscal decentralization in India consists of the constitutional amendments in 1992 to accord statutory recognition to the third tier of government. With constitutional recognition, separate schedules listing 29 subjects falling within the ambit of rural local bodies and 18 within the ambit of urban local bodies have been specified. Revenue and expenditure assignments of local governments are exercised concurrently with States' responsibilities. However, the actual powers and functions exercised by the local bodies depend on the extent to which States are willing to devolve. Each State has its own pattern of devolution and, in fact, there are wide variations in sub-State decentralization.

Thus, one billion people in the country are spread over 28 States. Below them there are over a quarter million local governments of which about 3,000 are in urban areas and the rest in rural areas. The rural local bodies or *panchayats,* in turn are in three levels–district, *taluk* (block) and village (see figure). Urban local governments consist of municipal corporations in large cities and municipalities, *nagar* (town) *panchayats* or notified area councils in smaller towns. Each State government is required to devolve revenue and expenditure powers to local bodies. Elections to these local bodies have to be held every five years and if the elected governments are superseded by States for any reason, elections must be held within six months of supercession. Each State has to appoint a State finance commission every five years to review local finances and recommend transfers to local bodies.

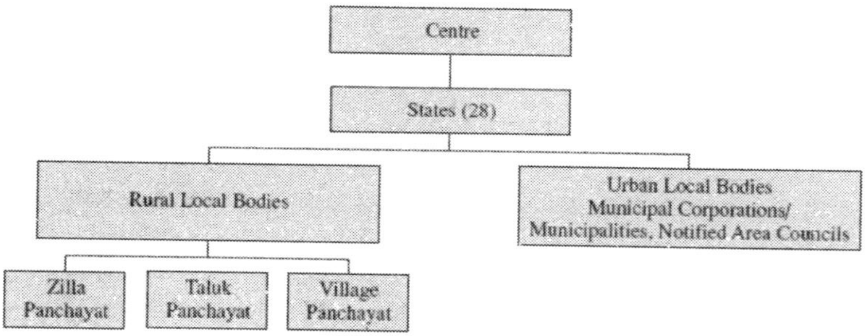

Figure Structure of Multilevel Government in India

Fiscal Assignment

An important feature of the tax assignment is its fragmented nature. While the tax on non-agricultural incomes is assigned to the centre, agricultural income tax is in the States' domain. Sales taxes on goods can be levied by the States but not taxes on services. Although the constitution is equivocal in stating that trade and commerce throughout the country should be free, the tax on interstate sales of goods levied by the centre and collected by the States impedes the interstate movement of goods. More importantly, the State list contains an item, "tax on the entry of goods into a local area for consumption, use or sale". This tax is called "octroi" and has been assigned to urban local bodies in a number of States. The levy of this tax has caused serious impediments to internal trade and has created several tariff zones within the country.

In addition to the above, there are a number of regulatory measures introduced as part of a planned regime that impede the free movement of goods and persons. Two examples will suffice to substantiate this: first, to meet the contingencies of food scarcity, restrictions were placed on the movement of foodgrains under the Essential Commodities Act; second, under the freight equalization scheme that existed for a long time, freight charges of many industrial raw materials such as coal, manganese and steel were subsidized to ensure supply at the same cost throughout the country. This has not only distorted industrial location but has also failed to strengthen forward and backward linkages in poorer, mineral rich regions of the country.

Assignment of taxes to the centre and States is guided by the principle of separation. However, there is considerable concurrency in the assignment of expenditures. This enables the higher level governments to push expenditure responsibilities downwards, particularly when faced with a severe resource constraint. Another consequence of this has been to create overlapping expenditure systems with both centre and States spending on concurrent functions. There are coordination costs and institutions are still not fully developed to cope with the problems arising from them.

Although the federal constitution of the country has enabled a considerable degree of fiscal decentralization upto the regional level, the devolution of powers and functions to urban and rural local bodies has been abysmal. Information on the finances of urban and rural local governments is not available. However, based on the information for 1997/98 provided in the report of the Eleventh Finance Commission, it is seen that despite constitutional amendments, fiscal decentralization has not gone below the State level States raise about 35 per cent of total revenues and after transfers command almost 55 per cent of the revenues for spending. On the other hand, local governments at both urban and rural levels raise a mere 0.6 per cent of GDP or 3 per cent of total revenues raised in the country. At their disposal, they have command over resources of just 2.1 per cent of GDP or a little over 10 per cent of revenues. Revenue and spending powers of rural local bodies are particularly abysmal. The quarter million rural local governments representing over 65 per cent of the population of the country raise only 0.04 per cent of GDP or 0.3 per cent of total revenues and after receiving transfers from the States, they have command over only 1.3 per cent of GDP or 6.4 per cent of total revenues. In fact, history shows that barring a few exceptions of States such as Karnataka, Kerala and West Bengal, decentralization is a phenomenon which is imposed more from the centre than initiated by the concerned States.

A related aspect of fiscal decentralization is the need to link revenue and expenditure assignments so that at the margin, the decision of the sub-national governments to spend is matched by their own tax effort. This is necessary not only to impart efficiency and accountability to sub-national spending but also to ensure macroeconomic stability (Bahl, 1999). However, in the Indian context, State governments are able to finance their expenditure programmes by softening their budget constraints in a variety of ways. Borrowing from public accounts, floating "autonomous" bodies to implement major projects and borrowing through them, borrowing through public enterprises and seeking overdrafts from the Reserve Bank of India are some of the important ways in which State governments have tried to soften their budget constraints.

In contrast, local governments have been facing hard budget constraints–in fact, they hardly have significant budgets. Their abysmal fiscal resources have resulted in poor service delivery. In the constitutional scheme, both revenue and expenditure powers have to be devolved to them by the States. However, in actual practice, as shown in the table, local governments have very few revenue powers. As regards expenditure functions, most States use them as implementing agencies. In effect, in many of the States, the functions of rural local governments consist of mainly implementing various schemes stipulated by either the central or the State government. Thus, despite constitutional recognition, in effect, local governments hardly have any independent fiscal powers.

Intergovernmental Transfers

A notable feature of intergovernmental transfers in India is the existence of multiple channels of transfer from the centre to the States. The constitution provides for the appointment of the Finance Commission by the President of India every five years to assess fiscal resources and the needs of the centre and individual States and recommend transfers. Finance commission transfers consist of mainly formula based tax devolution and grants-in-aid given to fill the gap between projected revenues and expenditures on the non-plan accounts. The latest, i.e. the Eleventh Finance Commission has recommended the transfer of 29.5 per cent of central taxes to States and the distribution is to be determined on the basis of a formula devised by the Commission. Grants are given to fill the post devolution gaps. Transfers given by the Finance Commissions constitute 58 per cent of the total central transfers to States.

With development planning gaining emphasis, the scope of the Finance Commissions was restricted to meeting States' non-plan requirements in the current (revenue) account. The Planning Commission became a major dispenser of funds to the States by way of grants and loans to meet their plan requirements. These too are distributed according to a consensus formula 6 evolved in the National Development Council (NDC). Transfers to State plan schemes constitute about 22 per cent of total transfers.

In addition to these two channels, various central ministries give specific purpose transfers to the centre and centrally sponsored schemes with or without matching requirements. There are about 190 such schemes at present, but in terms of assistance, the programmes on rural development and poverty alleviation, family welfare, primary education and nutritional supplements to school children are important. There is a good deal of discretionary element in these transfers. These transfers constitute 20 per cent of the total transfers.

Thus, although the constitution provides for an impartial institution and objective mechanism to resolve fiscal imbalances between the centre and States, the working of the system has brought in a great deal of subjectivity. First, the existence of multiple agencies making transfers has complicated the transfer system and has made it difficult to achieve the objectives of intergovernmental transfer policy. Although a significant portion of the transfers are formula based, the formulas themselves are not designed to offset the revenue and cost disabilities of poorer States. In fact, the gap-filling approach of the various Finance Commissions has serious disincentives for fiscal management. The States indulging in a lower tax effort and/or expenditure profligacy can show higher gaps and gain more grants. Moreover, despite the predominance of formula based transfers, the central government is able to exercise discretion through specific purpose transfers given for central schemes.

An important legacy of planning and the system of decentralization that has evolved over time is the existence of invisible transfers due to a repressed interest rate regime, origin-based cascading type consumption tax system and subsidized loans given to priority sectors (Rao, 2000). Invisible transfers in the Indian context also arise from the existence of inter-State tax exportation caused by the levy of cascading type origin-based sales taxes in the States. Another important source of such transfers is the allocation of market borrowings and central loans to States at subsidized interest rates. Providing loans to priority sectors at subsidized interest rates is another legacy of the planning regime that causes interregional resource transfers.

Transfers below the State Level

As mentioned earlier, in Indian fiscal federalism, decentralization below the State level is negligible. Local governments together raise only 0.6 per cent of GDP but spend about 2.1 per cent of GDP. In fact a quarter million rural local governments together raise a negligible amount of revenue. The State governments determine the system of assignments and the constitution provides for the appointment of State finance commissions by the States. However, similarity with the central transfer system ends here. Some States are yet to appoint finance commissions; in others the finance commissions are yet to submit their reports; in some others the report has not been accepted and the States have continued to make transfers on ad hoc basis. In some States the transfers are made on the basis of the recommendations of the finance commissions, but the recommendations are not based on scientific criteria for want of information and data on indicators of fiscal capacities and needs. There are also significant interstate variations in the functioning of sub-state fiscal decentralization.

Decentralization, particularly at the village level as envisaged in the constitutional amendment also provides for empowerment of socially backward classes and women. A third of the seats in village *panchayats* are reserved for women. The village *panchayats* are required to organize "*gram sabha*" or village assembly four times a year in which schemes are prioritized and the accounts are approved. This is meant to ensure provision of public services according to the preferences of the people. However, in actual practice, *gram sabhas* are not active; they are held less frequently and the participation in the *sabhas* is poor. Moreover, there are varying degrees of people's participation in different States depending on a number of factors such as the distribution of land holdings, social stratification and the educational levels of the people.

The most important shortcoming of the sub-State decentralization is that both assignments and transfers to local governments do not constitute much to give them any meaningful role in delivering public services. As already mentioned, lower level governments hardly have any revenue handles. In the absence of even basic information, a rational system of transfers has not been evolved. Further, as the amount transferred is negligible, the *panchayats* are involved mainly in implementing the schemes formulated by the central and State governments.

CONCLUSION

The challenges of fiscal decentralization should not be looked at from the narrow perspective of developing intergovernmental finance. This should be seen as part of developing a comprehensive and coordinated budgeting and fiscal system. Evolving a transparent and programme based budgeting system involves the development of an efficient tax, expenditure and intergovernmental finance system at the central and local levels. A systemic approach to fiscal decentralization also requires policies and institutions, on the one hand, and capacity-building of various institutions to implement them on the other.

Efforts should be made to evolve a decentralized delivery of public services, specifically removing the infirmities and impediments to the efficient functioning of a market-based system and of making a relatively smooth transition from plan to market. Rediscovering the role of decentralized governmental units in the context of a changed role for the government, severing the nexus between governments and State enterprises, removal of price and quantity controls, restoring market incentives, developing institutions to administer market-based instruments and policies and bringing in expenditures from all sources into budgetary discipline, are the major issues which need to be confronted to ensure equity and efficiency in delivering public services in the two economies.

References

Bahl, Roy W. (1999), *Implementation Rules for Fiscal Decentralization*, Working Paper No. 10, School of Policy Studies, Georgia State University.

Bahl, Roy W. and Christine Wallich (1992), *Intergovernmental Fiscal Relations in China*, Policy Research Working Paper No. 863, Washington, D.C., World Bank.

———(2001), *Fiscal Decentralization: The Provincial–Local Dimension*. Paper presented in the Seminar on Public Finance in Developing and Transition Countries, 4-6 April, Georgia State University, Atlanta.

Bird, Richard M. (2000), *Intergovernmental Fiscal Relations: Universal Principles, Local Applications* Working Paper 00-2, Andrew Young School of Policy Studies, Georgia State University.

Bird, Richard M. and Christine Wallich (1993), *Fiscal Decentralization and Intergovernmental Relations in Transition Economies,* Policy Research Working Papers, WPS. 1122. The World Bank.

Bird, Richard M., Robert D. Ebel and Christine I. Wallich, eds. (1995), *Decentralization of the Socialist State* (Washington, D.C., World Bank).

Bird, Richard and Francois Vaillancourt, eds. (1998), *Fiscal Decentralization in Developing Countries* (Cambridge, Cambridge University Press).

Breton, Albert (1996), *Competitive Governments* (Cambridge University Press).

Rao, Govinda (1997), "Invisible Transfers in Indian Federation", *Public Finance/Finances Publiques*, Vol. 52, No. 3, pp. 299-316.

Rao, M. Govinda and Tapas Sen (1996), *Fiscal Federalism in India–Theory and Practice*, Macmillan India, New Delhi.

Ma Jun (1995), "The Reform of Intergovernmental Fiscal Relations in China", *Asian Economic Journal*, Vol. 9, No. 3, pp. 205-231.

Malme J.H. and Joan M. Youngman, eds. (2001), *The Development of Property Taxation in Economies in Transition*. The World Bank.

Wong, Christine (1996), "Overview of Issues in Local Public Finance in the

PRC", in Wong, ed., *Financing Local Government in the People's Republic of China*, Chapter One, Hongkong, Oxford University Press.

Arzaghi M, Henderson J. V. (2005), Why Countries are Fiscally Decentralizing, *Journal of Public Economics*, 89 (2005) 1157-1189

Asian Development Bank (2006), The Working of State Finance Commissions by Ravikant Joshi Accessed at: *http://www.adb.org/Documents/Papers/INRM-PolicyBriefs/inrm9.pdf*

Bardhan, P. (2002), Decentralization of Government and Development *The Journal of Economic Perspectives*, Vol. 16, No. 4. (2002), pp. 185-205.

Bardhan and Mookherjee D. (2005), Decentralisation Antipoverty Program Delivery in Developing Countries in *Journal of Public Economics,* 89 (2005) 675-704).

Bardhan and Mookherjee D. (2005), Decentralization, Corruption and Government Accountability: An Overview in the *Handbook of Economic Corruption'* edited by Susan Rose-Ackerman & Edward Elgar.

Bardhan and Mookherjee D. (2006), Decentralisation and Accountability in Infrastructure Delivery in Developing Countries *The Economic Journal*, 116 (January), 101–127. Accessed from:

Dabla-Norris E, Wade P. (2006), The Challenge of Fiscal Decentralization in Transition Countries, Comparative Economic Studies, 2006 Accessed from: *http://www.palgrave-journals.com/ces/journal/v48/n1/full/8100063a.html on 13.1.2008*

Fjeldstad Odd-Helge (2001), Fiscal Decentralisation in Tanzania: For Better or for Worse? CMI Working Papers Accessed from: *http://www.cmi.no/publications/file/?872=fiscal-decentralisation-in-tanzania on 15.1.2008.*

INDEX

Q

R

S

V

W